OXYGEN

OXYGEN

OXYGEN
WILLIAM TRUBRIDGE

HarperCollins*Publishers*

HarperCollins*Publishers*

First published in 2017
This edition published in 2018
by HarperCollins*Publishers* (New Zealand) Limited
Unit D1, 63 Apollo Drive, Rosedale, Auckland 0632, New Zealand
harpercollins.co.nz

HarperCollins*Publishers*
Unit D1, 63 Apollo Drive, Rosedale, Auckland 0632, New Zealand
Level 13, 201 Elizabeth Street, Sydney NSW 2000, Australia
A 53, Sector 57, Noida, UP, India
1 London Bridge Street, London, SE1 9GF, United Kingdom
Bay Adelaide Centre, East Tower, 22 Adelaide Street West, 41st floor,
   Toronto, Ontario M5H 4E3, Canada
195 Broadway, New York NY 10007, USA

A catalogue record for this book is available from
the National Library of New Zealand

ISBN 978 1 7755 4134 9 (pbk)
ISBN 978 1 7754 9144 6 (epub)

Cover design by HarperCollins Design Studio
Front cover image © Richard Robinson: William Trubridge,
   Great Barrier Island, New Zealand, January 2017
Back cover image © Daan Verhoeven
Typeset in Sabon LT Std by Kelli Lonergan
Printed and bound in Australia by McPherson's Printing Group
The papers used by HarperCollins in the manufacture of this book are a natural, recyclable product made from wood grown in sustainable plantation forests. The fibre source and manufacturing processes meet recognised international environmental standards, and carry certification.

For my grandfathers,
Geoffrey and Maurice

Contents

The magnanimity of the sea, which will permit no records.

Herman Melville, *Moby Dick*

A NOTE FROM THE AUTHOR

FREEDIVING, OR BREATH-HOLD DIVING, has its roots in ancient cultures such as those of the Greek sponge fishermen, Polynesian pearl-divers and Japanese *ama*, all of whom have been holding their breath while harvesting the bounties of the sea floor for hundreds of years. The first 'official' records were set in the late 1940s, but in this era divers used weighted sleds to descend and inflatable lift bags to return, a modality called 'No Limits'. Nowadays, this style has been abandoned by athletes and the main governing body of freediving (the AIDA — International Association for the Development of Apnea) in favour of the more athletic disciplines.

The sport of competitive freediving as we know it today has existed in its current form for only about 30 years. There are three disciplines in which athletes compete for maximum depth (measured in metres below the surface):

- CWT (Constant Weight): the freediver swims down and back up wearing fins or a monofin, but cannot touch the rope (other than once at the bottom). Any weight worn as ballast must remain constant throughout the dive.
- CNF (Constant No Fins): the freediver swims down and back up, relying only on his or her own body for propulsion, and usually swimming with a kind of adapted underwater breaststroke. Any weight worn as ballast must again remain constant.
- FIM (Free Immersion): fins are not allowed, but freedivers can use the weighted dive rope to pull themselves to maximum depth and back to the surface. As for the other disciplines, any ballast weight must remain constant.

Holding the breath means stopping the intake of oxygen. From that point on, the freediver depends on the oxygen contained within the body: mixed with other gases as air in the lungs; attached to haemoglobin (inside red blood cells) in the blood; and stored in myoglobin within muscle tissue. As the apnea (breath-hold) continues, these stores of oxygen become depleted. When the body's stored oxygen falls below a certain level, the brain makes an executive decision and shuts down conscious activity — one of the biggest consumers of oxygen — in order to conserve what remains. This results in a blackout (loss of consciousness).

If an athlete comes to the surface and is very close to blacking out then they may suffer a loss of motor control (LMC). The freediver is still conscious, but cannot control a shaking of the arms and head while they breathe, and this state is commonly known in freediving as a 'samba' (named after the Brazilian dance).

If a blackout happens underwater and there is no one to intervene, it will be fatal 100 per cent of the time. This is why it is critical, in any depth of water, to always freedive with someone who is trained in safety techniques, and to use the 'one up, one down' system of diving (i.e. one freediver occupies the role of safety diver for the other). In competitive freediving the athlete is always accompanied by safety divers in the final 20 to 30 metres of their ascent, where the oxygen levels are at their lowest and blackout is therefore most likely to occur. If an athlete does black out underwater, the mouth and glottis clamp shut in a reflex action, keeping the lungs dry. They are brought to the surface by the safety divers, who then blow across the athlete's face to signal to the facial nerves that they are no longer underwater. This normally triggers recovery and a resumption of breathing, but if it doesn't then a safety diver can give a mouth-to-mouth 'rescue breath' to oxygenate the athlete's lungs.

Blackouts are clearly undesirable, but are neither painful nor (according to extensive medical research) damaging. Permanent damage to the brain or other organs does not begin until several minutes after a loss of consciousness, at the earliest, and this is more than enough time for the athlete to be returned to the surface by trained safety divers.

Before attempting freediving, breath-holding, or any of the techniques described in this book, readers are strongly encouraged to enrol in a freediving course where they can learn appropriate methods for safe practice underwater.

I'm not William Trubridge. I'm not an 'I am'.
There exists only a point of awareness,
wakefulness, seemingly contingent on the body of
a human man, drifting downwards into thin ink.

The heart of that falling body beats slowly,
shuffling thickened blood past the dormant brain.
With each beat the body sinks another length
away from the surface, away from the sun, away
from the air. Inside there is awareness — but
there is no content to the awareness, like a camera
filming in darkness.

Meanwhile, something is taking place. An unassisted
breath-hold dive to a depth no human being has ever
been to. A world-record attempt. Many people — in
the water, on the surface, in front of televisions and
internet feeds at home or at work — are completely
engrossed in the timeline of this dive. So, arguably, is

the subconscious mind — the autopilot — of the man attempting the record. But the shard of consciousness that is all that is left of him, of me, is unshackled, formless, empty.

Such detachment from identity and locality is actually necessary for my own survival. If I'm to swim to 102 metres below the surface of the sea and return by the same route, I don't have enough air to take the chattering monkey that lives in my head along for the ride.

An alarm from the depth gauge on my wrist sounds, sending a signal to the autopilot, which orders a subtle change in my position to ready my body for a turn. The rope in front of me changes pattern and texture; my left hand grips it, my right arm extends and its hand closes around a piece of material — a tag attached loosely to a round plate. The surface of the plate is exactly 102 metres below the surface of the ocean. I have the tag to prove that I've been there. Now I just have to make it back up.

*

Something has brought my brain back online. It was a sound, like a tiny, stifled sneeze. It came at the same time as my torso expanded, my ribs flared wide by my breathing muscles. That was involuntary as well: a 'breathing reflex' to try to pull fresh air into my lungs. There's no air where I am, though, which is why my mouth stays firmly shut. All the expansion does is suck my stomach further up under my ribcage.

I don't need to tell myself 'just keep swimming', since that is my body's default mode — it will continue on autopilot for as long as I am conscious. My strokes are, however, becoming laboured from the lactic acid pooling in my limbs. Attached to a Velcro patch on my leg, the fabric tag flutters with each kick and armstroke I take. If I can bring that little black badge back to the surface, swimming without fins or any propulsive assistance, and without touching the rope or any other diver, then I will set a new world record in the purest discipline of freediving: Constant Weight No Fins. All I have to do is stay calm, focused and, above all, conscious.

That squeak, though: it's not a good sign. It means that my inhale reflex was strong, strong enough to pull a tiny bit of air from my mouth past my glottis, making it vibrate. And I shouldn't be getting such strong breathing reflexes at this point in the dive. I still have so far to go before I reach air, and the oxygen I need to survive.

I've only just started ascending from 102 metres below the surface of the sea, and I feel as if I already need to breathe.

CHAPTER 1

WATER BUG

Waking to the sound of water

From birth, man carries the weight of gravity on his
shoulders. He is bolted to earth. But man has only to
sink beneath the surface and he is free.

Jacques-Yves Cousteau

THE TIME I WAS CLOSEST TO DROWNING didn't involve any
liquid water at all.

It is one of the first memories that I know for certain
is wholly my own, since I was the only one present. It
happened when I was four years old, in Suva, Fiji. The
yacht club there was playing the Bond movie *Octopussy*
on loop, and my brother Sam and I would while away
the days in that dusty, raucous room, while my parents
prepared our boat for the voyage to New Zealand.
The staff took a liking to us, and supplied us with
sodas, always with plenty of ice — a huge novelty for

9

children brought up on a boat with no refrigerator. On one of these sleepy afternoons I was toying with an ice cube in my mouth, melting it into a slippery jewel that skidded back and forth from one cheek to the other. Some errant movement of my tongue or jaw must have caused a ricochet that sent the frozen lozenge suddenly backwards, caroming off my soft palate to lodge firmly in the glottis. It was a snug fit, and the patina of melting water provided just enough lubricant to make sure there was a good seal around the ice cube.

The body's first instinct when surprised is to inhale sharply, and in that moment I realised I could not breathe. Although I was a child who had already spent some time not breathing underwater, this moment still provoked a surge of terror that added a more systemic chill to the one happening in my throat. I couldn't cry out, and there was no one within eyesight to signal to. Instinctively I knew that if I tried to move I wouldn't get far before running out of breath. Whatever was going to fix the situation, whatever it was, had to happen right there, on that aluminium chair, in front of a waggish Roger Moore canoodling with his latest conquest ('Forgive my curiosity, but what is that?' 'Why, that's my little octopussy.'). And it had to be me who fixed it.

A level of gravity that I had no idea even existed took control of my mind and senses. Riding on the shoulder of that wave of terror was the recognition that this moment might not be followed by another if I didn't do exactly what was necessary. And what was necessary? My mouth stretched wide as my hand plunged in, forefinger extended. There was a gag, followed by another, as for the first time something other than food or water touched the back of my throat. When Sam and I were seasick, we were told that forcing ourselves to vomit using the same manoeuvre would ease the ailment, but I could never muster the willpower to do such a thing. Now willpower was an irrelevant luxury, superseded by the stark criterion of necessity. I felt the cold slipperiness of the ice cube with my probing digit, and slid the fingertip down between it and the wall of my throat. There was a sickening moment when the ice cube merely tumbled on its axis without relinquishing its position; then the seal was broken and it popped forwards onto my tongue, from where I seized it between my fingers and pulled it out as I gasped air into my lungs.

Even at that age I could appreciate most of what had happened: that a previously dormant, atavistic part of me had taken over in those moments, freezing out the panic centre of my brain so that it could act calmly and decisively. What I didn't know was that later in life I would spend so much time trying to replicate that same self-control in the face of an extreme urge to breathe.

Granted, I have never really felt as if my life was in grave danger during a training dive or even a world-record attempt. Nonetheless, once the urge to breathe sets in then in every instant of a voluntary apnea (breath-hold) there are two branching choices: the first where you allow yourself to become *affected* by the hunger for air — a route that quickly descends towards agitation and distress; and the other where you acknowledge the sensation happening to your body but manage to remain detached and non-reactive — or, better still, choose to experience it as a signal from your body to relax more deeply. After all, the sensation itself is caused not by a lack of oxygen, but almost entirely by an accumulation of carbon dioxide. Even just the solace afforded by this important piece of knowledge can help to placate the clamour of urgency felt by the body. When we can respond to suffocation with equanimity, we are truly on the path towards maximising our breath-holding and hence our aquatic potential.

It always amazes me how early some people's first memories are — it's not uncommon to hear someone relate their impression of an event that occurred in their first year of life. This is especially hard for me to comprehend, since in my case an early memory is any in which my height is less than 6 feet. I wonder whether in some cases memory extends even further back, and one might even be able to recall what it was like to be suspended in the sea of amniotic fluid within the womb. Research suggests we can. Babies begin to learn their mother tongue in the womb, within which sounds and phonemes are clearly audible. There are many cases of children possessing rudimentary memories of events that happened before they were born, such as one girl who asked her mother about a minor car accident, and subsequent argument between her parents, and was told that she had still been in the womb at the time. Twins have been observed playing games with each other across the membrane curtain that divides them. It's been shown that the same soft music that soothes a baby in the womb will also be preferred following birth. It stands to reason, then, that we might also have a similar preference for some kind of warm-liquid suspension that matches our memory of the pre-birth experience.

Although not everyone may be able to access such early memories, they will always be present and can on some level be triggered. In the same way we may find a smell familiar but not know where from, or an event during the day can reunite us with the memory of a dream we were previously cut off from.

And what about the experience of being in the womb itself? Would that be similar to a free fall into deep water?

*

I took my first breath in the north of England: a home birth in a cottage on the Northumberland fells that border Scotland. The sea was nowhere in sight, but like every human to date I had spent the first nine months of my existence underwater, adrift in amniotic fluid. Perhaps my preference for an aquatic element had developed even by then, because I had no intention of exiting the womb until Linda, my mother, decided to speed things up by forcefully ingesting two cups of raspberry tea, made from the pulped leaves and stems of the bush (she ate the pulp, too). I needn't have feared, though — it wouldn't be long before I would return to a far larger sea.

Conceived in the twilight of the 1970s after, I'm told, a night of celebration at a Caribbean-themed party, I first saw light in May of 1980, a week after smallpox had been declared eradicated for good and while ash was still billowing from a fiery Mount St Helens.

It was a volatile time in Great Britain, too. While *The Empire Strikes Back* was opening in cinemas everywhere, Her Majesty's empire was fighting a tactical battle against the growing Red Star of the east (sorry, Margaret Thatcher — the analogy doesn't quite stretch to you being Princess Leia).

The freediving world record in the year of my birth was exactly 101 metres, set in a dive made in 1976 by Frenchman Jacques Mayol (inspiration for the movie *The Big Blue*). Mayol descended with the aid of a weighted sled and was pulled back up by an inflated lift bag. At the age of 30, I would make my first attempt at the same depth with no propulsive equipment whatsoever.

My father, David, made bespoke wooden furniture in a workshop in a field a short walk from our cottage. Linda kept my older brother, Sam, and me fed, warm and dry in a building that was remote, cold and wet. That was in the summer, mind you: in the winter it was completely cut off, freezing and snowed in.

In 1982, when I had seen 20 moons and probably as many sunny days, my parents took the daring plunge of leaving behind their gloomy but safe and dependable rural English life to embark on an open-ended journey across the seas; to sail west from Europe and not look back. Both my parents had travelled extensively before they met, and after tasting that bountiful life they had become terminally discontented with both the cold and sunless climate of northern England and the cold and sunless rule of its iron lady, Thatcher. It was such a radical move for the community and culture they inhabited that the local newspaper wrote a feature article on our family, entitled 'Into the Unknown', making no attempt to hide an almost funereal view of the send-off. The article did help secure a good price for the house my father had reconstructed from a ruin, however, and this paid for a 45-foot single-masted sailing boat with just enough money left over to see us through the first leg of our journey to the Caribbean; David had made loose arrangements for employment there. The boat, *Hornpipe*, was a sturdy steel-hulled vessel built in Brisbane and was named after an English sailor's dance. She was being kept in Puerto Banús, in southern Spain, so the first leg of our journey was overland, in a dying Morris Marina van. It was February, and we drove through a frozen midwinter landscape to catch the ferry to the Continent. Somewhere on the long drive down through Spain the van did finally die, but was kept by David in a state of suspended reanimation, in part by the opportune placement of my potty under a free-flowing petrol leak.

While my father had sailed in Europe, neither of my parents had any experience of long ocean crossings at the time when our family set sail from Gibraltar in the spring of 1982. It was Saturday the thirteenth of March. My mother recalls her feelings:

> Shot out of the Mediterranean through the straits
> of Gibraltar we were pitching and corkscrewing
> in an energetic sea, surging upon a rising easterly

gale on the first day of a voyage that might take
us around the world. Sailing downwind with
the current, it was a sliding slope with no way
back. We could not return to windward or the
comfortable house and business that we had sold
and abandoned. The mast vibrated as the sails
strained and our bodies tensed in response. From
below, a repetitive percussion of tins, jars, pots
and pans resounded from the galley. My hopes
of freedom were drowned under waves of fear as
I realised that we and our helpless children were
no more than flotsam and jetsam on the relentless
heaving sea.

As for my father, he was finally fulfilling the epitaph 'Cast
out into the deep' that was written on the tombstone of
his father, Geoffrey, who had died from a lingering war
illness when David was only 10 years old. Both of my
grandfathers had been officers stationed overseas in the
Second World War, and both had struggled in different
ways upon their return to England. My maternal
grandfather, Maurice, had wanted to continue travelling
and see more of the world, but was confined to the English
Midlands by dependent parents and a wife who was
afraid of flying. In a way, our adventure was a realisation
of what he yearned for but could not do himself.

To the question 'How do your parents feel about your freediving?', I often answer that the expedition they embarked on all those years ago was every bit as daring, taking place as it did in an era before long-range weather tracking, GPS navigation (my father used a sextant to take sightings of sun and stars to calculate our position and plot our course) or satellite communication. So they can relate to the desire to venture out into unexplored territory, and to the feeling that the risk of living a cloistered and unfulfilled life is greater than the risk of incident.

Of course I remember nothing now of that Atlantic crossing distinctly, but there's no denying that those amorphous tracts of time spent surrounded by nothing but ocean made a great impression on me. The fair-skinned toddler who looked out from the confines of the boat's cockpit at the start of each day and remarked 'Sea, sky' did not completely understand what he was looking at, but it was becoming a familiar environment, a homely one.

Nowadays the sight of the sea is a solace to me, and the source of a rejuvenating energy. When the stress of competing or my emotional life reaches a tipping point I escape to the nearest piece of coast and walk along the shoreline, or just sit and watch the moving water, the waves that paw and rake at jagged rocks. The sight is mesmerising, and without requiring any concentration on my part it induces a meditative state: a break in the mental recursions and emotive feedback loops that can plague our waking minds. It is no coincidence that our species spends so much of its holidays and free time by the sea, even those who have never experienced its calming and cleansing embrace to the degree that I have. It will always have a symbolic presence for many.

In Santa Teresa di Gallura, Italy, during the first years of my freediving career, I would spend the summer evenings on a granite shelf overlooking the bay, performing lung exercises and long sessions of *pranayama* (slow yogic breathing, with breath-holds between extended inhales and exhales). While my eyes were closed I could hear the slop and gurgle of gentle waves fragmenting among the boulders, and when I opened them at the end of the session I saw, each time as if for the first time, a liquid-crystal surface stretching forwards beneath me and condensing onto the horizon, upon which the sun was lowering its orange yolk.

*

When we finally made landfall at Antigua in the Caribbean, I had spent the preceding 5 per cent of my life at sea, out of sight of land, and probably couldn't remember much of what came before that. I had learnt to walk during the passage and wasn't too impressed when I had to learn to walk all over again on dry land, which was so static underfoot that it threw me off balance. Meanwhile, our parents' euphoria at arriving and a free rum-punch party combined to reverse the responsibilities, and Sam and I held our parents' hands and guided them back to the dinghy. 'No Daddy, don't be silly! Stop falling in the water!' Somehow we made it back to *Hornpipe*.

We spent almost two years in the Caribbean, mostly in the British Virgin Island of Tortola, and this time awakened a fascination with the underwater world and the creatures that dwelt there. A waterproof book of the fish and corals of the Caribbean had become our bible, and for my first exploratory paddles into this realm I was buckled into a buoyancy vest to keep me on the surface. I wore it at almost all times, including to bed, so when one day I jumped into a pool without it on I was surprised to go straight to the bottom. My mother had seen it coming though, and she hit the water, fully clothed, a fraction of a second after me, ready to fish me out.

The flotation aid made a brief revival 24 years later, after I had set my first world record in freediving. The captain of a day-cruise I was taking with my girlfriend in Nassau, Bahamas, insisted that everyone snorkelling must wear a lifejacket, and he didn't budge when I told him I

One of my earliest yoga lessons with my mother in the Caribbean.

Hornpipe at anchor in the windward islands of the Caribbean.

was a freediving instructor. 'You want to get in the water, you're wearing this!' My girlfriend couldn't stop laughing at me for the rest of the day, but thankfully it happened before social media, so the photos never surfaced.

After the Caribbean, the Panama Canal was the birth canal for my long-term memory — the means by which I emerged from a state of being enclosed in the womb of the present, equally oblivious to past and to future. According to study on self-recognition by Daniel Povinelli, it isn't until about three years of age that children begin to grasp the temporal dimension of the self: we learn that who we are isn't just what is experienced *now* but also what was experienced *then* and what will be experienced *tomorrow*. So, the Pacific is where I have my first memories. We sailed on a connect-the-dots course from Panama to the Galapagos Islands, French Polynesia, American Samoa, Tonga and Fiji. I had learnt to swim in the Caribbean, but in the Pacific I learnt to dive. Even if at first it was only for a few brief kicks and a squeak to clear my ears, I became not just a surface-level observer but also a fully immersed participant in the underwater world.

The sea contributed to every role in the survival of our family and the upbringing of myself and my brother. It was our means of transport, our source of protein, our playground and our classroom. Our longest ocean crossing was the 5500-kilometre passage from the Galapagos

Islands (where I met wizened, leathery tortoises born during Queen Victoria's reign), to the Marquesas Islands in French Polynesia. We made good speed through an area where sailing boats can easily spend weeks becalmed on glassy seas, but the crossing still lasted for almost a month out of sight of land. When we arrived at Fatu Hiva, at dawn, a reception of frolicking dolphins coincided with the exact moment that the sun rose above the island; set against the relief we felt at finally making land, not even this breathtaking scene was overly dramatic.

In Tahiti I went to a local kindergarten, and learnt French nursery rhymes alongside the Polynesian children. We participated in night-time hunts for giant coconut crabs, foraged for sugar cane and heart of palm, and made a boat horn out of a Triton's trumpet shell. By the age of five I could shin up a coconut tree or the wooden mast of a friend's boat. With a gang of other boat kids we came across a sea snake on the beach, and in a frenzied *Lord of the Flies* moment threw stones at it until it was dead — an event I am eternally repentant of, but which shows just how feral we could become.

Sam and I slept in the forward cabin, in bunk beds that ended at the door to the anchor locker in the bow of the boat. When we were sailing through heavy seas this part of the boat pitched the most, but the lumbering motion as *Hornpipe* crested waves and crashed into troughs could be sedative and cosy. Especially when we were on a port tack, which meant that the boat was leaning to my side of the cabin, and I would fall asleep wedged in the V between my bunk and the wall.

While snorkelling, Sam and I kept a constant lookout for new seashells to add to our collection; especially that Holy Grail of shells, the precious golden cowrie. When, years later, I finally gazed at one, locked in a glass display case of a dusty museum in Suva, it inspired more awe in me than perhaps any other artefact could have done at the time. As a naturally competitive second child, I was always trying to catch up to my brother, Sam, and became mired in dejection when the two and a half years between us created a barrier to my doing something that he was able or allowed to do. On one occasion in Tortola, my brother and parents returned, from snorkelling on the reef, to the dinghy where I was waiting and Sam immediately gushed 'I saw a shark!' — I didn't miss a beat with the reply: 'I saw a whale.' (In fact the biggest mammal I saw, by land or by sea, was King Tupou IV of Tonga, at 200 kilograms the world's heaviest monarch, when he paraded past in a golf cart during a local festival.)

Never was my frustration at my limitations more acute than when my parents and Sam all swam underwater to reach Mariner's Cave in Tonga. Legend had it that a beautiful princess in fear of her life had been hidden there by her lover until he could escape with her to Fiji. It is a very easy swim-through to reach the cavern, but after hearing my father explain carefully to Sam what he would need to do I said that I would not try it myself. Once again I was confined to the dinghy. It's very likely that in pining after that missed experience I planted the seed of my desire to prove myself in the depths. When, 23 years later, I swam through the arch at Dahab's Blue Hole — a feat several orders of magnitude more difficult than Mariner's Cave — it felt like I had finally appeased that despondent boy waiting behind in the dinghy.

We encountered another of our childhood legends several times when our boat crossed paths with his. Benoît was a Frenchman, sailing with his wife, Martine, and small daughter on the boat *Crysalide*. I don't remember anything else about him other than his capacity to freedive to the then mind-boggling depth of 90 feet (27 metres). Now, of course, my sense of scale underwater has changed completely, but back then this depth was abyssal. If Benoît had described how at 90 feet he had encountered an angler fish with a light on its head, swimming through the wreck of a German U-boat, we probably wouldn't have been incredulous. Our father had been able to disentangle an anchor at

60 feet (18 metres), and even this was a fact that we proudly relayed to the other boating kids we met in our travels. For us, 90 feet was the pinnacle of human achievement — for all intents and purposes the floor of the ocean. It's possible that it was the biggest distance I could comprehend at that time — if someone had told me that one day I would be diving four times as deep, then, aside from the fact that I couldn't yet do multiplication, I would have had no way of fathoming such a depth.

After our final Pacific stop, in Fiji — the site of my near-drowning on frozen water — my parents steered the boat south towards New Zealand, in search of employment. When we arrived, in the spring of 1985, I had no memories of a climate that wasn't tropical. Woollen sweaters knitted for us by our grandmother were itchy, and the water was cold and murky, making it boring for snorkelling. Sam and I had become accustomed to being able to play all day in the water and on the beach, but in New Zealand we had to find replacement activities. *Dungeons & Dragons* filled most of the gap, and our dice and character sheets spilled over into making swords and armour with which to roam the hillsides of Parekura Bay in the Bay of Islands, where *Hornpipe* was anchored. Forts were built, a thick marsh was turned into a labyrinth, and some passing cars may have been the targets of clay missiles ... My brother also taught me how to play chess, which ticked two boxes in the growing list of my appetites: mental challenges, and something you can beat someone else at. Apparently, Sam hasn't won since.

We alternated between periods attending Russell Primary School, where I played goalie for the losingest soccer team in the district (the Bay of Island Sharks), and completing Correspondence School study packages, which we could finish before breakfast so as to have the rest of the day free to play.

The Bay of Islands is a beautiful nook in New Zealand's wild coastline. Urapukapuka, Moturua, Motukiekie and other smaller islands are protected from the ocean swells by the Cape Brett Peninsula, creating peaceful coves and inlets that we would explore with the boat on weekend trips. David was taking his first steps in making furniture in New Zealand, a path that would lead to him becoming one of the country's most respected designers. When he knocked off at five in the evening he would walk down from his workshop to the shore, and whistle to get our attention on the boat. I delighted in my important role of rowing the dinghy ashore to fetch him while he waited, eating oysters off the rocks. Making wood carvings of animals alongside my father in his workshop, I learnt that the initial ecstasy of inspiration will never last to the end of a task. After its energy was exhausted by the first gleeful hour of chiselling, then if patience and discipline didn't take over you'd be left with a hacked-at block of wood that only half-resembled the intended camel/giraffe/whale. Watching David steadily shaping elaborate works and an even more elaborate lifework, in the same way that he steadily devoured mountain ranges on long hikes, I observed the archetype of patience and discipline. Thanks to my father, I have never reneged on a training session, nor quit when results were discouraging.

Linda taught relief at Kawakawa High School, taking the school bus for an hour along dusty roads on the days when she was alerted by an early morning call to the boat's radio. She also kept the boat functioning as a mobile house for three messy males and set nets in the bay for kahawai fish, though often caught stingrays that she would haul onto the beach to untangle, before chopping the wings up to batter and fry. Linda, who hand-sewed stuffed animal toys, quilts and costumes for my brother and me, and consummately praised us for whatever we did while also propelling us to something greater, represented a distillation of altruism that inspires me to this day. By coaxing and encouraging us — to write a little clearer, to paint a little more attentively, to play a little more fluidly — she taught me that there was always more inside: more creativity, more potential, more depth. Thanks to my mother, I believe in myself and the infinitude of our capacity for whatever we set our minds to.

*

In 1988 we left the New Zealand winter to sail once more as a family among the islands in the Pacific. This time I would be old enough to start testing the boundaries between daring and stupidity.

The first leg took us to the Isle of Pines in New Caledonia, and Sam and I resumed our days of snorkelling and island-exploring as if we had never left the tropics. We accompanied David when he went spearfishing, and I saw my first reef shark. On one of the atolls we found a sandy underwater bank that sloped steeply downwards from the shore to an unknown depth in an almost identical fashion to the edges of Dean's Blue Hole, which I would discover 17 years later. Sam and I took turns daring ourselves to swim further and further down the bank, hands outstretched to skim the soft incline, for a few more seconds, a few more kicks, before turning and sprinting to the surface.

One day we found turtles lying upside down on the beach between the hulls of an outrigger canoe, their flippers waving feebly as they waited to be served for dinner at the nearby restaurant. No one was around, so we flipped the turtles — which were too heavy to carry — onto their bellies, and pushed and cajoled them down the beach with whispered cries of 'Go, quick! Freedom awaits!' When all three were safely back in the water and swimming off into the bay (without, I was disappointed to note, any sign of gratitude), we swam back out to the boat to excitedly inform our parents of our successful campaign. Whereupon they quickly upped anchor and moved a few bays down the coast — after all, when the turtles were reported missing the locals wouldn't need a Sherlock Holmes to notice sets of children's footprints next to the tyre-track marks left by the turtles.

Sam was the model older brother, a responsible and eternally patient companion. He was also the creative designer of our games and roleplaying then as he is now in theatrical productions that challenge the expectations of his audiences. We fought, but probably less than most siblings. It hadn't taken us long to figure out that with so little space on *Hornpipe*, friction was not an option. Our father was not very forgiving of spats between us: if there was ever any conflict back then, regardless of who was at fault, we would both be thrown overboard (provided, of course, that we were at anchor!). One such time we ended up on a beach, sulking in the shade of an island pine. One of us began digging a hole in the sand, and was mirrored by the other. Gradually, and without communication or maybe even any conscious decision by either of us, the two holes veered sideways, converging until we broke through to create a tunnel between our two pits. And in that moment the morning's petty squabble was purged.

From New Caledonia we sailed to Vanuatu, and there for the first time I started to take notice of depth measurements. *Hornpipe* had an old Seafarer echo sounder, which buzzed and popped as a flickering red dash indicated the depth in feet and fathoms on a big green dial. 'Our scion of the depths, herald from the ocean floor,' Sam later called it. If we managed to dive to the bottom below the boat and grab a rock or handful of sand as testimony, then we would quickly climb on board to consult the sounder. There was very little resemblance to the kind of freediving I do today. Our fins were thick and rigid rubber triangles. The masks were basically rubber cylinders with a flat glass window: all of its internal volume would have to be refilled (equalised for pressure) every 10 metres, using air from our kid-sized lungs. We were oblivious of the concept of a 'breathe-up' (relaxed preparation before a dive), and would babble away as we trod water, right up to the moment when one of us gasped an inhale and jackknifed under the water.

Like frantic tadpoles, we would waggle our fins (and our arms, too, when the legs tired) and crane our necks towards our target on the seabed. There was no time to spare at the bottom: one hand flailed out to seize a fistful of whatever it made contact with (stone/sand) before the process reversed in an even more frenetic ascent back to the surface.

On Vanuatu's Hat Island (Eretoka) we reached the zenith of our abilities, and what would be my nadir of depth for the next 15 years. I had been diving regularly to 10 metres and wanted more of a challenge, so Sam and I snorkelled into an area where the sea floor had taken on a different kind of hue: darker and more monochromatically blue. It made us nervous just to gaze down, but eventually I was the first to try. All I remember is that when I turned at the bottom and, for the first time in the dive, looked back towards the surface, it was not where I expected it to be. It was remote. There was Sam, a lonely silhouetted shape; there were the waves on the surface, but they looked like ripples. There was, no doubt, alarm, panic, frenzied limbs and a burst of relief upon breaking the surface and sucking in fresh air. Sam looked appalled as he realised that he would now have to attempt it as well. Once again I marvelled at how small he looked when, after a flurry of kicking, he turned at the bottom. On his way back to the surface, one hand clutched the rock he had plucked from the sea floor while the other tore the mask from his face, as if he wanted to tear away the remaining water that covered him.

On that day the shaky red dash of the echo sounder settled on 45 feet, a depth of 14 metres, and we would wear this statistic like a badge in conversations with other boating kids for years to come.

Also in Vanuatu, on the near-mythical island of Tanna, the site of a very active volcano, Mount Yasur, that pulsed with an orange glow at night, we experienced what was probably our most terrifying sealife encounter. Soon after anchoring in the waters of Port Resolution, Sam and I jumped in the water with snorkelling gear to explore around the boat. The water was slightly turbid and brooding, with a mostly barren sea floor of volcanic boulders. We were swimming across the surface, gazing down on this unfamiliar seascape when I realised that one of the distant boulders was actually mobile, and moving rapidly towards us. The huge grey mass was the biggest living thing Sam and I had ever seen in the water: a 3 metre long slab of fat and muscle, with the doughy, amorphous face of a bulldog — or a dolphin that had been punched very hard in the nose. It was a dugong, or 'sea cow', a close relative of the hippopotamus and elephant that grazes on the sea floor, and may have inspired legends of mermaids due to the human resemblance in the way they breastfeed their young. The wonder at seeing something so massive moving so agilely through the water turned to alarm when the beast continued to swim purposefully straight towards us. What must have been close to half a ton of spongy flesh collided with our tiny bodies, pushing one then the other of us clean above the surface as we scrambled at the water, shrieking and gasping through our snorkels. As quick as we could, we swam back towards the boat, darting on angles to try to avoid the dugong's repeated attempts to bunt us with its massive snout.

Later we discovered that this male dugong had been a resident in the harbour for years, and its over-zealous interactions with humans were probably an increasingly desperate attempt at finding a mate. The locals would feed it with cabbages and other vegetables thrown from the rocks. For light entertainment they would throw the dogs and children in too: after hitting the water they would surface screaming or yapping, and pound the water back in to shore to escape from the dugong's amorous advances.

Tanna was one of our last stops before sailing back south towards New Zealand, on what would be the last ocean passage we made on *Hornpipe*. Before setting sail we climbed to the rim of the volcano and gazed down on that red sea of molten rock that had birthed our planet. It burped and spat fat globs of golden liquid, busy in the process of forcing solidity and permanence into the surrounding expanse of ocean. Terra firma was about to force itself back into our lives in a similar fashion.

*

In 1991 Sam and I settled into schools and Linda and David settled into jobs in Hawke's Bay. On attending my first day at a full-size school my social inexperience was keenly felt, and I was too busy trying to catch up to my peers, and discovering a passion for chess and sports, to really notice *Hornpipe* drifting out of our lives as she languished in the harbour before eventually being sold. Her features will never fade in my memory, though, and even from a distance I would recognise her immediately: the homely lines and colours of her hull, the tight curves of her sails on a beam reach, the intimate trickle of water past her steel hull when she was under way, her two cabin windows like softly smiling eyes, the rhythmic patter of her halyards at anchor during the night.

It's hard to say whether I would have become a freediver had I not spent almost all of my childhood on and under the waves. I can't imagine my life without those alluring depths, but neither can I imagine that a William who stayed behind to live out his childhood in the northern midlands of Britain would ever have been drawn to the oceans with such magnetism as I was in 2003. In all the time between that last Pacific trip in 1988 and my return to the underwater world 15 years later, those blue volumes were constantly calling me back; that much is now clear. The omens and messages line the years like a trail of breadcrumbs. Perhaps it would be more accurate to say that it was a deeper part of myself doing the calling: sending a message up through the layers of consciousness until it arrived in my awareness as an instinctive decision or cryptic piece of imagery. Quiz me at the end of a training session or a meditation in front of the water, and I might answer that, in the final analysis, the two entities — the sea and my subconscious — are one and the same.

CHAPTER 2

THE SIREN'S CALL

*Glimpses of blue between
the macrocarpa trees*

The sea, once it casts its spell,

holds one in its net of wonder forever

Jacques-Yves Cousteau

WERE THE MESSAGES CALLING ME BACK to the ocean
postcards from my future or reminders from my past?
Or were they both: twin bodies of history behind and
unrealised potential in front exerting the same tidal force
on the present?

Before my tenth birthday, I attended a horse-riding
camp in the heart of New Zealand's rural Northland. I
loved the horses and their readiness to trust and bond
with us capricious humans, but I didn't find the same
acceptance or loyalty among my young peers at the camp,
including the best friend I had travelled there with. In

37

one traumatising experience, I was asked by the group if I had ever touched a girl. I had no real idea what that meant, but fearing ridicule I made up a story about a time I had 'felt up' a classmate during a school trip to one of the islands in the Bay of Islands. The story went that we were standing in waist-deep water when the girl and I both ducked under and the alleged touching occurred. I don't think anyone really believed my story, as some of them asked me to repeat it, possibly for amusement. It's telling, nonetheless, that when I was put on the spot the fabrication that my mind felt would be most convincing involved being underwater, as if I held myself to be an authority on what might and might not happen there.

It wouldn't be the only time I would lie about encounters with the fairer sex in order to fit in. I arrived at every milestone well behind my contemporaries, and although I did my best to conceal the gap I doubt that I was very convincing.

When I converged with public education, I discovered that operations which my mind performed with ease and alacrity were not all the status quo. I was good at chess — better, it turned out, than anyone my age in the region. I won prizes in maths, English and science. A Hawke's Bay newspaper ran an article with a picture of my wistful 12-year-old face gazing into the middle distance, alongside the caption 'Casualty of the

Education System'. Apparently the local schools hadn't been providing enough of a challenge for students who were ahead of the syllabus. The article infuriated my intermediate-school teacher, who was forever after on the lookout for any slip-up I made that might debunk the article. It also provided fodder to the class bullies, who taunted me with the moniker 'gifted child'. I escaped into chess, and into sports in which I was much less 'gifted'. I played tennis, badminton and cricket, but never fully grasped the concept of training — I just assumed that the others had better natural ability than me.

One of Hawke's Bay's main attractions in the 1990s was a waterfront concrete compound called Marineland, which kept a variety of aquatic mammals, including a handful of common dolphins, as the main attraction. Even as an 11-year-old child I was aware of a creepy incongruity between the tiers of worn bleachers, the unyielding cement and the tacky murals, and the sleek, mercurial beings they enclosed. No doubt harbouring a fantasy that they might recognise me as one of their own, I pestered my parents until they bought me a ticket to swim with the dolphins, but the experience was anticlimactic. They were defeated animals, resigned to a monotony of task-and-reward behaviour, and for them I was just another task. The fact that a dolphin's jaw curves into a playful smile is cruelly ironic in creatures confined to the least smile-worthy existence imaginable for such an intelligent species.

It's every freediver's dream to swim with dolphins across an open seascape, tumbling and cavorting in three dimensions. Science has recently determined that, after humans, they are the most intelligent animals in the world (surpassing chimpanzees), and in India the ministry responsible for the environment has declared all cetaceans (dolphins and whales) to be 'non-human persons'. When you interact with them in the wild and witness the way they study you with their gentle eyes, or watch their rascally antics during play, it's difficult not to feel the bond of one conscious soul reaching out to greet another. There are tours that offer the chance to swim with wild dolphins, and if this is done respectfully then it can be a genuine and authentic experience. Dolphins communicate continuously, and a lot of this is through touch. In the same way that we would recoil from contact with a prickly hedgehog, smooth-skinned dolphins find our spindly and sharp-ended fingers creepy, and are suspicious of the explosive and haphazard movements of our limbs. So in the wild they approach and observe, and if they feel safe then they will spin and turn, coming closer little by little. I've been lucky enough to experience this kind of encounter, with bottlenose dolphins in Honduras, Atlantic spotted dolphins in the Bahamas, and even with the threatened Hector's dolphins of New Zealand. It is a magical and life-affirming experience; I doubt that anyone who has been blessed with such an encounter could feel comfortable with the idea of dolphins being treated as an entertainment commodity.

*

By my early teens I had become thoroughly immersed in the world of chess, playing at a local chess club that met every Wednesday night, as well as studying Grand Masters' games and puzzles in my spare time. The regional championships were held once a year over a long weekend, and although everyone played in a single group there was a junior prize for those under the age of 20. When I was 14 I played for close to 16 hours over a two-day period to win this title. After returning home and planting the trophy on the kitchen table, I was surprised to find myself bringing up and expelling the entire contents of my stomach. It was a well-timed revolt from my physical body for having been confined so long to a seat in front of a chequered board, while my brain commandeered every last resource for its marathon of concentration. Looking back now, it's clear to me that although I enjoyed the mental challenge, my mind was only one of the organs that had been placed at my disposal and I wasn't content or complete unless I was using the full set.

At school I enjoyed swimming, but there was no swim team and the local club didn't attract my attention. Each year there would be a School Swimming Day, where all the students showed up at the local pool for races and games between the four school 'houses'. I would place third or fourth in the breaststroke events, behind the club swimmers. My technique was merely what I had taught myself swimming in the ocean, and so in each stroke I was spending too much time underwater, gliding forwards with arms outstretched before 'leaning' on my hands to pop my head up and take a breath. It's perhaps the most pleasurable way to swim breaststroke, but definitely not the quickest! I was entered in the 100-metre butterfly event as well, since — in a field of three — any finish would secure a podium place. When I turned after 50 metres and found myself sinking deeper with every kick, I realised why there had been few takers for this event. Somehow I spasmed through to the wall, but from that day on butterfly and the dolphin kick were anathema to me. When I began freediving it took me years to purge my attitude to this kick, which is indispensable for the discipline of Constant Weight or CWT (where a monofin is used for propulsion).

At around the age of 16 I was roused by the winds of vanity, and these led me in two directions: acting

As Alonso in my brother's production of Shakespeare's *The Tempest*. I am surrounded by sea nymphs Meredith Rimmer (left) and Amber Sainsbury (right) while talking to Chris Hodder's Gonzalo. Sea nymph Fiona McCallum consoles David Passmore's Antonio in the background.

and working out. It started with the realisation that my arms were basically just uniform tubes of flesh, and my stomach (though flat) was soft. To the former I administered smooth cannonball rocks, lifted 50, then 100, then 200 or more times by each arm, while my stomach was targeted by some kind of 1990s ab-buster gizmo. This practice was soon transferred to the gym, where the rest of my muscles tried to catch up on the head start given to my biceps and abs. By the time I left school for university I had definition, and didn't mind showing it. At the same time, I had been acting in supporting roles

Taunted by sea nymph
Amber Sainsbury.

in school productions (Lane in *The Importance of Being Earnest*, and Egeus in *A Midsummer Night's Dream*). My acting took off at the University of Auckland, where I joined my brother's first theatrical work as director-designer: Shakespeare's *The Tempest*, set in a swimming pool (Auckland's Tepid Baths). The pool was divided into stage and backstage by a hung sail, and a platform in the centre formed Prospero's island. My first entrance as the shipwrecked King Alonso was by swimming underwater from behind the sail, to surface, spluttering at centre-stage, as the storm was rendered with turbulent water and crazed lighting.

Although I was taking a degree in the sciences I fell in with the university theatre group, Stage Two Productions, that Sam had helped to form. More productions followed, mostly Shakespearian; I had roles as Lysander in *A Midsummer Night's Dream* and The Dauphin in *Henry V*. By my third year I had become president of Stage Two, and was overseeing several productions a year. I tried to cross over into acting roles in television, but talent, looks or (more likely) a combination of the two was lacking, and when the pattern of rejected auditions became undeniable I started to lose interest.

At that point in my life, although I had shown interest, and at times promise, in a variety of pursuits (chess, cycling, piano, debating, tennis, cricket, art, acting and cryptic crossword puzzles), I had never completely grasped the concept and necessity of training. Perhaps I had been duped by the 'gifted child' article into seeing all abilities as gifts: once I learnt the basics of a discipline I would discover to what extent I was naturally talented, and then that would be more or less my level. This changed when I started rowing during my final year at university. I was talked into joining the North Shore Rowing Club by my high-school friend Michael Trousdell (who would later prick my ears for the first time with his talk of freediving). The oldest of four giant brothers (although at 6 foot 6 inches he was the second-shortest), Michael kept his thick black hair cropped short and had a Fibonacci spiral tattooed on his shoulder. He was majoring in engineering, with minors in beer-drinking and snowboarding, and his loyalty and virtuous example have made him a strong inspiration in my life as well as a lifelong friend. We would rise at 4.30 a.m. to drive out to the rowing club in Greenhithe, from where we sculled through morning mists and past moored yachts, as far as the Auckland Harbour Bridge and back (a 24-kilometre round-trip). It was calming to be back on the water, and to feel its paradoxical state of being firm yet yielding, even if this was through the intermediary of an oar. Our slender crafts glided over a mirrored surface, propelled by a combination of legs extending and arms heaving on the oars. In this movement there is a striking similarity to the no-fins discipline of freediving, in which leg and arm phases are accompanied by periods of gliding in the water.

In the evenings we would lift weights at the university gym, ending the session with 10 kilometres on the 'erg' (stationary rowing machine) before I ran a few kilometres home to my apartment in Newmarket. My strength increased and my technique improved, and my trial times for 2-kilometre rows and 10-kilometre ergs got steadily shorter. I witnessed my body becoming stronger and more fit; I felt the refinements in balance and speed of the boat. For the first time, I appreciated just how important training was to success in any sport. And not just any training. It's one thing to submit yourself to the drills and regimens set by a coach, with the primary goal of 'getting through' the training — ticking the box, as it were. It's quite another to perform the same drills and regimens while focusing every moment on improving efficiency, controlling the mind and pushing yourself as hard as you can. I call this 'proactive training', and it may have been the most important feature of my career in freediving. Although I was lucky enough to train with and learn from many incredible divers, I never once had a formal coach–athlete partnership. Instead, I cracked the whip against my own back, and all the training programs, daily schedules, and decisions about depth and progression, diet and recovery were determined by myself — perhaps with consultation from others but ultimately with autonomy. At 100 metres below the surface we freedivers are more alone than almost any athlete on the planet, and need to be unequivocally at ease with this fact.

The first seed of appetite for training and driving my own self forwards was sown in that mild surge of enthusiasm for rowing. However, when I discovered freediving several years later I would commit every part of myself to this method, and to the idea that only through meticulous and sustained practice could I become all that I could be.

*

At university I was mostly taking papers in genetics, with a view to catching the cresting wave of technology in that field. The Human Genome Project was nearing its conclusion, and it looked like the next tech bubble was going to be written in the letters A, C, G and T (these denote four subunits in DNA, the order of which determines genetics). But towards the end of the degree course I started to lose interest. It was difficult to admit this to myself at the time, as there weren't any other obvious careers offering themselves as replacements. Nonetheless, my subconscious was already rebelling against the prospect of being a scientist. In fact, it might have been rebelling against everything about my rational, conscious mind, as evidenced by these words, which seemed to appear on the page in front of me one day in my own handwriting:

Trapped with my thoughts in the court of my head,
but the jury is dead and the plaintiff has fled.
There's no escape from this mental self-rape;
the disease of my reason is directed at treason and
the only defences are senses, so stimulate them.

Stimulate them I did, with the requisite university program of pub crawls, tequila blow-outs and spotties on the stove (a way of smoking cannabis). Not to mention what we did on the weekends ... As fun as it was, it was obviously not a fulfilling way to pass the time indefinitely. Without drink or drugs, that kind of blissful gratification can only be reached by an accomplishment that follows a certain amount of effort or anticipation. With these substances, I felt like I was reaching into my brain to press the pleasure button, bypassing the normal process of essay and attainment that it takes to experience those kinds of feelings. It felt like cheating. I wanted to experience the same sensation but with the fulfilment of knowing that I had taken the authentic route to get there.

It's significant that we talk about a 'calling' when describing a strongly magnetic vocation. If you pay attention then you might actually hear it calling for you, in many subtle ways. I'd even say that it's really a part of ourselves (one falling under the umbrella of the 'subconscious') that is more in tune with our true desires, or *dharma*, that is doing the calling. So it was when the words for a short poem formed in my mind on the dance floor of an Auckland night-club. A friend had talked me into going out as an alternative to going to bed, so I was sober, which made it an eerie and alien experience. I was too alert, too self-conscious. In more recent times I've felt that same sensation — being almost *too* present — in the minutes leading up to a record attempt or competition dive. That night, the only way I could escape the feeling was by fixating on the music and on a video being projected on one of the walls of the night-club. It showed graphics like a screensaver, which seemed to zoom into a morphing image without any point of arrival. I was able to shake off my hyper-alertness while I plunged into the music and those flickering images, and from that empty-minded state these words arose:

> *I have a relationship with the depths*
> *They beckon me beyond my means*
> *Cold, dark, vacant pressure*
> *Forever night, muted dreams.*

Even to me it seems that this could only have been written by a freediver, or at least someone with fervent dreams of becoming one. But at the time I had no such dreams. If you'd asked me, I might even have confused a freediver with someone who somersaults from cliffs into the water. Nonetheless, I felt those words and the gleam of significance they arrived with. I repeated them to myself while I danced, until they were firmly memorised and I could write them down when I got home.

But what kind of relationship with the depths did I have in those days? I lived in a flat renowned for its student parties, above a busy Newmarket street; I studied retroviruses and vector fields by day, drank beer and chased indifferent party girls by night. The only time I held my breath was after inhaling balloons filled with nitrous oxide (laughing gas) from whipped-cream chargers. Most of the time I wasn't consciously aware of anything lacking in my life, so it alarmed me a good deal when a perceptive friend suddenly stopped short in mid-conversation to exclaim, 'William, you're turning into a munter!' The indignation I felt at her words only demonstrated their nascent truth.

No, there was no relationship with the depths being had. Not in those years.

I did have high aspirations for myself, and felt, viscerally, as if I could only be satisfied by a truly singular accomplishment — but would never have admitted it, or had any idea what kind of accomplishment it might be. I was besotted with Alana, a girl in her senior year at university, who didn't need a dead-end romance with a confused man-boy but was kind enough to tell me, 'You'll go on to great things, I know it.' In the summer of 2000, when she visited me with friends at my parents' house, I tried to impress her by swimming, underwater, two laps of the 25-yard pool (equivalent to 47 metres DNF — 'Dynamic No Fins') at the private school where my mother taught. Before this, I hadn't swum more than about 30 metres underwater and still didn't know a thing about freediving, or even that such a sport existed. Turning after the first lap I felt the primal scream for air, made all the more intolerable by the fact that air was there, so tantalisingly close, above my head. I remember thinking that completing the second lap was the hardest thing I'd done in my life. Afterwards, when Alana asked me — with flat indifference — 'Was it worth it?', I didn't know what to say. Now I know that, yes, it was worth it.

All of the breadcrumbs that brought me closer to the gingerbread house that is freediving were worth it. For instance, there were the times when my brother and I would hold our breath while the family car was being driven over bridges. This was normally a matter of seconds, although the Auckland Harbour Bridge was a challenge that at first appeared insurmountable but was nonetheless met at some point, just as depths in my career have passed from the distant horizon of possibility into the rear-view mirror of the accomplished. Then there was the New Year's Eve (2001) rock concert by the shore in Napier. Friends I had gone to the party with had all hooked up with girls, and I wasn't relating to the crowd around me. On a whim, just before midnight, I walked outside the venue and down to the beach, stripped to my boxers and jumped in the sea. As the distant crowd chanted out the countdown, I took a breath and ducked underwater for the final seconds, re-emerging in a new year. I didn't become a freediver that year, or the next, but in hindsight it seems as if that night was a window to my future.

It took a year working as a scientist before I finally pulled the pin on that career path. The year was spent at Genesis, a genetics laboratory in Parnell, Auckland. Most of the work involved sequencing (reading the genetic code) of samples from New Zealand's agriculture and horticulture industries. I started in a small team of five that ran the sequencing machines, and progressed to leading the team by the end of the year. As much as it was a stable job and lifestyle, I felt I was betraying the caller and the dreamer in myself. I shifted liquids from one 96-well plate to another, added, removed, centrifuged and ran electrophoresis gels, and at the end of it the computer listed a stream of letters like AAAAGTGCAACAATGGTA CTTGGGACTAGCCTAGCATAT, which was recorded in a file somewhere. But what did I have to show for my time other than the pay cheque I received every two weeks? Of course, I was on the bottom rung of the science ladder, the idea being that with time I could climb to a point where I would engage more of my mind and creativity in genetic research. The next rung that was being offered was a place in an *Arabidopsis* (rock cress) phenotyping project. But I'd lost any vestige of patience, and so in the summer of 2002 I planned my escape: the OE (overseas experience) to Europe, with no fixed date of return.

*

I started by travelling to Samoa, one of the few Pacific island groups that we hadn't visited on *Hornpipe*, and a convenient stop-over on the way to America. At Auckland airport, my close friend Dwayne Cameron came to see me off and handed me a pellet of cannabis wrapped in tissue paper. Although I swallowed it right there before going through security, the tissue must have insulated its contents for a while, as the weed didn't kick in until the wee hours of the morning when I had already landed on the main island of Upolu. I drifted through the sleeping capital of Apia and sat on a beach listening to the portable CD player I had bought for the trip, waiting for sunrise when a tiny plane would take me across to the more rural island of Savai'i.

Once landed, a colourful, jouncing bus took me around the north coast road to where I would stay for a week in a collection of *fales* (huts) that adjoined the beach. At night, the gentle noises of wavelets folding onto the sandy beach stirred up memories from my childhood.

It felt right to be there. I didn't do anything during the day other than snorkel in the lagoon or hike up through the jungle to try to get a view of the island, but I was deeply satisfied and at home in a way that I could never be in a city or laboratory.

I spent the second week on the main island, living in Apia and being adopted by a group of *fa'afafine*, Samoa's third-gender people who embody both masculine and feminine gender traits, and have formed an integral part of the Samoan culture since at least the early twentieth century. They were the most fun-loving people I had ever met, and showed me the best beaches, swimming holes and bars on Upolu. One of the group, Candida, mentioned an underwater swim-through that connected two sea caves, and immediately I became fixated, bombarding her with questions: How deep was it? How far across? Was it dark? She eventually agreed to take me there, but it was obvious that she was concerned about my safety. The two parallel caves cut back in from the shore into the rock, and we were able to wade into the southern cave to the point where the swim-through started. Ducking under, I could see the glow of green light, and without thinking I started to swim towards it. After the second stroke my head collided with a bulge in the ceiling, eliciting a moment of panic; but it was okay, I was already nearly through. The distance was probably less than 10 metres and not very demanding at all, but it was still rewarding to pop up in a completely different cave among a group of confused swimmers. A minute later, Candida arrived in a frantic commotion — terrified of swimming through herself, she had run around to the other cave entrance to find out what had become of me.

*

From Samoa I flew to Los Angeles to rendezvous with Michael, who had completed a season of snowboarding in Jackson Hole, Wyoming. We drove to Tijuana in Mexico, arriving at 3 a.m., slept in the car and were woken and extorted by a policeman, took a look around town and decided to drive to Las Vegas, where we were extorted instead by street hustlers, croupiers and plastic-tasting breakfast buffets, before driving back to Los Angeles with our tails between our legs. I think my dislike for big cities might have been born around this time. Michael flew home to New Zealand, while I practised diving into the pool off the second-floor roof at Backpackers Paradise in Inglewood. I asked another backpacker to take my picture from the water as I dived over him, and took a slightly bigger run-up. I easily cleared him — and the deep end of the pool: soon after I hit the water my face encountered the concrete gradient where the bottom of the pool sloped up towards the shallow end. The tip of my nose was pressed flat against my right cheek, the sensation accompanied by the cracking of gristle. This break has meant that my left nostril doesn't ventilate as well as the right, making it more prone to infection from airway viruses. Now most head-colds and ear infections begin on the left side of my head, and my left sinuses are more prone to lingering inflammation. Since all these conditions make it impossible to equalise pressure in my middle ears or sinuses, and hence to freedive, that one foolish high-dive has probably been responsible for weeks or months of lost training and competition dives over the course of my career. The accident brought a conclusive end to any kind of aerial stunts for me. From then on I had more respect for gravity, and all my diving would be underwater.

After a road trip to Vancouver and Calgary I flew to London, a kind of default city for vagabond Kiwis in need of travel cash. It would be my base for the next nine months, during which time I worked as a porter/valet in a small Kensington boutique hotel, Blakes, that was frequented by celebrities wanting to maintain a low profile. There I earned more in tips than my wage as a scientist in New Zealand, and I started thinking about where I could travel to next. London, in fact megalopolises in general, were not for me — that much was clear. At 3 a.m. one

Saturday night I found myself at a North London house party, surrounded by a heaving mass of shirtless ghouls, pupils dilated and teeth grinding in time to some soulless music. I looked around and realised that I was as much a member of this crowd as any. 'I have to get out of here,' I told Michael — the only person I knew at the party. He seemed relieved at the suggestion.

Michael had arrived in London fresh with stories of a month in Thailand, where he had studied to be a scuba-dive master. In the same centre there had been some people practising 'freediving', and when he talked about them, and about the current champions such as the Italian Umberto Pelizzari, my attention was captivated in the same way it had been when Candida mentioned the underwater cave swim-through in Samoa. This was the intersection in my life when the world of freediving — a world that had been bustling along without my knowing it, a world with its own history, protagonists, rivalries, records, tragedies, cultures and myths — made its presence known to me. In the following days and weeks, I read interviews with the top freedivers, looked up definitions for *pranayama* and other techniques they employed, held my breath on my bed (my first attempt was a pretty ordinary 2:15 — 2 minutes 15 seconds) and dreamt, wondered … what would it be like?

CHAPTER 3

RETURN

Chasing light beams down into the abyss

He is at one with every swarm of lime-green fish, with
every coloured sponge. As he holds himself to the
ocean's faery floor, one hand clasped to a bedded
whale's rib, he is complete and infinite. Pulse, power
and universe sway in his body. He is in love.

Mervyn Peake, *Titus Groan*

THE DOOR TO WHAT HAD JUST BECOME my ex-flat in
Wimbledon, London, closed behind me. I carefully
unfolded a square of tissue paper and took its contents
between thumb and forefinger: a pill that looked like a
biscuit crumb—small, misshapen and earth-coloured.
My mother had given it to me the year before, one of three
she had received from an emissary of the Dalai Lama.
They were known as 'compassion pills', and had been
created and blessed by Tenzin Gyatso, the fourteenth in

the line of Dalai Lamas (*dalai* is a Mongolic word for 'ocean' or 'big', while *lama* is Tibetan for 'guru'). I'd been saving this compassion pill for the right moment, which was now. The January air was clear and crisp with frost. As the crumb dissolved beneath my tongue, I shouldered my backpack and set out for the train station.

It was 2003, the year I returned to the sea — and found freediving. When you lie on the surface of the ocean and gaze into its depths, you have no idea of what is contained in that void below. Likewise, I had no idea where this voyage back to the Caribbean would take me. I had a flight booked to Belize, with the vague intention of following the coast of the Caribbean Sea down the Central American isthmus. En route I spent two nights in Miami, where I bought wetsuit, mask, fins and a flimsy pole spear; my evenings were occupied with drinking and courting South Beach girls (even the Dalai Lama's magic can't cure all vices!).

In Belize, an airport bus took me and some scuba-diving tourists to the port, from where a motorised skiff ferried us to the nearby islands scattered among the offshore barrier reef. The long, narrow powerboat swept in broad turns between low, mangrove-covered cays as I listened in my headphones to Tracey Carmen's chanted cover of 'Song to the Siren'.

*

Like most Caribbean islands, Caye Caulker had a pretty side, where the bars and backpackers' spilled onto the beach, and a more run-down backside of mangroves and shanty homes. I had a bed in the cheapest backpackers', where the beleaguered matron raved and ranted at her guests for their messy habits. She would inevitably win each battle, but I suspected that with a complete refresh of guests every few days she was never going to win the war.

I wasn't there for the customer service or the beaches, however, and quickly found a scuba-dive company that didn't mind me tagging along on their trips. On the first day we were taken to a site in 15 to 20 metres of water. The guide led his retinue of tourists down to the bottom, columns of bubbles ascending from each cluster of hoses and aluminium tanks. I watched from the surface, breathing through my snorkel, wondering whether I could reach the same depth. To my surprise, on my first attempt I swam all the way to just off the bottom, and spent several seconds there gazing around. I was floating above a landscape of undulating coral ridges, separated by strips of sand that filled the valleys between them. Fish flickered, bounced and soared in the midwater, swarmed and spun above distinct coral outcroppings, or slunk through coral hedges and shady gullies. Surface waves split the sun into flickering beams that tattooed erratic patterns of light over the whole scene.

I absorbed the sight, and for a moment my mind was a silent observer. Three years previously, living in that urban student flat in Auckland and with no physical escape other than lifting grimy weights in a basement gym, I had felt like I was 'trapped with my thoughts in the court of my head'. Now, as I held my breath and absorbed the underwater vista, I had broken free, for the briefest moment, from that unsolicited podcast, that relentless stream of internal dialogue. I was my naked self behind my mind.

Into that empty space my ego was quick to expand, pointing out that since I was at the same depth as the nearby scuba divers I could flaunt my newfound aquatic prowess to them in many creative ways! So I shadowed them on the surface, and for the rest of the session swam down to startle the group from behind, cruise disinterestedly past in front of them, or appear magically inside a wreck they were exploring. I was thrilling over the ease and naturalness of unencumbered underwater movement, and wanted an audience for it. Afterwards, aboard the dive boat, the guide scolded me as he swung his tank and buoyancy jacket onto the deck: 'Stay out of my way when you're doing that — it spooks the guests.' For the rest of my time in Belize, and subsequently in Honduras, I kept a respectful distance from any scuba divers. When we did encounter each other on occasion, rounding the corner of a submerged buttress or approaching from opposite directions of a coral alleyway, it was like coming across a busload of package-tour sightseers while hiking in the forest.

Instead of the scuba divers, I played with the full-time residents of the sea — like sting-rays, nurse sharks and barracudas. The rays looked like stealth bombers as they approached, hovercrafting inches above the sandy seabed. In a game of underwater chicken their bluff is easy to call — at the last minute they would wing up and glide over the top of me, revealing soft white underbellies broken only by a quirky mouth like that of a mischievous child.

I visited the Great Blue Hole, a murky aperture in Belize's reef that only really looks good in aerial photos. As the sun set on each day, I practised the yogic breathing exercise *pranayama*, sitting on the end of a long pier that extended towards the waves breaking over the barrier reef. After half an hour with my eyes closed, concentrating on slowly measured inhales, exhales that were twice as slow again, and a hold between the two that was twice the exhale, I would open my eyes and witness a scene that seemed almost *too* real. For a period my gaze had no focal point or periphery:

I could take in the sight of everything in front of me, all at once. The waves, reflecting the evening sun and forming a flickering pattern that gradually compressed into the crisp line of the horizon. A pelican, resting atop an old dock post, its bill smugly tucked into its ruff. The scarlet clouds that blushed the twilight sky over the ocean ...

I had made arrangements to meet with Dwayne, who had been in Los Angeles pursuing his acting career. One day, as I walked back to my hostel, I heard a hiss from the bushes — and there he was, the friend I called 'Snake' due to the influence he'd had on me in Auckland. We took a bus into the depths of the Central American jungle, to Bullet Tree Falls near the border with Guatemala. There a different kind of water, the cabbage-green Mopan River, slid through the steaming jungle, bearing Dwayne and me afloat on our inner tubes with bottles of warm beer in our laps. I felt like Bilbo in his barrel, drifting through Mirkwood.

Belize was fun, but expensive, and there was nowhere close to the islands where I could reach deep water. Scuba divers I talked to recommended that I travel to the Bay Islands in Honduras, where prices for rooms and meals were in single digits. (Honduras was the name allegedly given to the area by Christopher Columbus in 1502 and literally means 'depths'.)

Nowadays I wouldn't travel without an itinerary, but when I set off for Honduras from Belize I had only a vague idea of how to get there, and that could be summarised by one word: south. From Belize City a bus took all day to travel a hundred miles down the coast to Punta Gorda, which was the end of the line as far as roads were concerned. To continue into Guatemala required a boat, but the next to leave wouldn't go until the following day. So, I walked down the dusty streets past greasy chicken-fry stalls and the occasional convenience store until I found a place advertising rooms. There were cockroaches on the walls even before I turned off the lights, and the bed was made up with damp sheets stretched over a landscape of broken springs. Later that year I would sleep on a granite slab with only a towel for bedding, so this was by no means a low point.

The boat ride across to Puerto Barrios in Guatemala took about an hour, and from there I negotiated a taxi to take me to the border with Honduras. A bribe and a bus took me onwards to San Pedro Sula; this seemed like a pretty shady city to me at the time, and I held my bags close while waiting for my connection. I would later find out that San Pedro Sula is the most violent city on earth, with 187 homicides yearly per 100,000 people (over 100 times the rate in Auckland). The bus from there followed the coastline, which in this part of Central America runs east–west, to La Ceiba, the main Caribbean port of Honduras. After a night in a backpackers' with huge open rooms that reminded me of dormitories at school camp, I bought a ticket for the ferry to Utila almost directly north. The smallest of Honduras's three 'Bay Islands', the locals are descendants of English, French and Dutch pirates, including Henry Morgan, who used it as a base for his raids on gold-laden Spanish armadas returning from the New World.

*

Huddled together off the protected western end of Utila lie a series of tiny football-field-sized islands called The Cays, which have become a kind of *Waterworld* community of fishermen and boat builders. It's impossible to know the true shape of these tiny islands, covered as they are by a mass of tightly packed houses that all front onto the same central walkway. Bridges connect the islands, and the houses are backed out over the water on poles, with their toilets at the rear. A cool sea breeze blows over your nether regions as you soil the clean blue water below.

As I walked past the playground of the tiny school, children taunted me with the name 'Miguelito', for reasons I never deciphered. They also taunted an old man who was unlucky enough to live next to the school, and who answered the rocks the children threw on his roof with brayings of broken Spanish insults to their mothers.

I lived with some scuba instructors on a tiny island called Little Rock, squared off with cement walls and connected to the main walkway by an actual drawbridge. I slept in my bed perhaps twice; the hammock outside under the stars was a far more luxurious, air-conditioned and mouldable nest. In a hammock you need to lie on a slight angle in order to be flat, and when you do this the edges of the hammock curl up around you to create a kind of cocoon that you can line with thin bedsheets to protect against mosquitoes. I relished the sensation of being immersed in nature while I dreamt: the wind in the willowy casuarina trees, the slap of the waves, the creaking of boats at the dock. These sounds became familiar and soporific. I was like a parrotfish, which in the evening finds a coral alcove and secretes a mucus sleeping bag around itself to shield it from predators and parasites. Next to us, a formidable lady operated a fishing business employing a dozen or more 'Caribs', an ethnicity descended from African slaves who had bred with Native Americans. They somehow all slept in a tiny shack not much larger than a bedroom. We were woken one night to find one of these men stealing the stereo and CDs from our living room. Startled, he abandoned his loot and jumped into the sea to swim the short stretch back to his shack, and was gone the next day on an early boat.

Each morning the dive boat would arrive from Utila town to pick up those staying on The Cays, and would continue on to the north side of the island, where the best dive sites were. Our captain was John Wayne. Although born the same year as me, he had consumed twice the quota of years, teeth and rum. But he kept the old dive boat and its diesel engine running, and drove it prodigiously, once managing to surf it over a shallow reef by perfectly timing his approach to coincide with the swell and ride its steep face across to deeper water.

Honduras is where, over the course of two months early in 2003, I became a freediver. I was always the first off the dive boat and into the water, quickly pulling on mask and fins while the scuba divers were shouldering their heavy aluminium life-support. Choosing a direction that normally followed the shoulder where the reef drops from shallow to deep water, and which is a kind of coastal highway for underwater life, I would set off in search of a new discovery, be it sea creature, coral garden, grotto or swim-through. Barracudas would stalk behind me, gunmetal tubes of muscle that can accelerate faster than any other fish. Ocean triggerfish kept a wary distance but were intrigued by my descents, and I would often find that they had followed me from the surface

Gliding above the reef of Utila, Honduras. (*Adam Laverty*)

to 30 metres or more down. Groupers and moray eels rested their chins on the thresholds to their lairs. Tiny electric-blue fish swarmed with small wrasse above coral heads, waiting for mouths to clean.

In many dive sites there was a maze of sandy gullies through the reef, and these were my favourite places to enjoy being underwater. The depth was only 10 metres and after relaxing and breathing on the surface I would slowly swim to the soft seabed. There I was barely negatively buoyant, meaning that I could lie almost weightless on the sand, resting on my feet, knees and elbows. Tiny fish with cartoon eyes would swim out on bouncy trajectories from their safe spots to have a closer look at this massive interloper. Shrimp with limbs like glass spindles rummaged through the sand along the edge of the gullies. The closer you looked, the more activity, life and vivacity there was to see. Just as enjoyable was closing my eyes and surrendering to my environment, trusting it and its populace. In these moments my consciousness would go inwards. The sensation of not requiring breath, of being completely integrated into the underwater world, could last minutes.

At other times I ventured out from the sheer drop-off that marked the edge of the reef. I would spend a few minutes floating over the bottomless water, before duck-diving and swimming to just below the level of the adjacent reef table. There I stopped finning, and let my negative buoyancy draw me deeper. In front of me I watched the underwater cliff face, draped like a

The scuba gauge I held in my hand in order to tell depth during my first year of freediving.

Christmas tree with bright sponges and sea fans, slip past at increasing speed. Spotted eagle rays soared past a distant outcrop. I plummeted down, changing my trajectory with subtle movements of my tail-fins. The decision as to when to turn and come back up was made by consulting two things. One was a crude scuba gauge measuring depth in feet, which had been popped out of the 'octopus' of a scuba rig. I held it in my hand, glancing at it periodically to check the position of the needle. The first 30 feet (9 metres) were shown in blue, the next 30 in green, 60 to 90 feet (18 to 27 metres) was yellow, and this was where I would become negatively buoyant and stop finning. From 90 feet (27 metres) onwards the dial was orange, and here I imagined I was entering the 'danger zone'. I felt the pressure of the water column above me as a constriction in my diaphragm and windpipe, and had to make an effort to equalise my ears and my mask, which was being crushed onto my face. I didn't know it then, but my lungs had been compressed to their residual volume, which is the volume of air that remains after a full exhale. To continue below this depth means that the lungs are reduced to volumes that are physically impossible to attain by exhaling on the surface. The day I saw the needle pass into the red zone deeper than 120 feet (37 metres) — red because it is beyond the limits of recreational scuba diving — filled me with a sense of both awe and pride at having visited such a profound stratum of the ocean. In my career I would reach a depth more than three times as great, but I wouldn't have believed anyone who told me that at the time.

The other meter I would consult to determine when to turn back towards light and air was an internal gauge. Our bodies' levels of carbon dioxide rise while we hold our breath, in concert with the falling level of oxygen. Carbon dioxide is the waste gas of cellular respiration and stimulates the urge to breathe, provoking a suffocating feeling when we resist it. However, with time and familiarity we can learn to make peace with the sensation and use it as an indicator of how far we are through our reserves of oxygen. This is why it is so important not to over-ventilate (breathe too deeply or rapidly) before a dive, as the signal to return to the surface may come later than normal — when you have used up too much oxygen and don't have enough left for the return journey to the surface. Only through gradual increments over the course of weeks and months, and through learning how to read my body more accurately, could I feel confident in inching that needle a little further round its dial; in waiting a little longer, sinking a little deeper, before turning back for the surface.

The ascent is where we freedivers pay for our free ticket down. As soon as I turned upright I had to push hard with my fins to counter gravity's pull on my negatively buoyant body. I kept my hands by my sides and was careful never to look upwards, which would break my streamline as well as possibly cause alarm if the surface appeared further off than I expected. Gradually the ambient light increased, and the reef wall in front of me passed from the slumber of deep blue to lighter greens, yellows, and finally the shortest wavelength colours of oranges and reds. Pillars of exhaled bubbles extended from the location of nearby scuba divers. John Wayne, my safety diver for the day and himself a proficient freediver, appeared in front of me, studying my face for signs of difficulty. Each surfacing, and there were hundreds during the two months I spent in Honduras, was a rebirth, a whoop of exultation for the journey I had just completed, and a surge of excitement at what I had discovered, within myself as well as within the waters I penetrated.

Once a week there would be a night dive, which offered a completely different experience of the underwater world. At night, shrimps, lobsters and other scavengers inherit the reef, while the daytime reef-grazers like parrotfish sleep in their mucus cocoons. The beam of an underwater light would pick out tiny transparent fish and crustaceans, and bigger nocturnal prowlers like jacks and barracuda would flash through the beam to grab at these suddenly illuminated morsels.

At first I couldn't ignore an awareness of how small the window of light I created was, and how much of the water around me was an unknowable black. When paranoia bubbled over I would swing my light beam around to slash at the shadows, expecting to see — what else? — a shark, but there was never anything there and I gradually grew calmer.

The first time I switched off my light, the sensation of fear-tinged surrender was exhilarating — a delicious flutter below the sternum. Underwater darkness is blacker than anything above the surface, since, like ink or pitch, the darkness has a liquid medium. The water isn't just dark; it is darkness as a *substance*. Coordinates in this empty nothingness are picked out by phosphorescent organisms that are excited into light by movement. After swimming to a sandy bottom at 15 metres I would turn off my light and ascend with arms stretched out above me. Streams of phosphorescent sparks were ignited by my fingertips and cascaded in a flurry down my body. I was travelling at warp speed through a river of stars and galaxies that collided with the glass lens of my mask and ricocheted into my peripheral vision. As I burst through the skin of the water's surface my journey ended, and the stars congealed into the fixed constellations of the night sky above.

This was my life for two months. It seemed as if my childhood life on the boat had been spliced seamlessly with this new experience of the water; as if the intervening 15 years had never happened. Such is the timeless quality of the ocean. One night early in my stay I had one of those dreams that are so vivid and heavy with meaning that they seem more like a visitation. My oldest childhood friend, Damien Duff, appeared and told me repeatedly, 'Stand in your dream,' before shaking my hand and vanishing. I forgot to e-mail to ask him whether he was okay, or at least whether he had developed powers of witchcraft that allowed him to infiltrate others' dreams, but I never forgot the message he delivered. It was a confirmation that the life I had begun was my *dharma*, my 'personal legend' as Paulo Coelho's alchemist calls it. This was my dream, but to inhabit it I would have to stand true, and weather the winds of opposition that challenge us in our course. As the Māori proverb says,

> *Tama tū, tama ora (He who stands lives)*
> *Tama moe, tama mate (He who sleeps dies)*

I swam with dolphins, sharks, turtles, eagle rays, moray eels and one very bashful little seahorse. I lay blissfully in sandy-bottomed caves where groups of scuba divers would come across me, become alarmed and attempt to shove a regulator in my mouth. I came face to face with a whale shark as it ascended under the boat in the same moment that I dove into the water. These slow-moving leviathans are the biggest fish in the sea, and were easy to locate as they followed the balls of bait fish, which in turn were indicated from a distance by diving seabirds and jumping tuna.

In a group e-mail at the end of my stay in Honduras I wrote, 'On my last day I asked John Wayne to take the boat a way offshore, and jumped in with a dive instructor, Adam Laverty, for surface backup. I took a few hundred breaths, jackknifed, flapped down to 152 feet [46 metres], turned around, shut my eyes and hurtled back up again. The extreme pressure, panic and exhilaration on breaking the surface are going to take some getting used to, but I am taking a course with the world champ, Umberto Pelizzari, in Sardinia which should address these. My hair has been bleached the same light brown that my skin has been tanned to, so I am now a universal shade of shit. I am also growing a 24-carat mullet to remind me of home, or at least Henderson. In short, I look like your typical Kiwi travelling tramp.'

I celebrated breaking the milestone of 150 feet (46 metres), as well as the end of my stay on Utila, with a night at Bar in the Bush, where I guzzled the local brew (somewhat misleadingly named Salva Vida, or 'lifesaver' in Spanish) until I ate the napkin along with my burger and danced a Scottish jig ... or so I'm told.

*

My time in Honduras had re-acquainted me with the underwater world of my youth, and introduced me to the concept of freediving as a sport. I knew that if I wanted to pursue it further I would need to learn from an expert. Together with my close high-school friend Michael Trousdell, who had first grabbed my attention with his talk of freediving, we planned to attend a course run by the Italian maestro Umberto Pelizzari. Pelizzari was the greatest freediver of his generation, having set world records in all disciplines throughout the 1990s before retiring in 2001 and founding a school called Apnea Academy.

I met Michael where he was living in Valencia, and we trained for several weeks in a pool there ahead of the course. During this time I made the commitment to quit alcohol, caffeine and all foods with added sugar. These three pillars of modern nutrition definitely add a lot of colour to life, but they can also blur its edges. To become a better freediver, the energetic systems I would need to enhance have biochemical pathways that operate behind the scenes, with subtle and continuous use of adrenal glands, liver, spleen, nervous and cardiovascular systems, and more. Alcohol, caffeine and sugar gatecrash these organs and make a mess all over the walls and carpet for someone else to clean up. As a Kiwi it was a hard thing to give up drinking altogether, but luckily I wasn't in New Zealand when I did it. Sugar was a struggle too, but I soon found that I appreciated food more for its nutritional content, and relished a bunch of crimson grapes or a glass of freshly squeezed orange juice not just for its sweetness but also for the sensation that goes with absorbing nature's bounties, unfiltered and unprocessed. Within several weeks I found I had more consistent energy and attention throughout the day. I slept better and was more stable emotionally. Most importantly, I could tolerate greater training loads and recover from them more quickly.

During this time training in Valencia, I also suffered the first blackout of my freediving career. It's a story worth telling, not just for a laugh but also because it shows how different an experience it is to what one might imagine. We had been doing dynamic apnea (breath-holds where the goal is to swim maximum distance underwater in a pool) after having first exhaled all air from our lungs. On this occasion I was attempting to swim a full lap of the Olympic pool (50 metres) for the first time with empty lungs. It's not an exercise that I now consider worthwhile, but back then I was a rookie full of ideas. As you would imagine, when there is very little oxygen stored in the lungs your body depletes its stores of oxygen in blood and muscle very rapidly. At 20 to 30 metres into the swim I was feeling this deficit already, but continued swimming. At around 40 metres I clearly remember looking up, seeing the wall not too far away, and thinking, 'I can make this.' Then I was sitting on the edge of the pool, looking back at the same wall about 5 metres away, thinking, 'Not only did I make it to the end, but I turned and came back another 5 metres!'

'Wow, did I just swim 55 metres on an exhale?!' I asked Michael, whose hands were grasping me in a strange way under my armpits. Then I realised that there was someone else also holding me — a very flustered Spanish lifeguard. My reality turned upside down. Michael explained: my strokes had got weaker and weaker, ending with my hands stretched out while still doing tiny strokes with my fingers only. He had jumped in at that point, and had pulled me unconscious to the surface. The lifeguard, seeing a limp and ashen-faced swimmer being manoeuvred to the side of the pool, catapulted himself into action. He sprinted around the pool edge, yelling *'Ayuda! Ayuda!'* before grabbing my arms and yanking me onto the pool deck. If I had come to a few seconds later, then it would have probably been with his lips clamped on mine and stale air being forced into my windpipe. As it was, I was half-seated on the side of the pool, facing back towards the direction I'd been headed, and my brain had seamlessly stitched together the earlier conviction that I would swim the full lap with the fact that I was now evidently 5 metres beyond it.

There is very little warning of a blackout, especially if the initial carbon dioxide levels in the body are low. Neither is there really any memory of the event afterwards. If we don't dream during a blackout (and some freedivers do actually have short, time-bending dreams, where they manage a full storyline in the 5 to 10 seconds that they're unconscious) then there is nothing to mark the event — just like if it wasn't for dreams then we wouldn't remember anything of sleeping. A blackout experience is very different for safety divers, who go from watching their buddy holding his or her breath to what feels like trying to bring a zombie back to life. Hypoxia (low oxygen) and decreased circulation to the skin suck all the colour out of the freediver's face, and when unconscious the eyes will naturally roll upwards into the skull. Although medical science confirms that oxygen levels at the time of a blackout are still three times greater than the threshold for brain damage, it is still difficult not to be affected by the sight of someone who looks like they've just been dredged up from the bottom of a lake.

To date this remains my only blackout in dynamic apnea, a discipline where you are able to surface whenever you choose — meaning that it's really only stubbornness that will cause you to over-reach. Diving in the ocean is a different scenario: we must determine the difficulty of the performance when setting the depth of the line before the dive, or at the latest halfway through the dive when choosing to turn. At that point you're committed to the swim, and if you realise you've made even a small error in judgement, in most cases there's nothing you can do about it. So, you keep swimming in the knowledge that should you have a problem your safety diver will be alongside you to assist and bring you to the surface.

After this incident we were banned from practising apnea in the pool where we'd been training. Luckily, our trip to Sardinia for the course with Umberto wasn't far off. Writing about the trip afterwards, Michael and I renamed ourselves after the clumsy detectives in the Tintin cartoon books: Thompson (Michael) and Thomson (me). 'The journey from Spain to Sardinia started as optimistically as our fresh mullet haircuts, when our rental car was double-upgraded from a bubble to a little diesel buggy. After refuelling with petrol we ground to a halt close to the French border, where Thompson (with a p) was sent under the car to drain the petrol, and demonstrated his concern for ecology by soaking the petrol up with his hair. An hour later Thompson and Thomson were back on the road, racing into Marseille to catch the ferry. Since they hadn't reserved beds for the overnight crossing to Corsica, they ended up sleeping on the ship's bar room couches. The ferry staff had the politeness to leave the air-conditioning set to sub-zero, and Thomson (without a p) had the politeness to rehang their fine curtains after using them for bedding.'

Santa Teresa di Gallura is a sleepy fishing village by winter and a booming holiday resort by summer. It is at the northern-most end of the Italian island of Sardinia, and faces the French island of Corsica across a 12-kilometre-wide strait. After we'd arrived, the next day and the rest of the week were spent under the tutelage of Umberto Pelizzari, who would become my most influential mentor in freediving. He is also a dedicated exhibitionist, as the Japanese student who left her camera unguarded aboard the dive boat found out! The course was intensive, and invaluable for its coverage of both technique and theory. Using the weighted sled, which eliminates energy expense on the descent, I became comfortable at 50 metres. With Umberto diving alongside me, I managed an unassisted (No Fins) dive to about 35 metres.

The end of the course and Michael's imminent twenty-fourth birthday were two good enough reasons to break our seven-week wagon ride, and get 'on the rip' Kiwi-style. Six pints later, and halfpint-without-a-p-Thomson dropped straight out the bottom, leaving Thompson (without his p's or q's) abashedly pouring the G&Ts that an Englishman was shouting into a handily located pot plant. After that, Thompson returned to Spain and I was left to fend for myself in Santa Teresa, with rental prices skyrocketing as the Italian summer holiday kicked in. An apartment that costs €300 to rent for a month in the winter can be €1500 *per week* in the height of summer. I was determined to stay on in Santa Teresa, to continue training and be close to Pelizzari's school, but I found

Practising *pranayama* on a familiar rock above Santa Teresa beach, Sardinia, Italy.

myself without anywhere affordable to stay. To the left of the village a peninsula adorned with smooth granite boulders extends north into the strait. I left my luggage at the dive school and walked to the end of this promontory, where a slab of rock and two beach towels made my bed for the night. The experience showed me how determined and impassioned I was in the path I was pursuing. Although the night was mostly a succession of uncomfortable and damp awakenings, I remember it fondly; perhaps because it was the moment when I first placed the realisation of my dreams above creature comforts.

After that night I moved between grubby accommodations, sharing with South American restaurant workers, until the flocks of Italian holiday-makers had returned to Milan and Rome, and prices dropped again. By September, Santa Teresa had quietened back into a tranquil Mediterranean seaside village. I continued my training in the bay, with long dives to the sand bottom at 30 metres, or apnea hiking (breathing once every 10 to 30 steps) along the tracks of Punta Contessa, a seaside nature reserve next to the village.

I was learning Italian as quickly as I could, since I had noticed an opportunity: Pelizzari's freediving manual hadn't been translated into English, and there were no good English books on freediving. Uncommonly for languages, Italian actually follows the rules it lays down, with very few exceptions, making it mathematical and easy to learn. Within four months I was reading Paulo Coelho in Italian. Although my spoken Italian was still very poor, written translation mostly requires comprehension of the source language and a good command of the language you're translating into, so I knew I could handle a technical text on a familiar subject. Nonetheless, when I called Umberto (who had returned to Milan for the winter) to propose myself as his translator, I was nervous that my stammered Italian and thick accent would make my offer laughable. To my surprise he accepted, and this expression of faith in my abilities was one of the greatest gifts that he gave me. Suddenly I had my first job in almost a year — and not a moment too soon, as I had reached the point of paying attention to what came after the decimal point on bank transactions.

As the incessant nor-westerly winds settled in for the winter, I settled into a rhythm of working long hours on my laptop interspersed with sessions of yoga, apnea hiking and breath-hold training, with perhaps a cold-water dive if the wind relented. Small poetic encounters defined my experience of living for the first time mostly alone in a foreign country. A nun, somewhere inside a pyramid of white with a skylight for her chocolate African face, passes a weather-beaten Sardinian with a white captain's hat and a stick. The two stop and say a few words to each other before the nun signs the cross over the sea-dog and they continue on their separate ways. A group of schoolboys pile into the library where I am vacillating over an Italian–English dictionary the size of a double bed. Three advance to my table clutching a picture-book biography of Pelizzari, which they pore over, whispering excitedly. When I tell them I'm writing an English version of his freediving manual, they look at me as if I am a messenger from Neptune.

An overzealous (but rather good) fireworks display is released from the village castle, but it's still too dry and windy, and when the brush catches fire, half the surrounding hillside is burnt to a crisp. The 130-kilogram owner of the *frutteria* bags my mushrooms, grapes and panini before chucking in a box of peanuts as a *regalo* (gift) — he remembers I don't eat sweet food. As I am getting out of my wetsuit, a fisherman asks me whether I saw any fish in the bay. I reply that where he's sitting, he has more chance of catching Osama bin Laden. He smiles and doesn't look at all bothered. I find a fragment of pottery, including a handle of what might have been an urn, lying on the sandy seabed outside the bay. I have no idea how old it is, so it holds its worth a secret, sitting on my mantelpiece. In the midst of so much water, a seahorse floats alone close to the surface, its journey mostly determined by the currents and the waves. I stop and float a while next to the tiny *Hippocampus*, watching it and wondering if it sees me in the same way I see it, as company.

One of my only acquaintances was my landlord, Tiziana, a slim and elegant Sardinian property manager in her early thirties, with a candid but fun-loving personality, whom I would see once a month when paying the rent. Just before I was due to leave for New Zealand she surprised me by inviting me out for pizza, and although little happened that night, a romance bloomed. It endured several months by e-mail until I returned to Santa Teresa in 2004 and eventually moved in with her. This was my first long-term relationship, and although over the next four years our differences gradually became inescapable until we eventually parted in 2008, it helped me to shed a lot of the crude and selfish ways left over from my youth.

*

Towards the end of 2003, on a windy late-afternoon walk, I found myself on a granite buttress of rock looking west across the Mediterranean Sea that was alive with white-caps. The wind was a nor-wester, of the type that in Italian is given the name *tramontana*. I would later give this name to my house in the Bahamas, as it was the *tramontana* that drove me from the Mediterranean to look for calmer waters, to ultimately arrive on Long Island, home of Dean's Blue Hole. Although it confounded my training in the sea, that Italian wind was invigorating, as if it contained an abundance of what in yoga is called *prana*, or life-force energy. It filled my nose, mouth, ears and eyes, and the gusts buffeted my body as I stood and contemplated what lay ahead for me. I now knew that freediving was my passion and my path. I relished the idea of dedicating myself to it, of giving over every aspect of myself in the quest to redefine human aquatic limits.

At night I dreamt of a man who went through life breathing only when necessary, like a dolphin, and who had removed the hair and ears from his body in order to be able to glide naked to unfathomable depths: 100 metres and beyond. At that time the world record in unassisted freediving was 60 metres, a depth that had blown my mind the year before when I'd seen the video of Finnish freediver Topi Lintukangas powering himself down and up with just his hands and feet. Lintukangas had been a professional triathlete who had crossed over to freediving, and reached this depth after only a few years of training. I believed that if someone trained relentlessly, for a longer duration, then depths beyond 60 metres must be achievable. I was 23 years old on that autumn day in Sardinia. As the wind bled salty streams from my eyes, I set myself the goal of reaching a depth of 76 metres, or 250 feet, by the time I was 25. It was an audacious goal — the world record with a monofin was only 10 metres deeper. If I had announced this goal, people would have said that I was presumptuous and deluded; after all, I was a nobody in the sport, a 40-metre diver who had never even competed. So I resolved to tell no one, to keep my dream a secret until it had become reality.

If ever in my career there was a moment of crossing a line into total dedication, then this was it. It was both a liberating and a precarious moment. When we admit to ourselves that we are fully committed to something, the shore we set out from slips over the horizon behind us. We finally cast off many of the doubts that were holding us back from making that commitment, but their place is suddenly filled with a keen awareness of the vast tracts of open ocean that separate us from the point of arrival.

I turned from that view, and made my way back to my rented apartment in Santa Teresa, thrumming with determination and anticipation of the year ahead. Despite my hopes, in 2004 my body would become practically allergic to the depths, and every ounce of my nascent commitment would be put to the test.

Dean's Blue Hole, Long Island, Bahamas. At 202 metres of depth, it is the second deepest Blue Hole in the world and provided the perfect location for my 2007 world-record attempt.

Freefalling into Dean's Blue Hole in the purest discipline of freediving: Constant Weight No Fins. I still recall with clarity the morning that I walked onto the beach and came face-to-face for the first time with that lens of deep blue water in the corner of the sandy lagoon. *(Igor Liberti)*

CHAPTER 4

SETBACKS

Cold nor-westerlies and lingering colds

In sports, words are words, explanations are explanations,
goals are goals, but only performance is reality.

Harold Geneen (paraphrased from quote on business)

AT THE START OF 2004, I thought I already knew all about freediving. By the end of that year, however, I had realised that I knew as much about the sport as a seagull flying across a pitch knows about the game of cricket. Sometimes it takes a while to graduate to the level of complete beginner.

Having exhausted my travelling funds, I returned to New Zealand for the first time in two years, to await the proceeds of the translation job I had just finished. During this time my training centred on a theory, proposed by Australian diver Sebastien Murat, that it is more efficient to dive after having exhaled about half the air in the lungs, a technique used by some of the deepest-diving aquatic mammals such as sperm whales and elephant seals. The difference between them and us, as I would later discover through conducting my own research into the topic, is that these species have been forced into exhale-diving as a way of saving energy in the long run. Living in cold climates, their bodies are already buoyant with insulating blubber, and if they filled their lungs with air as well then the descent would become too strenuous and the overall energy required for a dive to a given depth would skyrocket. To compensate, oxygen storage systems have evolved in these mammals' blood and muscles: tissues that are incompressible and therefore don't contribute to buoyancy. An elephant seal stores 96 per cent of its oxygen in its red blood cells and in myoglobin organelles embedded in muscle tissue — and only 4 per cent in its lungs. By comparison, we humans typically store 28 per cent of our oxygen in myoglobin and haemoglobin combined; although that can increase with training, we will always still be reliant on oxygen stored in our lungs. Furthermore, a fit freediver has very little body fat, and can actually make a dive more energy-expensive by exhaling! Our physiologies are much more similar to those of warm-water aquatic mammals like dolphins, which inhale before diving.

However, I was then oblivious to these differences

as I trekked backwards and forwards across my parents' garden while holding my breath with half-empty lungs. This exercise, known as apnea walking, is popular among those who don't have access to depth or a pool. It is also fairly easy to push any given repetition to the point of wetting yourself, passing out, or both (which makes a private garden a better setting for it than a public courtyard).

*

As the New Zealand summer started to give way to frosts and cold southerlies, I packed my dive gear into a giant canvas carry-all and boarded a flight back towards Europe. I would stop first in Sharm El Sheikh, in Egypt, where an Italian training camp and competition was being organised by the Apnea Academy. Around 200 freedivers, from newbies to seasoned champions like Umberto, were all eating, diving and lounging on the coast of the Red Sea, in a massive all-inclusive resort called Coral Bay, so large it had minibuses to shuttle guests from the restaurant to their rooms.

The lengthy travel had left me recovering from a cold, so after arriving I was straining to dive with residual congestion in my nose and sinuses. The repercussions of this critical mistake would haunt me for many months to come. A freediver's airways must be in pristine condition in order to equalise the ears and sinuses during a dive. Any small blockage means a rigid cavity that won't be in communication with the lungs and can't be pressurised to match the surrounding water, resulting in barotrauma such as burst eardrums and bleeding sinuses. It's further testimony to just how clueless I was that I thought I would be able, on my first deep dive with a monofin — not to mention my first ever dive in competition — to reach a depth of 55 metres: 5 metres deeper than I'd ever been with bi-fins. I basically assumed that the monofin worked like a video-game power-up — as soon as I strapped it on, I would get an instant bonus to performance. About 10 minutes before my 'Official Top' (the zero time at which a freediver's performance must begin), I donned the borrowed fin for the first time and realised that I didn't stand a chance. My attempt to send dolphin-like undulations down my torso and legs into the blade of the fin would have looked like a porpoise beached on hot black sand. The fibreglass plane of the fin buckled and warped as sporadic forces exited into it via my feet. Luckily I had enough sense to return the fin to its owner and slip into some more familiar bi-fins instead, with just minutes to spare.

Down I went. Normally I can equalise without having to squeeze my nose shut, but with the congestion

I had to keep my hand on my nose for the entire descent. I strained to force air into my sinuses, which squeaked and whistled each time the air passed through their narrowed channels. Little did I know it, but the negative pressure caused by my incomplete equalisation of my sinuses was causing capillaries in the walls of these cavities to burst, and blood was combining with the congestion to create a kind of jelly doughnut mixture in my nose. Moreover, a leak in my mask was causing it to fill with water, and when I finally and almost miraculously found myself turning at the bottom plate and grabbing the tag (the marker used as evidence of depth), things really started to get messy.

If you exceed your personal-best depth by a significant margin, you can never be at your most relaxed during the ascent, especially when things have been going wrong up to that point. My particular level of relaxation on that day would have fallen somewhere between finding a scorpion living in my wetsuit, and finding out the same thing after having put the wetsuit on. As I powered towards the surface my mask took on more and more water, infuriating me to the point where I wrenched it clean away from my face. Meanwhile, as the air in my sinuses expanded with the drop in pressure it strained against the congealed blood/mucous clot that had formed. I felt a curious movement behind the bridge of my nose before the clot was ejected in a messy burst. Blinded as I was with no mask, I was spared the look of alarm in my safety divers' faces when they met me at 20 metres. I rocketed past them, oblivious as to my depth, and had erupted halfway out of the water, blood pouring from my face, before I finally stopped finning. To the amazement of the judges, I was still conscious and able to complete the surface protocol. If freediving was judged aesthetically, like high-diving is, then I would have been given a big fat zero; but as it was the judges showed a white card (for a legitimate performance) and I earned 55 points (one for each metre) for my team, as well as the second deepest dive of the competition.

With clean white card performances from my team mates Gianfranco 'Jimmy' Montanti and Fabien Pallueau, we were in first position overall. However, I would soon destroy any cause for optimism with an over-reaching performance in the second part of the competition: static apnea. My team mates had impressed upon me the importance of being conservative, as a simple 4:30 (4 minutes 30 seconds) breath-hold would have secured us first place, but my ego wasn't about to let me settle for such a paltry time when I had a personal best of more than 6 minutes! Sure enough, somewhere just shy of 5:30 I found myself coming out of a major samba (pre-blackout state) amid the realisation that I had just thrown our medal chances out the window.

I later found out that prior to the competition, Umberto Pelizzari had asked his close friend Jimmy Montanti to form a team with me, telling him '*Occhio, che ci scappa il morto*' ('Watch out, or this one might "buy the farm".'). It would have inflamed me to have heard this at the time, but now, looking back on how I was diving at the time, I would definitely side with him and am grateful for his discreet concern. Jimmy was a swim coach and lifelong spearfisher from the Egadi Islands, off the western tip of Sicily. He routinely piloted his RIB (rigid inflatable boat) to a sea mount 50 nautical miles (about 90 kilometres) from land, between Sicily and the coast of Africa. There he would spear giant grouper and amberjack to share with friends at endless summer dinners that spilled over onto the narrow communal streets of Marettimo.

*

After the competition in Egypt, I was tormented for the rest of the summer by sinus inflammation that just wouldn't go away. I was paying the price for having forced the issue during the competition. The passages connecting my sinuses to my nasal cavity were completely closed off, meaning that most of the time I couldn't even dip my head underwater without a piercing twist of the invisible knife lodged in my brow. I tried antibiotics, nasal sprays, cortisone pills, and cortisone injections into my buttocks (begrudgingly performed by Dwayne, who was visiting from New Zealand). Tiziana even took me to a local Sardinian *maga* (sorceress), who scrutinised the way oil drops coalesced in a bowl of water and pasta in order to discern whether I had been the subject of a *malocchio* (evil eye). Nothing worked. The gremlins squatting in my forehead refused to budge. There is no greater torture for a freediver than to be kept out of the water, trapped on the wrong side of that mirrored divide.

However, I was determined not to let adversity triumph over me, and kept myself to a strict dry-training regimen. Resistance training at the gym, lung-stretching exercises, exhale static apneas and *pranayama* were all regular elements. On the secluded promontory of Punta della Contessa I would practise apnea sprints: a more rigorous version of apnea walking that I had devised and which I performed on an inhale. At the top of a small hill, I would take a full breath in, then run down the hill as 'deep' as I dared before turning and running back up to my 'surface' starting point, where I could breathe again. The process would be repeated every 2 minutes or so, for as many repetitions as I could muster.

So it went on for most of the summer, with only

small periods when my sinuses might allow a brief window of diving before closing up again. It wasn't until October that my blueless period came to an end. During an Apnea Academy Instructor Course that was held in two parts, split between Pisa and Sharm El Sheikh, the Academy's ENT (ear, nose and throat) specialist, Stephano Correale, prescribed me a cocktail of drugs that evicted those lurking germs once and for all.

Finally freed from the mucosal glue that had kept me stuck to terra firma, I didn't take long to reinflate my over-reaching hubris. The day after the course finished and I had graduated as an instructor, I decided to put the months of dry training to the test with an attempt at a 45-metre CNF (No Fins) dive. I performed a series of exhale breath-holds to warm up, then relaxed for 10 minutes before starting the attempt. The descent felt dreamy, liquid and peaceful, and despite being deeper than I'd ever gone without fins I stayed relaxed. Nonetheless, a tiny voice told me I had better turn about now. So I did, and with that the tables turned. Breathing reflexes contracted my torso in increasing frequency, and I fought against the impulse to swim more quickly or look towards the surface. Jimmy was safetying me, and when he met me he could see the agitation in my eyes. I made it to the surface, took one breath and blacked out, falling backwards in the water where Jimmy supported me for several seconds until I came round again. The slowly dawning realisation of what had happened, the resultant embarrassment and disillusionment, the mixture of alarm and, maybe — yes — a touch of ridicule on the faces of my course-mates crowding the water around the platform, all left me wanting to sink back under the surface to escape the earthly vices of expectations, judgements and reputation.

Over the following days, as the wound in my pride slowly knitted over, I began to reassess my approach to freediving. The training I was doing occupied long hours, and took me regularly to the precipice of low oxygen saturation, but it didn't feel like I was training for a sport. I had avoided any and all forms of cardiovascular exercise, on the grounds that I didn't want to increase my muscular capillarisation and mitochondria content, both of which make the body a more oxygen-greedy machine — great for long-distance running but a liability for freediving. This left me doing very little in the way of physical exertion. To improve performance in any sport, the muscles have to be taught how to complete movements autonomously (muscle memory), and be trained to develop the specific strength required (muscle tone). The process takes literally thousands of hours of repetition, and in the case of freediving this means pool training. We could of course achieve the same results with repetitive shallow freedives, but even these carry a risk of decompression sickness; plus the effect of moving up and down the water column, subjecting the body to oscillating pressures, can be extremely debilitating, requiring much longer recovery periods for an equal distance of swimming. So there was no escaping the fact that I would need to swim laps to develop my technique and power-to-weight ratio.

In 2003, a trio of Scandinavian freedivers had smashed the records in pool freediving (dynamic apnea), including a powerful no-fins swim of 166 metres by Stig Severinsen. The following year he visited Santa Teresa with a film crew to shoot an episode in a mini-series about his attempt to break the no-fins depth record, which then stood at 62 metres. Seldom reluctant to talk about himself or his methods, Stig had given me valuable information about how he'd made gains in the pool through intensive training tables that involved countless short underwater swims with gaspingly quick recoveries between them. Among many benefits, these tables adapted the body to extremely high levels of hypercapnia (high CO_2 levels in the blood). As the recovery time between laps wasn't sufficient to off-gas the CO_2 created in swimming the lap underwater, the level of CO_2 would gradually rise to the point where the urge to breathe was present even at the start of each lap.

When I travelled back to New Zealand at the end of 2004 to spend the summer with my family, it was with a new resolve to start again from 'first principles' and build a foundation of strength, technique and CO_2 tolerance from which I could launch my forays into depth. It's the upside-down version of the approach used for centuries in mountaineering, where alpinists develop their skills over years of climbing at lower altitudes, then acclimatise with brief trips to medium altitudes before making the final push for the summit.

*

In that humiliating dive at the close of 2004 I had returned from 43 metres without fins to a blackout on the surface. Barely a year later, in the waters of the Bahamas, I would be diving to 76 metres in the same discipline. 2005 was the year that I discovered how to train, and raced up the slope of a steep learning curve to cement myself as a contender for a world record.

It began in New Zealand with daily pool sessions and exhale static apneas — for which I forbade myself any kind of warm-up so that I would have to deal with the full force of an early urge to breathe. Indeed, for all of my maximal apneas, whether in pool or in depth, I eliminated any breath-hold warm-ups altogether, in order to enhance the dive response when it was finally triggered. Just as in other survival reflexes (such as the fight or flight response), the mammalian dive reflex has been demonstrated to be most acute in the first exposure to a breath-hold dive. Thus, it made sense to go into a maximal dive 'cold' in order to get the most out of the reflex's oxygen-conserving effects.

Exhale static apneas are a rare constant in my training regimen, which has evolved greatly over the years. One of the more curious discoveries I've made in freediving came from observing the way my body intuitively responded to these breath-holds. I perform them in a seated half-lotus posture, focusing on staying calm and still throughout, which equates to an attempt to avoid the spasms of breathing reflexes. Breathing reflexes are the body's involuntary attempts to suck air into the lungs by contracting the intercostal muscles, which run between the ribs, to expand the ribcage. As the freediver doesn't allow air to enter the mouth or nose, the result is that the abdomen is sucked up under the ribcage to compensate for its expansion; this can almost look like an invisible punch to the stomach. It had been necessary to avoid these intercostal contractions during my initial practice of *pranayama*, a form of yoga that concentrates on slowing the breathing with long inhales and even longer exhales, to the point where each breath can last well over a minute.

When I later began doing exhale static apneas, I tried to conserve the same state of stillness throughout the breath-hold. My mind didn't know the process by which my body was achieving this, and I never stopped to analyse it at the time. It wasn't until some years later, when I was reading about *bandhas* in a yogic text, that I realised I had been employing them unconsciously during exhale breath-holds. *Bandha* means 'lock' in Sanskrit; the three principal locks are *jalandhara bandha* (a slight drawing of the chin down and backwards to put pressure on the neck), *uddiyana bandha* (an expansion of the ribcage that also raises the diaphragm) and *mula bandha* (a contraction of the pelvic floor muscles). In an exhale static apnea, after breathing out almost all of my air (to just above residual volume), there would be a brief relaxed period where I didn't experience any urge to breathe. Then, as the urge came on, I would observe my body very gradually, by tiny degrees, straightening the spine and engaging the three *bandhas*. The stronger the urge to breathe, the more I would tense those three points, but also the more the rest of my body (arms, legs, face) would dissolve into greater relaxation. The result was that of a central, vertical line of tension where the *bandhas* were stacked on top of each other, from my head to the base of my spine, with the rest of my body around it slipping away. My hands rested limply on my knees, but I had no sensation of either body part. The yogic texts talk about experiencing the body as the thin stem of a lotus flower, and this describes the effect perfectly.

Later I would discover that these three *bandhas* could be substituted with a single one that takes place in the mouth. This particular *bandha*, which I call the tongue lock, is only mentioned in one or two of the most obscure yogic texts I have come across. Again, I discovered by accident that I had been performing it unconsciously during deep CNF dives, and I attribute much of the calmness I am able to maintain in the ascent from maximal dives to this one small technique.

Returning to exhale static apneas, when I used the three *bandhas* (together called the great lock) — and especially when I combined them with the tongue lock — this resulted in a rapid and dramatic bradycardia (slowing of the heart rate), to as low as 25 to 35 beats per minute (the average resting heart rate of an elite athlete is 50 beats per minute). My explanation for this is that the body is no longer being tricked into thinking that the breath-hold is over by the breathing reflexes themselves. In a breathing reflex, or 'contraction', stretch receptors in the intercostal muscles detect that there has been an expansion of the ribcage, and they figure that this must mean that air has come into it. 'Don't worry!' they tell the brain, 'We just took a hit of air — fresh oxygen should be on its way up to you any time now!' This is why there is a temporary feeling of relief after each contraction, followed by a rapid decline back to the sense of suffocation as the brain realises that it's been duped. The mini-hiatus is a nice thing to have during a hard breath-hold, but it's also responsible for sending mixed signals to the part of the brain that governs the dive reflex. If the breath-hold is finished, then there's no point in carrying on with bradycardia, peripheral vasoconstriction, splenic contraction and everything else involved in conserving oxygen. So the dive reflex occurs by fits and starts, as the body responds to the conflicting messages from contractions. In contrast, when doing exhale static apneas without contractions, there is no respite to the gradual intensification of the urge to breathe, but neither is there any interruption to the body's response to this urge, and oxygen is conserved.

These are some of the methods and ideas that began to form during that pivotal year of 2005. I performed the techniques mostly unconsciously at first, as by-products of commands I gave myself (like 'sit still!' and 'look for the hard part and focus on that'); then, as I became aware of what I was doing, I was able to analyse and have an active role in developing them.

I say that 2005 was a pivotal year because it was one in which I saw a rapid spike in results; 2008,

2010 and 2016 were similar periods of improvement. However, I do feel a pang of injustice in favouring these particular years over others. It's easy to train and motivate yourself when you're on a roll, but a lot harder to persevere when it seems like you've hit a ceiling or an insurmountable road-block. Years like 2004, 2006, 2012 and 2014, although they involved mostly setbacks and disappointments, were probably in truth the most pivotal years for me: those years when my mettle and self-discipline were truly challenged, when I made it through the winds of adversity without losing headway and could then sail on upwind with the more favourable breezes of easier years.

In April 2005 I travelled back to Utila, Honduras, where I had planned another phase of depth training. I had come to the island in 2003 as a complete beginner, so when I returned as a freediving instructor capable of diving well past the recreational scuba limit, abstemious and with a strict diet, I found myself on the outside of the social bubble of backpacking 'dive bums'. Not that I wasn't still a bum myself, of course! I would sleep in airports rather than pay for hotels during long lay-overs, lived during the summers in the house of my Italian girlfriend and teetered at the limit of my credit card. However, somewhere along the line I had had my last night of furious drinking and deranged dancing at some bawdy nightclub followed by passing out in a corner of the car park.

I spent my days in Utila quietly, using a kayak to paddle to a point off a coral wall where I could train in 45 metres of water. This depth quickly became comfortable in CNF, to the point where I could even spend 30 seconds lying on the silty bottom before beginning my ascent. Often a lazy school of ocean triggerfish that showed absolutely no interest in me on the surface would follow me down for the entire dive, for reasons I could never decipher. Their grey diamond shape and triangular fins could make them resemble a shark when caught out of the corner of the eye, but after a while I got used to having them around. Their curious faces, with puckered white mouths that looked as if they were wearing dental braces and dark eyes that rolled around in leathery grey skin, gave them a goofy, bashful look. In all my time diving in Utila I never once saw a single shark, not even a reef shark, and I now know that this is testimony to the devastating effect of shark-finning in these poorer nations of the Caribbean. At first I would sometimes get the 'shark jitters' in the water and look around constantly, but by the end of my time there I could happily close my eyes while resting on the bottom, without any real apprehension.

*

The summer in Italy that followed was very different to the previous year. I took care of my ears and sinuses, and was able to continue my progress in depth training. Before long I had maxed out the depth available in the waters of Santa Teresa, and was even doing short pauses on the sandy sea floor at 53 metres, much to the concern of my safety diver waiting on the surface. The lack of depth beyond 55 metres and the frequent interruptions when the *maestrale* (cold nor-westerly wind) blew foaming swell into the strait led me to investigate flights to the Red Sea for a session of depth training. Mike Lott, an English student in the freediving course I had helped Umberto to teach, and whom I had kept in touch with afterwards, was living in Dahab, Egypt — a low-cost version of Sharm El Sheikh about an hour's drive north through the desert. Mike invited me to join him to dive in Dahab's Blue Hole, which is a Mecca for European freedivers looking for warm water and reliable conditions coupled with a cheap cost of living. Mike was a long-time surfer and recent convert to freediving, and made a living writing computer code. His unruly mop of blond hair hid half his vision; it also hid him from the world somewhat, a position he seemed to prefer. In the following years he would become my most loyal training partner and safety diver, travelling with me for weeks and months at a time to support world-record attempts, and all for no pay.

We stayed in the small stone building Mike was renting on the outskirts of Dahab. Egypt in August is a furnace, and the nights offer little respite. With no air-conditioning and only a weak fan for cooling, I would wake at night in a puddle of sweat, toss and turn to try to position myself on a dry portion of the bed, then fall back into a soupy sleep. The taxi rides we took to the Blue Hole were no more comfortable. Most of the time we were sandwiched into the back of a jeep, clutching our

My most loyal friends and crew members from my early years of freediving.
From left: Nic Rowan, Mike Lott and Michael Trousdell.

dive gear on our laps as the vehicle bounced and rattled over a vicious unsealed road. At times it seemed like the surrounding desert would have offered a smoother ride than that rutted track. Alongside it, dispassionate camels toted tourists in the same direction and at almost the same pace, and we passed herds of goats feasting on piles of cardboard.

I'll paint a rough picture of Dahab's Blue Hole, if only so that the reader can contrast it with Dean's Blue Hole in the Bahamas, which I first visited later that same year. The Dahab Hole is a shaft, easily reached from the shore, that descends into the reef to a depth of 92 metres. Water can enter the hole both over the top of the reef, which is always underwater, and through a tall opening (known as the Arch) that makes a connection at 55 metres down between the Blue Hole and the open sea. A collection of restaurants crowd around the access to the Blue Hole. A floating pier extends from the shore out into the deeper water, supporting a waddling file of be-flippered Italian, Russian and English snorkellers, with all the belly fat but none of the coordination of a penguin march. These same snorkellers, trucked up from Sharm El Sheikh on fleets of Toyota Land Cruisers, would prove an all-round hazard in the water, whether to themselves (they swam either poorly or not at all), to the living reef (which they trampled over when they became exhausted from trying not to drown), or to the freedivers training in the centre of the Blue Hole (onto whom they would clutch for flotation if they couldn't make it as far as the reef). Many a relaxed breathe-up was ruined by careless or floundering snorkellers, and many tempers burst at the sight of delicate staghorn corals, which take years to grow, being snapped underfoot by those who became stranded.

Scuba divers, with whom freedivers also shared the limited underwater space of the Blue Hole, could also be a hazard. During a deep freedive, looking in the direction of motion would compromise one's hydrodynamics, relaxation and equalisation, so the freediver keeps the head aligned and sees only the rope next to them. If an oblivious scuba diver decided to use one of the freediving lines to hold onto during a decompression stop, then some kind of collision was almost inevitable. That meant a ruined freedive, followed by a heated altercation as soon as the scuba diver surfaced. In one of the worst cases, a scuba diver being tongue-lashed by a fuming, red-faced Danish freediver pulled out his dive knife, in what he probably thought was a defensive measure. Luckily, things de-escalated rapidly from that point on.

Absent the human element, Dahab's Blue Hole is a beautiful dive site. Reef fish, abundant in shape and colours, populate the shallow rim and sides of the hole. This provides a beautiful vista, especially during the freefall phase of the descent, when you can relax and watch the coral walls and resident fish-life gradually slide by. Beginning at about 45 metres, if you're facing the right direction, you can witness one of the most incredible underwater spectacles: the Arch. This huge passageway frames a view of the open water of the ocean, and what a view it is. A single colour, blue, in its most pure and radiant form, it speaks of emptiness and completeness, untold volumes and possibilities.

My training in Dahab started strongly, and on just my second dive I had turned in front of the Arch at a depth of 57 metres and swum back to the surface to set a new personal best without fins. The next day I aborted my first dive after straying too far from the line and grazing the rock wall. But on the second attempt I reached 60 metres, equalling the depth that had been a world record when I first began freediving two and a half years earlier. That record had inched up to 66 metres; then, in April of 2005, it had been flung all the way to 80 metres by the Czech freediver Martin Štěpánek. Many freedivers considered that mark unbeatable. After all, only a few years earlier Umberto Pelizzari had signed off his unparalleled career with a world record in Constant Weight to the same depth, wearing metre-long carbon fins. I had been astounded and, if we're being honest, just a little demoralised by Martin's incredible dive, but I didn't share the view of it being unassailable. I had seen the video, and thought that his swimming technique was careless and left a lot of room for improvement. If Martin wasn't realising the full potential of efficiency underwater, then someone who did could swim deeper still.

Over the remainder of my time in Dahab I gradually increased my dives to 65 metres, a depth that was approaching the limits of my tolerance to hypoxia (low oxygen) at that time. As well as this spurt of progress in maximal depth, there was another experience that Dahab's Blue Hole introduced me to: narcosis. Narcosis in diving is a state of stupor, drowsiness or euphoria, caused by the way that gases — principally nitrogen and carbon dioxide — interact with our nerves at high pressure. Scuba divers, who keep their CO_2 levels constant by exhaling, are mostly affected by nitrogen narcosis, at depths greater than 30 metres. This is one of the reasons why the recreational limit for scuba diving is 40 metres: if the mind is severely impaired by narcosis, then the diver might lose track of time and not monitor their depth or gas levels. In freediving the absorption of nitrogen into the body's tissues is limited, but the accumulation of carbon dioxide, which cannot be off-gassed, is much more pronounced.

Combined with the pressures experienced at depth, high levels of CO_2 can bring on a state of wooziness. This starts off being dreamy and pleasant, but on deeper and longer dives takes on a more sinister tone, and may even result in hallucinations. I would start to experience this in 2008, when I first dived past 100 metres in the Free Immersion discipline, sometimes in complete darkness. For now, in Dahab, the narcosis was of the pleasant variety. It dampened most of the urge to breathe in the ascent and shortened my perception of time, to the point where it felt like the ascent was abridged and there must have been some kind of mistake made with the line being set too shallow. Gradually, over the years, my tolerance to CO_2 increased and so did the depth at which I would become 'narced'. I even developed a training exercise that targeted 'narcosis resistance' and as a side effect provided a shortcut into the most refined state of consciousness — a kind of yogic *samadhi*-like bliss — but that came later, and in a different Blue Hole.

*

While in Dahab I had asked my peers whether they had ideas about places anywhere in the world with good conditions for training during the northern winter. It may seem strange that on a planet covered mostly by water there is such a small selection of dive sites adequate for freediving training, but we're a fussy bunch! The water must be warm, or our lean bodies start to shiver in our thin wetsuits; it must also be clean and clear, to leave enough light at depth to see the line. Currents and swells are impractical, and this rules out most exposed areas; the remaining sheltered areas are almost always too shallow. The site can't be too remote from shore either, or boat transfers consume too much time and fuel. The ideal freediving location would be a bottomless pool in the corner of a tropical lagoon, right next to a white sand beach that you can drive right up to. As it turns out, there *is* one such place in the world, and it was Sebastien Murat (proponent of the theory of exhale diving for humans) who tipped me off to it. Although he hadn't dived the site himself, he told me of this little-known Blue Hole on a remote Bahamian island where he had been a dive master several years previously: Dean's Blue Hole; at the time the deepest known Blue Hole in the world, at 202 metres.

My ears were pricked. I knew that if I could train consistently for several months in good conditions, I would be able to improve on the 65-metre mark I had reached in Dahab. When I returned to Italy I tried to research Dean's Blue Hole, and Long Island where it was located. There was almost nothing on the internet other than some ambiguous photos of the surface of the Blue Hole. I communicated with a resort on the island, but despite lengthy questioning still couldn't ascertain whether there was something critically wrong with the site. Did the shaft of the Blue Hole go straight down, or at an angle? Were the currents just on the surface of the lagoon, or did they move the water column vertically? The fact that no one had yet freedived the Blue Hole kept me thinking that it was flawed, that if it sounded too good to be true then it probably was. As it turned out, however, Dean's Blue Hole was even better than it sounded.

Before travelling back to the Caribbean I consolidated on my progress with a dive in Syracuse, Sicily, at a competition in memory of the freediver Rossana Maiorca, daughter of the great Enzo Maiorca. There was no CNF category, so I competed barefoot alongside the other CWT divers who were wearing fins and monofins. To this day I can still picture the wide-eyed face of the scuba diver stationed at 65 metres when he saw me freefalling towards him and the base plate. I was told afterwards that he was the club's veteran, who had seen 'everything there is to see underwater', but I had given him the surprise of his life, as he could only think that I must somehow have lost my fins on the way down without knowing it, and he was going to have to intervene to take me back to the surface! That dive, my second ever in competition, would prove a milestone for me, and the words I wrote in my journal motivated me for many dives to come: 'On the 18th of September 2005, when you were tired from the sun and sea of the previous day, when a black cat had crossed your path that morning, when there were waves and current and countless other niggles, you performed a personal best to 66 metres. You overcame the negative psychology and influencers. For, after all, the dive is up to you, and you alone.'

*

I arrived with Tiziana in the Bahamas at the start of October. The monosyllabic owner of the apartment we were to rent collected us in a single-cab utility truck. We stopped at a sparsely stocked supermarket to buy provisions, and the meagre selection of canned goods, weevil-infested grains and wilting vegetables began to convey an idea of how barren Long Island was at that time. For two of the next three nights we ate corned beef with onions and potatoes. The apartment was next to one of the most beautiful beaches on the island, but its beauty was the bait in a mosquito trap for humans; the mosquitoes were, according to the locals, at their very worst during this period. Returning from the beach, we would have to break into a run to outpace the whining black nebulae that formed above our heads — and this long before sunset. A local man I met later that week drove his pick-up truck with a bottle of Guinness and a can of full-strength DEET insect repellent, in side-by-side cup holders. Before opening his car door he would take a swig of the Guinness, scrunch his eyes and mouth closed and spray the DEET (which will melt plastic) liberally across his face.

With such a plague of marauding bloodsuckers trying to get in, our apartment was not the impregnable haven it needed to be. The window nettings were torn and punctured, and the buckled aluminium window-frames displayed wide breaches that mosquitoes could sail through in double file. We were a kilometre from the main road, with no neighbours, phone or other means of communication. Somehow we survived the night, and the following day received a dying old truck that we rented for a few days, at an exploitative price, before we could find better lodging and transport. Those first days were the antithesis of the image of an island paradise that the Bahamas invokes. Tiziana was at the limit of her tolerance for hardship, and I wasn't far behind. Within a week of landing I was at the only place I could find with an internet connection (a telephone store where the shopkeeper begrudgingly stepped aside to let me use her desktop computer and 14.4 kbps dial-up modem), writing e-mails to contacts in Hawaii and elsewhere to enquire whether I could escape and train where they were instead. Looking back, it's fortunate that the difficulty connecting to the outside world meant that by the time I received any replies I had already met a kindly local couple with a rental cottage and spare car, and with the generosity to help us adjust to the many trials of life on a secluded island.

Long Island is a very different place now. In part due to the exposure that freediving has brought it, tourism is better catered for, with a variety of hotels, apartments and villas available. High-speed internet, cellphone towers, better-stocked supermarkets and farmers' markets provide for most of the creature comforts of our age, and the bountiful shallow seas around the island mean that seafood dinners are easy to obtain. In 2005, however, the only thing that kept me on the island was Dean's Blue Hole. I still recall with clarity the morning of 7 October that year, when I walked the few steps from the end of the grass-and-sand road onto the beach and came face to face for the first time with that lens of deep blue water in the corner of the sandy lagoon. It was a brooding liquid mystery that swallowed the light from the sky. Limestone cliffs collared the hole on three sides, creating a natural amphitheatre with an abyss in place of a stage.

As I swam from the shore out over the edge, where the rock cuts far back underneath to form the second-largest known underwater cavern in the world, I found myself gazing down into a darkness more impenetrable than the depths of the open ocean. It's impossible not to be awed, and not to feel just a little trepidation, when suspended for the first time over the centre of Dean's Blue Hole. Nietzsche noted that the abyss also looks back into you, and I needed no leap of imagination to feel that giant iris of deep water penetrating my mind and reading the thoughts, hopes and expectations lying therein. Right from the first day, I realised that Dean's Blue Hole could not have been designed more perfectly for freediving, and that more than anywhere else on the planet it would enable me to unlock the aquatic potential that was in my species; that was in myself. I felt those possibilities, and the turbulence of dreams and aspirations they triggered, as I gazed. And then I lifted my legs, spread the water with my hands, and let my body follow my eyes downward, past the lip of the hole to where the chamber opens and the side walls retreat into the shadows. Suspended in that underworld I turned in a slow circle, taking in the immensity of the volume of water it contained, and only sensing the untold greater mass of inky liquid lying beneath. Everything was muted: light, sound, thought and identity. I felt naked

Reaching for the surface in Dean's Blue Hole. Diving without a wetsuit is the most exhilarating way of moving through the water. (*Igor Liberti*)

and intensely alone, but I also felt a sense of belonging. In 2003 I had found my calling, but in 2005 I had found my home.

I settled into my new quarters very easily. The perpetual twilight of the depths beyond the rim of the Blue Hole became familiar and soothing. Within two weeks I had hit 70 metres, and because of the simplicity of the training I was able to follow the deep dive with a training table of six to eight dives to 32 metres with short recoveries. In the evenings I would do yoga or exhale static apneas, and on rest days I explored the island or swam from shore to spear fish and lobsters on the shallow reefs.

On Boxing Day of 2005 I dived to 75 metres with no fins, and on 8 January 2006 I reached the goal of 76 metres (250 feet) that I had set for myself in 2003, when the world record had been 63 metres. When we attain a goal, we sometimes reward ourselves with a pause in which to recover and reflect. This is all very well and necessary, but pauses can turn into standstills, and as time passes waiting for new motivation, the prospect of beginning again becomes more and more daunting. In freediving my foremost intention has never been to set a record or reach a certain depth, but rather to try to come as close as possible to human aquatic potential, wherever that may lie. Pretty numbers that took my fancy when

I knew comparatively nothing about freediving (like '250 feet by age 25') had little to do with that goal, and were just way-markers that indicated my progression. Even today, I set my goals as far out as I dare into the dark waters of possibility. In the words of Ellen Johnson Sirleaf (Africa's first elected female head of state), 'The size of your dreams must always exceed your current capacity to achieve them.'

So, the day after I dived to 76 metres I was back in the water, repeating the dive plus a training table after it. I had already set a new target of 92 metres, and the marketing department in my brain had come up with a catch phrase for it, to make it sound even more appealing to my ego: '300 feet, with two bare feet and one breath of air.' Of course, I didn't mention this new goal to anyone, just as I had also kept the previous one to myself. Together with the fact that, most likely, it would have been ridiculed, I had discovered that the inner fire that stokes motivation is best kept that way: internal. If I trumpeted my goals to all those I crossed paths with, then they would of course congratulate me for being so bold and aspiring ('Really? You want to dive how deep?? Wow, that would be amazing!'), and that premature praise could satisfy my brain's reward centre and breed complacency. Instead, if I told no one then the only way I could show them my intention was through realising it. A blacksmith knows to keep the forge door closed to build the heat that can shape iron.

I did, however, allow myself to start contemplating a world-record attempt for the spring of that year. A colleague, Riccardo Mura, who ran a freediving centre in Sharm El Sheikh, agreed to host and organise a record attempt in May, as part of an Italian Apnea Academy freediving jamboree. Suddenly I found myself considering an entirely new prospect in the sport: freediving under the scrutiny and expectations of judges, spectators and media. I knew there was still a lot of work to be done before then, so concentrated on bringing my focus back to the task at hand.

For many of my training dives I was joined by American ex-pat Charlie Beede, who lived on the island with his Bahamian wife, Joyce. A real estate agent by trade, Charlie had spent his life on and in the water, as a surfer in Hawaii in the 1980s and '90s and then as a commercial spearfisher in the Bahamas while he waited for his broker's licence to be approved. As well as safetying my deep dives, we would go on spearfishing trips together to the Jumento Cays — a chain of flat rocks that stretches west 60 nautical miles (111 kilometres) from the coast of Long Island towards Cuba. They form the boundary between a deep tongue of the Atlantic Ocean and a vast area of shallow, sandy-bottomed water peppered with coral heads and reefs. These are the lobster grounds, where Long Island fishermen make their living fetching up the prized crustaceans.

Spearguns are illegal in the Bahamas, which makes Hawaiian slings the only way to hunt fish underwater. The sling is essentially an underwater slingshot; it requires brute strength to pull the rubber back and release it, propelling a free steel shaft through a hole in the handle of the sling. A primitive form of hunting, it requires greater skill to hit and land the fish so limits catches, taking pressure off fish stocks. Some fish, such as groupers and hogfish, were still very easy to target, but the prizes were the more timid mutton snapper, or free-swimming mackerel and permit.

In March I was joined on the island by Mike Lott and his Danish friend Timo Jattu, who was an avid spearfisher. After training in the morning we would go in search of a new area of water in which to hunt in the afternoon. We'd take turns pushing an old ice chest to store the fish in, out of reach of the sharks. The Bahamas is one of the few countries in the world that has made illegal any form of shark fishing. This wise move has ensured healthy shark populations, which in turn guarantees thriving reef ecosystems. It also means that there is always a shiver of Caribbean reef sharks on the prowl, hoping to steal the fish off your spears. They were easy enough to keep at bay as long as we were able to collect the speared fish, bring it quickly to the surface and throw it straight in the ice chest. Things got dicey, however, when we were being followed by a half dozen or so sharks that had become increasingly frustrated from watching the skewered groupers and snappers vanishing literally into thin air above them. And things got downright hairy if the ice chest, containing the day's haul of fish plus several litres of seawater mixed with said fish's blood, capsized in a rogue wave. On several occasions we had to turn away a toothy opportunist with a jab from the blunt end of the spear, although I don't think we were ever close to being bitten ourselves. There is an increasing understanding of sharks, however some people still retain the notion that they are voracious aggressors that will attack anything with a pulse. The reality is that sharks are mostly timid, cautious, and selective in the way they feed. It is only in extreme circumstances that they might confuse humans for their prey, and even then the confusion seldom lasts beyond the first taste. Granted, with all the fish blood in the water these did classify as extreme circumstances, but we were still able to keep control of the situation by showing confidence and dominance, and the sharks acquiesced to this enforced hierarchy in the same way that wild cats, dogs and other animals do. If you ever find yourself snorkelling in open water in the presence of a shark, and you haven't been spearing fish, then I encourage you to stop and watch its graceful and languid movements for as long as you can. However, if you're not comfortable with its presence then the best method of driving it off is to duck underwater and swim, with purpose, straight towards it. Even large tiger sharks will be spooked by the intimation that they are your prey, and will scuttle off at high speed on an arcing route that allows them to keep you on one side of their vision. One caveat: don't try this in water with poor visibility or when swimming in an area frequented by seals — in those cases it is best to get out of the water!

On 15 March 2006 I completed a training dive to a depth of 80 metres, equalling the current unassisted world record, in a time of 2 minutes 58 seconds. I knew that there was a great difference between a casual training dive with friends and a record attempt under the scrutiny of judges and video cameras, not to mention spectators. Competition stress is a huge factor in freediving performance, and accounts for many divers struggling to reach depths that they have handled easily in training. It results in an elevated heart rate and cerebral activity, as well as stimulation of the sympathetic nervous system that governs the fight or flight response, releasing adrenaline into the body. All of this eats into oxygen stores before the dive has even begun. To break the world record I would have to dive to at least 81 metres, but to have confidence in attempting such a depth I felt that I needed a 'buffer' of several metres more in terms of what I was capable of doing in training. In short, there was still work to be done.

*

At some point during our spearing expeditions we added a black grouper and horse-eye jack to the ice chest, and to our dinner table one evening. We also shared some of this fish with our landlords. For months afterwards I would regret this act of imprudence. Of course I had heard of ciguatera (tropical fish poisoning), which is caused by the toxin ciguatoxin, but I had assumed it was only present in larger fish and that even if we did contract it we would be sick for a day or two and then recover, knowing not to eat that species of fish again. I was spectacularly wrong on both counts. Black groupers, known as gags in the Bahamas, are all toxic regardless of size, as are most jacks. Moreover, ciguatoxin is not a toxin that lets you off lightly. It is created by tiny organisms, dinoflagellates, present in the coral and algae of the reef and is ingested by the herbivorous fish that feed on the reef, accumulating in higher concentrations with every step up the food chain.

Ciguatoxin is a neurotoxin, and in humans gastrointestinal problems are only the vanguard of a host of more-sinister disorders such as severe headaches, muscle aches, weakness, paraesthesia (pins and needles) and, most interestingly, cold allodynia, which is where contact with a cold surface or liquid produces a burning sensation. Most of these symptoms were experienced by me and Timo, and some by Mike (who had become tired of eating fish for every meal so hadn't consumed as much of the toxic species). Over a period of several days, my training became taxing and unfruitful. I was having sambas on dives that had previously been straightforward, and feeling lethargic for the rest of the day. Something was definitely off, but I couldn't pin down the cause so we continued to eat fish while I tested different theories about the lapse in performance. Several days of complete rest didn't help at all, and the idea that it might be iron deficiency was ruled out by taking several different natural supplements like spirulina and chlorella, as well as eating the raw and still-beating hearts from the grouper we caught! It wasn't until I mentioned my symptoms in passing to our landlords that we discovered the truth.

'Ohhh, you got it too then!' exclaimed Ivan, an elderly sponge fishermen who had been blinded in one eye when he fell into a crab pit. 'That's ciguatera, that is!

We had it too, y'know, from the fish you gave us, but I didn't want to say nuthin' to make you feel bad!'

Unfortunately, there is no cure for ciguatera. Only time can remove the substance from the body, in a gradual process of detoxification. At this point there were only a couple of weeks remaining before I was committed to travelling to Egypt for the record attempt. I tried my best to find a balance between the rest required to rehabilitate from the sickness, and enough training to try to maintain (or ideally improve) my performance before the attempt.

There were more failed dives, and a few good ones, including the last dive before I left the Bahamas: a clean and lucid 82 metres. This dive gave me hope that I might be starting to overcome the ciguatera, but by then I had already committed another serious error. My flight arrived in Sharm El Sheikh on Saturday 6 May, with the record attempt scheduled for the following weekend. I had thought that a week would be enough time to acclimatise and recover from jet lag, but when the first two dives to (only) 74 metres resulted in a samba and a surface blackout respectively I realised that I had vastly underestimated the effect that the two days of travel and the change in climate, conditions and time zone can have on performance.

I took a step back and dived 68 metres, then 74 the following day, this time clean. With two days to go I set the mark at 78 metres, for what should have been my last dive before the attempt. However, a sled (used for weighted descents in training) had been left at the bottom of the rope, and when I turned at 78 metres one of its crossbars knocked my mask, flooding it with water. Unable to see, I had no choice but to abort the dive and pull myself up the rope. This meant that instead of resting on the twelfth, the eve of my attempt, I felt I needed to retry 78 metres to give myself confidence for an 81-metre dive on the thirteenth. I did so, and the dive was the easiest yet. I felt strong and positive even though I hadn't had a rest day since I'd arrived. It was clear that I was starting to adapt and recover from the travel, but was I ready to add another 3 metres, not to mention perform in the pressure-cooker of tension that results from an official attempt? The following day I would find out.

I was shuttled by launch to the dive boat, anchored in front of Sharm Club Resort in 200 metres of water. I had to be under the judges' surveillance for at least 45 minutes before the attempt, so I went to the top deck to listen to music while I waited. Umberto Pelizzari had agreed to be my deep safety diver, and he would meet me at 45 metres on my ascent. My other two 'safeties' were my most loyal training partners, Mike Lott and Jimmy Montanti. Michael, and Nic Rowan, my two best high-school friends, had travelled from Spain and England to support me, and their familiar presence did have a calming effect. Nic was warm-hearted and staunchly loyal, and although he had gone to university in Dunedin the three of us had remained close companions. He had the build of a sturdy rugby hooker, and despite being almost a head shorter than Michael he wouldn't concede that as any kind of advantage in the friendly rivalry between them. He was Costello to Michael's Abbott, and their constant banter lightened any occasion, even the preparation for a record attempt.

The time finally came, and I pulled on my new wetsuit, entered the water and swam the few metres to the rope, which was suspended from a boom over the port side of the boat. I tried to ignore the cameras, judges and many attentive pairs of eyes that watched me from the boat. But there was no way to remain unaffected by a situation that was completely new to me in freediving. I could hear my heartbeat striking a rapid staccato of alarm against my ribcage. My mind was racing, too, like a wheel spinning without grip, flinging out random pointless thoughts. I knew that the risk in such occasions was to over-breathe, ridding the body of too much of the carbon dioxide that is necessary for triggering the dive reflex and consequent oxygen conservation. So I laboured to drag my attention time and time again back to my breathing, resisting the temptation to take bigger or quicker inhales.

Finally I felt it was now or never, took one last breath and duck-dived to start my descent. The water soothes, and removes the stress of earthly worries, even in the most trying circumstances (such as a first-time world-record attempt). I felt at peace as I kicked and pulled the water on my way down towards the plate at 81 metres. Yet the damage had been done. My body was still recovering from the insults of ciguatera, travel and jet lag, and this, combined with the heightened level of excitement before the dive, meant that on a physiological level I had started the attempt firmly on the back foot. It might have been that no matter how well I swam, I literally didn't have enough oxygen molecules in circulation to complete the dive. Despite this, I felt good when I pulled the tag from the plate at the world-record depth. I still felt good when I met Umberto at 45 metres, and greeted him with a smile. But we don't feel the effects of oxygen depletion until towards the end of the dive. Soon after meeting Jimmy and Mike at 30 metres, the contractions started to rock my torso with urgency. At 20 metres from the surface my swimming style deteriorated and my pace increased as I frantically tried to cover the remaining distance separating me from the air my body craved. Just below the waves I took a last futile stroke and flailed my legs several times, which was enough to bring me to the surface — but I had already blacked out and the movements were unconscious spasms. Umberto supported my head above the water, removed my mask and blew across my face to stimulate the nerves that tell the body it is okay to breathe again. When this didn't work immediately, he covered my mouth with his and blew hard to force air past the spasming glottis and into my lungs. He had just surfaced himself from a dive to almost 50 metres, and later he commented that 'there couldn't have been much oxygen in that breath I gave you!' — but whether it was the thin trace of oxygen or the surprise at locking lips with another man, the effect was immediate and I quickly regained consciousness and started normal breathing.

The audience of concerned faces and their conciliatory applause reminded me of the time 18 months previously when I had blacked out among my peers at the end of the instructors' course, attempting a dive that I should have left for another day. The video crew who covered the attempt made a generous short film that was shown to a crowd of Italian freedivers attending the jamboree that evening. It discreetly cut the footage of my brief rescue on the surface, and ended with the caption: 'Next will be better.'

'Not all sporting careers debut with success,' I told myself. 'If I break the record on the next attempt then I can still go on to great things.' What I didn't ask myself was what would happen if I was unsuccessful again the second time around.

*

The planning for that second attempt began almost as soon as I returned to Sardinia and resumed training. It seemed almost self-evident at the time that with the ice broken by that first record attempt, then provided that I recovered fully from ciguatera the second time should be a charm.

Throughout June, July and August I trained long hours in the pool and in dry sessions of weight training, yoga and exhale static apnea. The harder I trained, the more rest became important as well. Our bodies need time to respond to training stimuli and make the physiological adaptations that improve performance, but they can't do that if new stimuli are already being piled on. I generally trained in a pattern of three days on and one day off, and on the rest day I looked for activities that gave the body a pause while distracting the mind. Writing, painting, playing chess or reading a book on the beach were all ways I could recharge my batteries for another round of pushing my body to its limits of tolerance for oxygen desaturation and carbon dioxide saturation.

I envisaged that if I kept all the conditions the same for the next record attempt, then the months of hard training (and ciguatera detoxification) would fill the gap between my last dive and a world-record dive. So in mid-September I travelled back to Egypt, in excellent physical shape and brimming with confidence. I started well, with two strong dives taking me straight to 68 metres, but on the fourth day I was appalled to detect the tickle of an itchy throat and the throb of achy legs, both telltale harbingers of a viral infection. Training was suspended, and I visited the local doctor to ask for whatever medicine might hurry the virus on its way. Anti-histamine and anti-inflammatory drugs along with 3 grams of vitamin C and a decongestant nasal spray were prescribed. They say that if you do nothing a cold will last a week, whereas if you take every possible medicine then it will last seven days. Sure enough, seven days later the tubes and chambers of my upper airways were clear once more, and back in the water I went.

With my depths increasing through the seventies, under the watchful gaze of Mike Lott who was coordinating this new attempt, the progression was on track. But something else was happening. My blood pressure had dropped, and this could make me lightheaded before dives, an ominous sign that I might also be more susceptible to blacking out. Even worse, my resting heart rate was faster than that of a dormouse. Thinking that I was dehydrated, I started taking a rehydrating powder containing, among other salts, 11 milligrams of anhydrous zinc acetate. In addition, I was becoming frustrated with the food served up at the buffet restaurant in the resort where we were staying. Not only did it lack variety, but also it was bland and completely devoid of salt. I asked the chefs to add more, and they obligingly did so while I watched, but there must have been a problem with the salt they were using, as it had little effect. In my diary I commented: 'The salt they use in cooking and put on the table might as well be talcum powder for all it salts: I poured some on my tongue and couldn't taste anything other than the rice they use to keep it dry.' So, I asked a friend to buy me some real sea salt from the market, as well as some good honey, since the brand used by the resort was hardly sweet at all.

Strangely, the new condiments were no improvement. I put it down to the general quality of Egyptian food, but at the same time I noticed that my mouth was producing saliva like I was some kind of frothing psychopath. And my blood pressure was continuing to drop. To test the severity, I asked Mike Lott to spot me while I took a full breath and stood up from the floor. A few seconds later I woke up to him holding me and patting me on the cheek. Who needs to dive to 81 metres when you can black out just by getting out of bed too quickly?

On 5 October I blacked out just before surfacing on a 76-metre dive. The next day I stepped things back to what should have been an easy 70-metre dive, and still had a samba on the surface. Now this was just plain stupid: I had done more than a hundred 70-metre-plus CNF dives (sometimes back to back on the same day), and it was a depth that should have been a walk in the park for me. Something was definitely up. It seemed that no matter how slowly and shallowly I breathed, I was still getting the pins-and-needles signs of over-breathing. After a day of rest, I decided to attempt another 70-metre dive. During the breathe-up I actually had to stop, exit the water to raise my CO_2 levels, then get back in and breathe extremely slowly, with 20- to 40-second apneas between inhale and exhale. Even then, I started the dive with slight finger-tingling. The dive was clean, albeit a lot more difficult than it ought to have been. There followed a sequence of training days where I played snakes-and-ladders with the bizarre physiological condition that was wreaking havoc in my dives, not to mention destroying my sense of taste. Every time I felt like I was starting to make progress and dive more easily again, I would have another difficult dive, surfacing on the edge of a blackout. It culminated with several clean and confident 78s, then two big sambas on dives to 80 and 81 metres.

But why stop at mere physical woes? After all, I'd shipwrecked on that reef in the previous attempt. A fresh form of persecution was provided by the coastguard informing us that we would not be allowed to anchor our dive boat at the site intended for the attempt. The reason: Hosni Mubarak, the president of Egypt, was hosting British prime minister Tony Blair in the resort next door, and for security all boat traffic was prohibited within a certain distance. Mike and I tried first to vent our anger and make ourselves look presentable before walking over to the adjacent property, where we asked to speak with the distinguished guests. Whether we were actually wearing shoes is a detail that escapes my memory, but it's certain that there were no trousers, let alone suits, in our wardrobe at the time. The guards on duty must have marvelled at the audacity of these two foreign drifters standing before them and requesting — or more likely demanding — an audience of their head of state. Of course we were turned away, and I doubt that the two leaders were ever aware of the debacle their presence had caused. At the time, it might have consoled us to know that their days of spending taxpayers' money on luxury getaways were numbered: the following year, Tony Blair would be pressured to resign over his role in what many saw as war crimes in Iraq, while Mubarak was found guilty of worse when the dust settled on his country's revolution, and he languished for six years in a military prison.

Because of the ban, we lost the first three days of our window for the record attempt. This meant that I would only have one day remaining, 27 October, to try to complete an official dive to 81 metres. My mother, Linda, had travelled from New Zealand for the event; it would be her first experience watching me freedive. Michael and Nic were back to help take my mind off the diving by recalling stories from our schooldays, but the comic relief took a fresh turn when they both came down with 'pharaoh's revenge' (severe diarrhoea) and supplied running commentaries of the logistics and pitfalls involved when two room-mates with volatile digestive tracts share a single bathroom. After weeks in Egypt I had guts of steel, but the same wasn't true of my nerves. The undiagnosed disorder, the setbacks and the failed dives had all undermined my confidence. I told myself not to think about the objective, but rather to concentrate on doing the best dive that I was capable of.

On the day itself, at 11.00 a.m., I walked with one of the judges down to the beach and swam the short distance out to the boat. The rescue boat wanted to pick me up to transfer me, but I was wary of their outboard motor, which was spewing carbon monoxide over the water. Aboard the dive boat, I escaped to the top deck again while the crew lowered the rope and got into position. At 11.30 I went down and entered the water, which was the signal for the two deepest technical-support divers to start their descent to 81 metres, followed by the two who would be stationed at 55 metres. A team of four video operators and two photographers also got into position to capture the attempt.

After about 8 minutes of gentle breathing I lifted my head, took the last breath and started to move forward for the duck-dive. It was at this moment that I realised my right arm was caught up in the cord attached to my snorkel. The air came out of me as from an unknotted balloon, and I had to repeat the last 2 minutes of my breathe-up. By this point a feeling of despondency had enveloped me, and if I'd had more experience I would have known to listen to the voice quietly advising me to call it all off. One of the hardest skills in freediving is to distinguish between instinct and fear. They both communicate through the same visceral channel — the 'gut' — but there's no return address to trace where the missive came from, and where it came from makes all the difference. Whereas fear is an emotive response that can be completely irrational or out of proportion with the threat (such as arachibutyrophobia — the fear of peanut butter sticking to the roof of your mouth), instinct is actually the result of a reasoning process that happens behind the veils of the constant mental conversation we have with ourselves. Our subconscious mind has access to more data and can work at a greater speed than our rational mind, which is limited to about the same pace that we can say words. But most of the time our subconscious isn't allowed access to the 'situation room' in our brain, so it has to send messages; and unfortunately these get delivered to the same inbox as all the spam we receive from our emotions.

In those last minutes before the dive began, I was clearing the emotional spam out of my brain every few seconds, and the soft-spoken misgivings of my subconscious were deleted along with everything else. At a guess, my heart rate was between 100 and 110, and despite breathing as slowly as possible I still had slight hypocapnic signals in my hands. When I started the dive, the seven descent strokes I take before freefall were over so quickly that I wondered if I had miscounted. Then, almost straight away, between 30 and 40 metres, I started to feel narcosis. Normally this begins during the ascent — not halfway through the descent. I kept a watch on the narcosis, ready to abort the dive if it became too severe, and this may have meant that I wasn't as relaxed as normal. With no way of knowing how deep I was, I kept on falling, trying to find the 'infinite regression' that I train through exhale static apneas. Finally the 75-metre marker flashed past, and I readied myself for the turn. Just above the plate I grabbed the line with my left hand, reached out with my right for a Velcro tag and slapped it onto my thigh as I pulled on the line to start my ascent.

I was telling myself that, one way or another, by now the dive had already been decided and all I had to do was swim. I felt the heat from a video camera light burn through my closed eyelids when it was thrust too close to my face by an overzealous cameraman. At this point I was still feeling okay — no contractions and plenty of strength — but, as always, hypoxia won't rear its ugly head until the finish line is in sight, like a wolf that waits by the door of your house for your return. Just below 30 metres Mike Lott came into view, and I waved my head from side to side to indicate that I wasn't sure I was going to make it. The last memory I have is of reaching for the line at about 15 metres and starting to pull for the surface, then feeling Mike grab me to help me ascend. It was the worst blackout of my career. I was unconscious as I was dragged from 10 metres to the surface, and didn't come round for another 20 seconds after that; long enough to have a short dream about something completely irrelevant that I forgot soon after.

To be there again, aboard another sinking ship as it headed for the bottom in a sea of disillusionment, was a hard reality to accept. The warm words of sympathy and encouragement from all those around me should have floated any old wreck, but I wouldn't allow it. Perhaps part of me needed to dwell for a while in that murky chasm, to let the experience of it seep into my skin so that I always could keep a part of it with me, as a reminder and as an incentive.

Sebastien Murat wrote a succinct e-mail that helped me to assimilate the disappointment: 'Success without some hardship doesn't make for good story, at least not with the script you've chosen; there needs to be hardship (continued) and failure (at least twice) before there can be empathy, support and rejoice. Otherwise, it's an empty experience, at least socially, which by the way is all that will really matter in the long-term, for those emotionally smart enough to work that one out. This is why many of the "guns" of the sport are like shooting stars: people are impressed by their feats, but quickly move on to the next spectacle. Aim for a lasting impression.'

So far, I had made no impression at all. Not just socially (which I liked to think I didn't care so much for, but then again I was never emotionally very smart either!), but also on the particular journey I had chosen: the quest to measure the depth of our species. My personal resources and self-belief were finite resources that had been all but consumed. The patience of my friends, who had supported me with their time and energy, was being tested as well, though I suspect that their loyalty might have outlasted my perseverance. I decided to admit to myself that my career in the sport depended on being successful on the next occasion. Third time lucky, third time's a charm; no one ever mentions anything about the fourth time around. No, it had to be the next attempt.

In this way my mind fixed on the concept of inevitability. It is one thing to say 'I'm going to do my best!' or even 'This time I'll do it for sure', but when we make the statement 'Next time it'll be inevitable', then *that* is in an entirely different category. It discounts even the most remote possibility — or, shall we say, even the possibility of there being a possibility — of an alternative scenario. Having made such a declaration, as I did, and having meant it, then I was locked into an entirely different mindset. I knew I would have to go far deeper than the current world record in training, and that I would have to ensure that the attempt itself replicated my training dives in almost every detail. I would have to insulate myself from any kind of sickness and any influence from the outside world. I would train and I would have patience, and when I was ready, when I knew that there could be no other outcome, then I would allow what was inevitable to have its day.

*

My taste never did come back after that time in Egypt, and I have never deciphered the cause, although some research showed correlation between the condition and the dubious Egyptian medicines I had been taking to clear cold symptoms. Ageusia is a very rare disorder, in which the tongue loses ability to taste salt, sour, sweet and bitter. All the other myriad flavours of the food we eat are actually perceived by our sense of smell, when the aroma travels up our retronasal passage and across our olfactory sensors (this is why food tastes bland when you have a cold). While I can still detect the nuances in flavour between blackberries and raspberries, I wouldn't have a clue whether either was sweet or sour. Both salt and sugar are like sand in my mouth, and I can only distinguish between them by the texture. All told, however, it is a painless sense to lose, especially since my training diet already prohibited any food with added sugar and I had also stopped adding salt to food when I learnt that it has absolutely no function in the body other than to make us drink more water in order to eliminate it. Now I rarely think about it, or perceive any lack in my experience of eating. The only complication might be if I were marooned in a lifeboat; in that case I'm sure I would be the first to start drinking the seawater, as in my mouth it is indistinguishable from fresh!

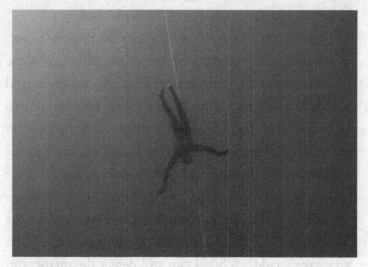
Descending towards 82 metres in Sharm El Sheikh, Egypt, September 2006. My body was still recovering from the effects of ciguatera poisoning, long travel and jet lag. *(Louisa Jane)*

Disappointment after my second unsuccessful world record attempt in Egypt. Linda (left) travelled from New Zealand for the event, and it was her first experience watching me freedive.

CHAPTER 5

CONFIRMATION

A *mantra* of *inevitability*

In wantonness of spirit, plunging down
Into their green and glassy gulfs, and making
My way to shells and sea-weed, all unseen
By those above, till they waxed fearful; then
Returning with my grasp full of such tokens
As showed that I had searched the deep

Lord Byron, *The Two Foscari*

CHEMISTS USE TEST TUBES so they can control the exact contents, isolating the experiment from any external influence. If they repeat the experiment with the same base materials, they can expect the same result. What I needed was a giant test tube to dive in. If I surfaced smiling from 81 metres on Tuesday, then dived again on Thursday under exactly the same conditions (of the sea and of my body), I should be able to expect a similar result.

Luckily, I had a 200-metre-deep test tube right under my nose: Dean's Blue Hole. Flying in safety divers and judges for a record attempt in the Bahamas would be more expensive than diving elsewhere, but at least I would not have to travel and change time zones myself. And I had hatched a plan to maintain even more uniformity between my training and the attempt itself. When the time came, I would tell my team that I needed a rehearsal before the big day, in which I would do a training dive to the attempt depth with all the judges and cameras in place. Of course the judges themselves had to be in on the plan, so that if it was successful they could register it as an official record, but for everyone else it would be 'just another training dive'. My team might have questioned why I didn't just make it an official attempt in case I made the dive; but at the same time, everyone knew that I had been trying to have my training replicate as accurately as possible the conditions of an attempt.

I won't bore readers with a blow-by-blow account of the road back to full strength and greater depths after the second failure in Egypt. Suffice it to say that within three weeks of that nadir of morale, I had returned to the Bahamas and was diving with renewed vigour and enthusiasm.

Another effect of setting a goal of 'inevitability' was that it lifted a ceiling on depth. I knew that achieving an

82-metre dive in preparation wouldn't suffice to make success in the record attempt *inevitable*: I had to go to 86, or deeper, in training. Invention is not necessity's only child: her first-born is the belief in the very existence of a potential solution. If it's imperative to us, then we have no choice but to believe in its possibility. Then, armed with belief, we go out and invent. I didn't stop to smell the roses at 80 metres, or at 82 or 84. I wasn't thinking about record attempts, competitors (of whom one, the Canadian William Winram, was also trying to break the same record), or the naysayers, such as AIDA president and judge of my previous attempt, Bill Strömberg, who had scoffed that I was 5 to 10 years too early for a world record. Anything that didn't relate to the technique and process of diving I was using was irrelevant to me.

I wrote glorifying e-mails to entice freediving friends to come and dive with me in the Bahamas over the winter, so that I would always have training partners. I analysed every dive, honed and refined every movement. And one day, in March 2007, I swam decisively to the surface from 86 metres, removed my mask and made an 'okay' sign to Tyler Zetterstrom, a Canadian who was safetying me, and knew that this time I was truly ready.

For this attempt there would be no extra cameras or photographers; the entire team numbered nine people. Below the plate at 82 metres, would be stationed two of the most experienced cave divers in the world, Brian Kakuk and Paul Heinerth, with rebreather equipment and lift bags that they could clip onto my wrist if I suffered a problem at depth. In midwater, at 55 metres, would be Charlie Beede and Michael Trousdell with twin tanks of regular air and extra lift bags. Mike Lott and Tyler Zetterstrom were my safety freedivers, ready to escort me to the surface in the final 30 metres of the ascent. Nic was stationed on the platform to film the surfacing, and the AIDA judges were Dimitris Vassilakis and Karoline Meyer.

When I walked out onto the beach on the morning of 9 April, only the judges knew that I was going to be diving for a world record. The atmosphere was relaxed, as everyone went about their business doing final checks. In the midst of the scene, a tiny seahorse — the first I had ever seen in the Blue Hole — was found clinging to one of the platform's mooring lines, its tail coiled tightly around the rope.

I was nervous and tense as I prepared myself on the small fibreglass platform that had been constructed for the attempt. I'm sure my heart rate was pushing three digits. But whereas in 2006 the feverish anxiety had permeated all the way to the core of my subconscious, this time there was a calm in the eye of the mental storm. It's easy for me to say now that I knew it was 'my time'. Is that really true though? I'm sure that if I'd been asked then, I wouldn't have claimed such a degree of certainty. We seem to resist admitting (to ourselves or others) any premonition of an agreeable future, lest we tempt fate to contradict us. However, this means that if the premonition is realised, we're left wondering whether it isn't just the distorted view of hindsight that created our memory of the premonition itself.

I was successful in tricking my team into thinking that this dive was just a rehearsal, and their relaxed behaviour helped maintain the illusion in my own mind. It really was like a training dive, and for most of it I was barely conscious of the significance of the occasion. Even the bizarre sight, during the start of my descent, of a large barracuda being chased at blinding speed by an even larger tarpon didn't disrupt my mental state. It wasn't until I had returned to the surface, removed my mask and handed the tag to the judge that it dawned on me. I turned to Nic, who was on the platform filming me, and said, 'Well, that was actually the official record.' His face displayed a brief struggle between jubilation and the indignation of a prank victim. 'You bastard!' he shouted. Meanwhile, beside me Mike Lott was laughing and claiming 'I knew it!' as he tried to push me back under the water while making it look like he was giving me a hug. We whooped and hooted together, letting out all our relief at having finally achieved what we had set out to accomplish a year before. It was made all the more special by having the same core group of the four of us who had stuck it out through three attempts.

The fourth member of that core group, Michael Trousdell, was still underwater with Charlie, Brian and Paul, so I dived down to where they were decompressing at 10 metres and tried to communicate the news using sign language. It was easy to trace the shape of a globe with my fingers, but for 'record' I resorted to miming a DJ, with one hand on my ear and the other scrubbing an invisible record table. Michael, who'd had 15 years of practice at deciphering my addled thoughts, was the first to twig, and he almost lost the regulator from his mouth as it widened into a broad grin. I shook hands with everyone, and tried to communicate my thanks for the role they had played in getting me to that upside-down summit and back again.

Back on the surface, I was amazed to discover the seahorse still gripping tenaciously to the mooring rope. The exhaust air from the divers was creating a blizzard of bubbles and powerful up-currents, but that miniature water dragon was still weathering it out, its long snout nodding like the bowsprit of a ship on high seas. I silently thanked the seahorse for its allegiance; soon afterwards, it unhitched itself from the rope and floated slowly away.

Having removed my wetsuit and mask, I ducked back under the water and thanked the ocean, too, as I do after all my deep dives. For a few seconds I open my eyes underwater and try to extend my awareness to the water on all sides of me. I have no reason to believe in an ocean god, or that the ocean is itself an entity. When I speak to it, thank it or, more commonly, just smile in its presence, it is with the understanding that on a certain level I am indistinguishable from the ocean, and am thus really only thanking myself. (More later on why I think this.)

There was nothing anticlimactic about finally claiming the world record, but I still wanted to prove to myself that I was capable of doing it without the mental trick of dressing the attempt up as a training dive. I also wanted to share a record attempt, from start to finish, with my team. And so, two days later on 11 April, I dived again to 82 metres and this time the team's celebrations required no cue.

The same day, the ocean kept for itself another world-record holder, French sled diver Loïc Leferme. During a training dive, the equipment he relied on to ascend had somehow malfunctioned, and by the time he could be brought to the surface he had drowned. In the 'No Limits' discipline, the diver descends with a weighted sled and ascends by inflating a lift bag using an air cylinder. Although only a dozen or so divers train in this modality, it has claimed the lives of four and seriously injured several others. None of the official freediving organisations ratifies No Limits anymore, and nowadays it is regarded by the freediving community as a stunt and a relic that the sport has outgrown in favour of the more athletic disciplines. Nevertheless, Loïc was a true waterman who was in search of *profondeur absolute* (absolute depth), within himself as much as within the ocean.

*

Having finally broken the world record, and proved to myself that I could play a role in discovering the extent of human aquatic potential, my mind turned to another lofty goal that had been making regular appearances in the showreel of tantalising dreams my mind displays as I drift off to sleep at night. The Dahab Arch. Its ethereal blue, framed by shaggy walls of coral and sponge, was an image I could not forget. It awed me, and haunted me with temptation, like the locked basement door in a horror film. There was a singularity to the idea of my freediving through it. A world record could be any depth, measured as a whole number of metres — and what was a metre anyway, other than an imperfect and fairly arbitrary division (one ten-millionth) of the distance between the equator and the North Pole? But swimming into Dahab's

Blue Hole, through its arch and ascending into the open Red Sea — *that* would be a unique accomplishment, like climbing a sheer rock wall for the first time.

There was also something transformational about the idea of passing through that portal into the open sea. Almost as if, wherever I went back then, I was still bounded by the walls and floor of an enclosed volume of water; to dare to pass through into that limitless empty blue might somehow yield access to a greater level of ability in freediving.

I began training specifically for the endeavour, doing drills of dives to 55 metres and then swimming an increasingly longer horizontal distance away from and back to the line before ascending again. I also announced on the freediving forums my intention to be the first human to pass through the arch with no fins (at this point, a couple of freedivers had made the trip with fins or a monofin), and set a date in July. This might not have been the smartest move, however, as it alerted the team of one of my few competitors, William Winram. Winram had been a Canadian national breaststroker, so had a clean and powerful technique for swimming underwater without fins. He had also made two attempts at the CNF world record, suffering logistical complications in the first and a blackout 20 metres below the surface in the second, which had taken place in Hawaii the week before my 81-metre dive. A narrow, goateed face and a long mane of sun-bleached hair gave him the look of a pirate, and his rascally antics and crazed toothy laugh confirmed the suspicion. In true pirate fashion, he snuck in ahead of me and stole the booty before I could get to the X on the map. In truth, William had only had idle intentions of attempting the dive, as after his deep blackout in April his confidence was low. Also, four harrowing root canal procedures had left air bubbles in his jaw that caused severe pain when subjected to the pressure of a deep freedive. He was persuaded to make the attempt by the Russian freediver Natalia Avseenko, who wanted to become the first woman to swim through with a monofin. Natalia bailed, but William carried on through; speaking about it years later, he said that in the moment when he committed to the crossing it was less about the arch itself and more about regaining trust in himself and his own abilities after the demoralising failures of the previous year. In the back of his mind, he felt that if he turned back then, his career was over.

My trip to Egypt was already booked, so I had to try to salvage some kind of purpose for it. I decided that the only way to make the dive even more pure (and difficult) would be to attempt it without a wetsuit, wearing only my Speedos. Hairy man-flesh is rough and wobbly material underwater, especially compared with the taut silicone-coated surface of my Orca wetsuit, so I would be wasting a lot of energy in both form and surface drag. Diving mostly naked would also expose my weakness to cold (I have poor stores of body fat, or 'bioprene', and get cold even in tropical water), and this would mean that I'd shiver my way through more oxygen stores before the dive even began.

The way my preparations had been going, I'd been confident that I would be able to swim the arch unassisted — but doing it *sans* suit made me more nervous. I started to fear that the project might go the way of most of my other Egyptian escapades, which cut my newly won confidence right back to the ground. That anxiety gnawed at the back of my mind until the day I arrived at the Blue Hole to attempt the dive, whereupon it sat up and sank its jaws right into the middle of my adrenal glands. From the shelter of a shaded restaurant on the beach, I watched as my support team set up orange buoys for descent lines to hang on the inside and outside of the Blue Hole, to give me references for the vertical parts of the swim-through. The distance between these two lines was terrifying. I literally had to sweep my head from left to right across the horizon to identify first one, then the other buoy. I'd been told by technical scuba divers that the horizontal distance I would have to swim to pass through the arch was 30 to

35 metres, but what I was looking at had to be at least 100. Later I would discover that there'd been an error in the positioning of the outside buoy; this was corrected just before my descent, but the image I carried in my head as I swam out to take position on the inside buoy was of a chasmic distance — an insuperable gulf that would have been difficult to swim underwater even just below the surface, let alone at 55 metres.

I told myself that I would swim to the arch, take a stroke or two into it, and then decide whether to commit or to return the way I came. I knew that I would have to be quick with my breathe-up, or risk descending into a fit of shivering from where I could never attempt a maximal dive. Sure enough, after barely a minute of lying relaxed on the surface, the first twitches and ripples had arrived. My nerves had teamed up with the cold, and with every breath they gained more control. 'What the hell, let's just go and have a look,' I told myself, and sucked a full gust of air into my lungs.

Without the buoyancy of a wetsuit it took just six easy strokes before I could feel gravity starting to take over. I tucked my arms to my sides and enjoyed the novel feeling of water flowing across the entire surface of my body as I picked up speed in the freefall. Through half-closed eyes I watched the walls of the Blue Hole loom out towards me as the diameter of the hole narrowed.

The delicate tendrils and filigree of the softer corals that adorned the structure made an elaborate tapestry that slowly slid upwards through my view.

My depth alarm went off to tell me that I was at 45 metres; I should be able to see the opening of the arch soon. I cast my gaze downwards — and there it was, that immaculate blue, coming into sight. By good fortune I was already oriented in the right direction, and wouldn't need to swivel to locate the opening.

Using a scull of my hands, I changed course to angle downwards towards that beckoning blue light. This put me in a belly-up orientation, but I had already visualised this when I had planned my swim, and over the course of two kicks and strokes I slowly rolled over onto my stomach. I glided past the first of two scuba divers stationed at the openings on either side of the arch. I had requested that no diver enter the arch itself during my dive, since bodies and exhaust bubbles could easily obscure or obstruct my path through it. The flip side to this was that if something did happen to me while I was in the very middle of the arch, then I would sink faster than the scuba divers would be able to intercept me, towards a sea floor that sloped steeply down from a depth of 90 metres into the abyss of the Red Sea trench. In that (I hoped unlikely) event, I had instructed them not to try to reach me. They were already beyond the limit of regular air diving, and to go deeper would expose them to nitrogen narcosis that could spell their end also. After all, this was the most dangerous dive site in the world. Over the 2002–2017 period, it claimed the lives of over 150 scuba divers (by comparison, Mount Everest took 120 climbers in the same period), and veterans refer to it as the Diver's Cemetery. The first of the victims were remembered by plaques on the cliff next to the Blue Hole, but once the tally started to mount up they stopped the practice — otherwise it really would have looked like a cemetery.

As I passed the first scuba diver, I felt the heat from the lights on his camera rig trail down my back and off my feet. From here through to the other side, I was on my own. A thrill like I had never experienced before passed through my body. 'I'm really in it!' I thought to myself. After all the dives where I'd witnessed the enchanting but foreboding spectacle of that massive gateway, now I was actually inside the picture. It was really happening.

Somewhere in the preceding moments I had subconsciously made the decision to keep going. I felt completely in control and powerful, and the uncertainty I'd had on the surface about the distance I would have to swim was quickly subsiding with the realisation that I was already halfway through and the ceiling was starting to slope upwards again. I was following this curve, to take the most direct route out, when I narrowly avoided colliding

The moment of committing to swimming through the Arch at the Dahab Blue Hole.

more than that in me. There was even the slightest sense of remorse that this epiphanic journey would soon be over. As I met my safety diver at 30 metres I slowed my strokes down, feeling as if for the first time the joy of parting the water above my head and sweeping it down to my sides in long, powerful flourishes. There was a rush of turbulence around my head as my body was propelled upwards towards the light with each stroke.

I broke the surface next to the buoy, took one breath while I removed my mask, then leant back into the water as I pumped my fist triumphantly into the air. There was something so innately *complete* about this dive, so satisfyingly conclusive. It had taken me through all three stages of matter: from air, down into liquid, then seemingly through solid rock itself, before returning up through liquid to air again. I was back more or less in the same place as where I had begun — on the surface of the sea beside the Egyptian desert — but I felt as if I had swum through into an alternate version of that world, one that presented open vistas of possibility in every direction. It was an immersion into confinement that ended with delivery into a limitless sea, having shed the restraint of all beliefs — my own and those of others. It was the ultimate rite of passage.

*

Shortly after returning to Italy and resuming a regular training pattern, I heard that Martin Štěpánek, whose record I had recently broken, was going to attempt to retrieve it with a dive to 83 metres in Egypt, in the same Blue Hole I had just left. The day of the attempt came, and news of Martin's successful dive quickly spread online. My ego felt a twinge as it found itself demoted to second-best in the world, but this was vastly outweighed by an almost jubilant wave of fresh motivation. Martin's success was a prime incentive for me to train harder and answer the challenge laid down, and on that same day I set a personal best in exhale apnea during my dry-training session.

However, the record was destined to be short-lived. When the official video was released the following day, I noticed that no tag had been used in Martin's dive. The AIDA rules had recently changed to require that a tag be retrieved from the bottom plate as proof of arrival at the announced depth, and both the AIDA officials and Martin (himself an AIDA judge) should have known this. Somehow I was the only person who picked up on the fault, and so it fell on my shoulders to notify AIDA that the record should not have been validated. I did so immediately, so that Martin would have enough time to re-attempt the record, since it would be better for AIDA, the sport, and my career if he did so. Instead, his team chose to dispute the overruling, and by the time the attempt was confirmed as invalid Martin had lost the opportunity to try again. It was a tense moment in the freediving community, with opinion divided between those who saw the tag as an irrelevant feature of an otherwise perfect dive, and those who argued that the reputation of AIDA was at stake if it allowed records to be given to dives that didn't satisfy its requirements. In the end, the critical detail in the AIDA jury's decision was the fact that collecting a tag from the bottom plate and attaching it to one's body, however simple an action it might appear to be, does in fact add a certain margin of difficulty to the dive itself. For my world record in the Bahamas I had used a rectangle of female Velcro as a tag, with a patch of male Velcro on the leg of my wetsuit to attach it to; this has now become the standard in freediving competitions. However, locating the tag, breaking it free from the plate and securing a good contact on the leg, all while executing a turn at the maximum depth, is still undoubtedly one of the most delicate phases of the whole performance. (Not to mention the niggling uncertainty during the ascent as to whether the tag is holding fast where you put it!)

Of course, with video cameras and accurate depth-gauges supplying fairly unequivocal proof of whether a particular depth has been reached, the tag has become more of a symbolic testimony. It harks back to the actions of the earliest freedivers, who dived to retrieve sponges or pearls from the sea floor. However, it also allows for a triumphant moment when the tag can be brandished to the judges and spectators as tangible evidence that, yes, I was there, and I brought this thing back to prove it.

I knew it wouldn't be long before Martin, or someone else, did exceed my depth with a valid performance. I wanted to be prepared for that day, with more in the tank so that I could respond in kind and maybe create the kind of storied rivalry with another athlete that had fuelled the careers of great freedivers before me: Umberto Pelizzari and Pipin Ferreras, and before them Jacques Mayol and Enzo Maiorca, whose feud in and out of the water was immortalised in the cult film *The Big Blue*. However, that ambition was only the spike of the marlin: the muscled fish behind it was my desire to go deeper than I or anyone else believed was possible, beyond even the 300-foot (92-metre) goal I had set myself; in short, to redefine our concept of human aquatic capacity. Whether another athlete was alongside me, leapfrogging my records with his, was a less important detail.

And so I threw myself back into training, swimming two pool sessions a day of endless 25- or 50-metre underwater laps, stretching, strengthening and refining my technique, and above all trying to get 'inside' the sensation of a breath-hold. 'Know thy enemy', the saying goes, but it's even better to make your enemy your friend. Rather than treating the crescendo of discomfort and agitation that comes during a breath-hold as 'pain' or 'suffering', was it possible to make peace with that sensation? To experience it without being affected by it? Or, to put it another way, could I stay calm while suffocating?

T. E. Lawrence (of Arabia) had a famous party trick where he would pinch a burning match between his fingers to extinguish the flame. When a colleague asked him for the secret, Lawrence smiled and replied,

'The trick, my dear fellow, is to not *mind* that it hurts.'
This same concept can be applied to the urge to breathe:
acknowledging it, but remaining impassive to it. This
is the challenge that I have set myself in my freediving
career, and it is a work without end, for there will
always be a deeper state of relaxation and equanimity
that is accessible. At times, when I sit and do exhale
static apneas with little or no preparation, so that the
CO_2 levels build very quickly into an intense urge to
breathe (with no respite in the form of the breathing-
reflex contractions), I tell myself that if only I can match
the intensity of my body's primal scream for air with an
equal level of mental serenity and composure, then I will
break through into a realm where I can continue holding
my breath indefinitely. Years, centuries, might pass,
and I would remain seated there, empty in mind and
suspended in body. Of course it's a fantastical idea, with
zero scientific basis, but it's possible for me to entertain
it just enough to inspire me to go a little longer, to strive
for a slightly deeper state of relaxation.

All the while, through all the hours and days I spend
in a state of hypercapnia, hypoxia, lactic acidosis and
hyperbaria, my body is making responses, adjusting itself
to be better equipped to respond to the stimulus. My
kidneys secrete a hormone to stimulate the production
of more oxygen-carrying haemoglobin (in my red

blood cells); my muscle tissues increase their content of myoglobin so as to store more oxygen when my blood supply is cut off by extreme vasoconstriction (narrowing) of my capillaries; my diaphragm and ribcage become more flexible to allow for my collapsing lungs, while the structures inside my lungs develop elasticity to allow for increases in air and blood content. Overhauling so much of the body's physiology is not a simple process, and this is why we no longer see world records being set or challenged by athletes who have only a handful of years of training and experience behind them.

*

It was possibly the most experienced and successful male freediver of all time who would next attempt to break the record I had set in April. On 21 October 2007, at the 'Triple Depth' competition in Dahab's Blue Hole, the Austrian Herbert Nitsch announced a no-fins dive to 83 metres. This time, there would be tags on the bottom plate. Also, this time I was present as a spectator, watching from the water next to the dive line as Herbert prepared himself in his trademark position: seated, rocking-horse style, on a large blue foam 'noodle'. He collected a sizeable portion of the Egyptian desert air into his cavernous lungs, then turned and started to swim down with armstrokes that were so relaxed and truncated they almost appeared feeble. Herbert's lung capacity is an incredible 10 litres, and he can increase this to 15 litres when packing (a technique that uses the mouth like a pump to force extra air in after a full inhale). This gave him the advantage of more oxygen stores, but also meant that he would have to work harder to overcome a greater positive buoyancy on the surface; alternatively, if he chose to offset that buoyancy by wearing lead weights he would pay the price for this by being more negatively buoyant at depth, where his lungs would compress from 15 litres down to less than 2. Herbert's lung capacity makes him less concerned about dive duration and swimming technique, and more focused on getting through the initial high-buoyancy phase of the dive without using too much energy and creating too much lactic acid, which could lead to muscle failure in the ascent.

By contrast, my lung volume is around 9 litres, even with packing, so I spend less energy battling against my positive/negative buoyancy in the dive but have less oxygen at my disposal. The advantage of this configuration is that over time, as I develop better oxygen storage in my blood and muscles (where it is dissolved and thus incompressible), I will start to get the best of both worlds: more fuel (oxygen) and less opposing force (buoyancy). There is an analogous trade-off in the sport of rock-climbing, where muscle makes you stronger (good) but heavier (bad).

The last we saw of Herbert was the flash of two white feet as he kicked out of sight at around 25 metres. There followed two and a half minutes of pregnant silence, as everyone waiting on the surface trod water in a circle around the dive line, scrying the inscrutable blue below us. I was torn in two directions: on the one hand, if I was to break the no-fins world record again in the future it would be a better story if the previous record belonged to someone like Herbert; on the other, I couldn't deny that I was feeling a kind of cloying hope that the record would remain unbeaten, that even such a great freediver as Herbert Nitsch would have difficulty going deeper.

The safety freedivers descended, and we could see them milling around at a depth of 30 metres for a few seconds before Herbert's shape appeared between them. He was swimming even more languorously than when he had started his descent, his arms only just clearing his head before he dragged them loosely back towards his sides. It was clear that his muscles were saturated with lactic acid — but his mind was still clear and, as he drifted up, allowing positive buoyancy to take over for the remaining few metres of the ascent, he calmly removed his fluid goggles, which are basically swimming goggles with lenses that permit underwater vision when flooded with water, so that he would be able to see clearly above the surface.

Two breaths after surfacing, and he was flashing an 'okay' sign to the judges. They showed their white cards, and the record was official: 83 metres. I joined in the applause and laughs of disbelief from the audience, telling myself that this was further confirmation of the great potential remaining in this discipline. Both Štěpánek and now Nitsch had dived to 83 metres, with comparably little specific training, and what I felt was marginal technique. This could only mean that we weren't yet close to the human limit.

Herbert would continue to dominate a few weeks later at the AIDA World Championships, held in Sharm El Sheikh. Once again the mysterious physical condition that I have experienced only in that location resurfaced, giving me a blood pressure in the basement and a resting heart rate through the roof. Several other athletes commented that they had exactly the same symptoms, but we never did identify what was behind it or even come up with a realistic hunch. The weather conditions weren't optimal, either, with large choppy waves and a slight current. From being able to dive in the mid-eighties in the Bahamas I was relegated to the mid-seventies in Egypt, and when I announced what I thought was a conservative 75 metres I still blacked out briefly after surfacing at the end of the dive. Meanwhile, Herbert correctly guessed that an announcement of 77 metres would be enough to win a second gold medal to go with the gold in the Constant Weight discipline he had won two days earlier. William Winram, who had also announced 75 metres, completed his dive for the silver medal; and third place went to the youthful Alexey Molchanov with a 65-metre dive, signalling that he was more than just the son of his mother, the great Natalia Molchanova, who was dominant across all the disciplines in both pool and sea.

*

I left Egypt empty-handed, and relieved of the world-record title. But I was in a very different state to how I had left the country almost exactly a year before. The record was still less than the depths I was capable of in training, and I intended to increase that margin.

My problem now was that I could not afford to keep attempting world records as stand-alone events in the Bahamas. After breaking the world record in 2007, I had been secretly disappointed to wake the following morning and *not* find at my door a queue of marketing directors from aspiring sponsor companies, waving juicy contracts for me to sign. Even when I solicited sponsorship myself there was a distinctly lacklustre response — it seemed that either the sport was too small or it was deemed too dangerous for most brands to be associated with it. My first sponsor was the wetsuit manufacturer Orca, a New Zealand company with its offices in Auckland, almost next door to where I had flatted during university. They supplied me with wetsuits for my first record attempts and then, in 2008, began to support me financially as well. Also in 2008 I began a contract with Suunto, a Finnish company that makes the most accurate diving and freediving computers, used by AIDA as the official gauges in records and competitions. The marriage of my 'athlete brand' with these two sports brands has thus far been a happy union of almost a decade, helped by the fact that both companies really do supply the best-quality products in their sector (and that's not just because I'm paid to say that (though of course I would say that too (no, but really it's true (promise!)))).

In 2007 I also began teaching freediving courses myself, in Europe and the Caribbean, under the school name of Vertical Blue. Between the first trickle of sponsorship money, the course fees and some odd translation jobs that I could fit into my spare time, I was able to sustain my training, travel and living expenses. However, even then a record attempt easily ran into five figures, and that was simply untenable as an annual expense. Additionally, there was an undertone of prejudice against record attempts among some in the freediving community. They felt that the opportunity to set a record should only be available during registered competitions — the same as for most other sports. In a competition, the exact time of day when you must start the dive ('Official Top' time) is decided by the schedule of the event, and the dive must begin within a 30-second window following that time. This was easy to adapt to; the major difference, that I had until then been exploiting, was that in a competition the use of a lanyard safety system was mandatory. The lanyard is a tether that connects the athlete to the descent line: on the athlete's end it is attached by means of a wrist strap or belt, while at the other end a large carabiner is clipped on to the descent line. The carabiner falls loosely along the line beside the athlete, but cannot fall further than the plate at the target depth. If the athlete fails to ascend, this can be detected by multiple means (a sonar device on the surface, feeling the rope for the vibration of the ascending carabiner, and failure to rendezvous with the safety freediver at a certain time) and the whole descent line is then hoisted by allowing a heavy counterweight attached to the other end of the rope to drop off the other side of the boat or platform. As it lifts, the bottom plate catches the athlete's carabiner and drags him or her to the surface with it.

This system is now standard across all competitions and record attempts, but in 2007 there was still the option to instead employ safety scuba divers, stationed every 30 metres along the rope with lift bags ready to clip onto the athlete. The difference for the athlete is one less piece of equipment, and thus one less source of drag during the dive. I had done comparisons between the two systems, and estimated that even with a minimalist lanyard the difference equated to at least 2 per cent. Given that we only needed to exceed a record by about 1 per cent (1 metre), this little handbrake could easily make the difference between success and distress. Moreover, I hated feeling like a dog on a leash during a dive, especially in a sport that was all about freedom. I felt that lanyards were an imperfect solution — added to which, at that time they had never been required to resolve an incident (it is hard to imagine a scenario in which a freediver might black out at depth, where oxygen levels are still high), but had in fact been the cause themselves of numerous incidents when the lanyard's carabiner became entangled with the bottom plate, abandoned fishing nets and lines, or even with itself.

Ultimately, though, there was no better solution for how to guarantee that a freediver couldn't drift off into the blue while far down and out of sight of the crew on the surface. Lanyard designs have also become more tangle-proof, and in recent years the counterweight system has indeed been used to save the lives of at least two competing freedivers. However, it's hard to know whether having the lanyard creates a false sense of security, which, had it been absent, might have meant that these rescued freedivers wouldn't have over-reached themselves in the first place.

Herbert's record was the first in CNF to employ a lanyard. Setting aside the safety debate, I felt that it was important for me to replicate this level of difficulty if I was going to exceed the depth. After all, I would be the first person to claim that a dive to 83 metres with a lanyard is more difficult than one to 84 without one.

The natural solution to both my budgetary limitations and the onus of diving clipped to the line was to host a competition in the Bahamas. That way I would only have to pay a share of the expenses, while still enjoying the perfect conditions of Dean's Blue Hole. At the end of 2007, I wrote to all my acquaintances among freediving athletes, inviting them to come to Long Island in April 2008 for an 11-day period of officially judged diving. It would be a competition under AIDA regulations, but rather than competing against each other the idea was for us to have a chance to attempt personal goals, whether those happened to be world- or national-record attempts or just personal-best dives. All expenses were to be divided equally between the competitors, and to keep these low we would take turns to be each other's safety divers. To keep it manageable I limited the number of entrants to 15, and quickly had that many takers — including many of the top-ranked divers in the world, such as ex-CWT world-record holders Eric Fattah and Guillaume Néry, Japanese champion Ryuzo Shinomiya, pool world-record holder and fellow Kiwi Dave Mullins, and the Russian Natalia Avseenko, who everyone was billing to take down the women's no-fins world record. William Winram would be there too, with a similar goal to me: something deeper than 83 metres without fins.

However, for the first time I was seriously training in more than just CNF. I didn't know how close I could get to the world record in Free Immersion (FIM), which stood at 106 metres, but I was curious to find out. I had made a key change to one piece of my equipment, swapping out a low-volume mask for fluid goggles. This eliminated the necessity to equalise the mask's airspace, which, although it is a small volume, still needs to be refilled eight times on the way to 80 metres.

In FIM, freedivers use the rope to pull themselves down and up during the dive. It is a very slow and relaxed, almost meditative form of diving, and since it uses exclusively upper-body strength it is a good complement to CNF. However, of the three depth disciplines it is easily the least technical and the least noteworthy, and I have sometimes questioned its inclusion in competition. After all, pulling on a rope is not something that normally comes to mind when we think of diving, to say nothing of 'free' diving! Nonetheless, I still enjoyed the sensation, and in my first training dives I revelled in how much easier it was to use a rigid point of contact to propel my body, with long, smooth pulls along the rope.

It only took me a few dives before I was hitting three-digit depths, and there was where the fun started. The extra ambient pressure and duration of an FIM dive took me to a level of narcosis that I had never before experienced. In scuba diving, narcosis is often called the martini effect because every additional atmosphere of pressure (added with each 10-metre increment in depth) has an effect equivalent to drinking one martini. Luckily it's not quite that bad in freediving, or with 10 martinis under my belt at 100 metres I would probably have had difficulty working out which way was up, or even remembering that that was where I needed to return to. The general sensation is of becoming more detached from your body, coupled with affected vision that can turn into hallucination. On one dive, I was watching my hand come up past my face, grab the line and then pull downwards, crossing with the other hand that was returning upwards to take its turn. I felt as if I should probably close my eyes to relax more, so I did; but I carried on seeing exactly the same thing: left hand, right hand, left hand, right hand ... I squeezed my eyes tightly closed so that I could feel my eyelids pressing against each other — yep, they're definitely closed — but it made no difference to what I saw.

On the worst occasion, I was diving with Guillaume Néry and his partner Julie Gautier, who was safetying me. It was an overcast day, and a strong easterly wind had whipped the ocean into a frantic swell that threw itself against the barrier reef, trying to break into the sanctuary of our lagoon. In the protected corner where the Blue Hole is, the water was barely ruffled, but the churning of sand out on the reef meant that visibility had been reduced to only a few metres. At depth the darkness was complete, and this can amplify the symptoms of narcosis. When I turned at a depth of 105 metres I knew straight away that I was in for a ride. For the first time, I wondered whether it might be possible to black out from acute narcosis, and this thought alarmed me. I began pulling harder with my arms, while trying to keep the rest of my body relaxed. At these depths, if you panic and try to get to the surface as quickly as possible then you will use up your oxygen long before you even reach your safety diver. And speaking of which, where was she? The comfort of meeting one's safety diver can be enough to induce a second wind on difficult ascents, and at that point that was exactly what I needed. With almost masochistic mirth, I noticed that my vision was now starting to go white, just as it does in the accounts of those who return from a near-death experience. And as if on cue, there was an angel descending into my field of vision, ready to escort me towards the light ...

All through these hallucinations my arms kept on pulling, doing what they had been programmed to do, and when I arrived on the surface, out of breath but still very much conscious, reality started to superimpose itself on my narcotic revelry. The whiteout had just been the return of light as I climbed into shallower water, where the sun's rays could still penetrate through the silt, and the angel had of course been Julie. She told me that I had been pulling a little quicker than normal and had given her a strange look, but other than that I had seemed to be doing fine.

*

It seemed to me that if I could learn to manage that state of deep inebriation, I would then be capable of attempting the FIM world record. Meanwhile, my CNF training dives were adding to the depths I had reached in 2007, and on 28 March, three days before the inaugural Vertical Blue competition kicked off, I surfaced cleanly from a dive to 90 metres. I was trying to keep my training depths a secret from any competitors, so I didn't talk about this dive with my safety diver or anyone else at the Blue Hole. Not until I had returned home, eaten a post-training meal and sunk into the couch with some music playing did it start to sink in. It wasn't just the milestone depth, or the fact that it was a strong and clean dive; the oceanic sense of fulfilment and gratitude that I felt in that moment came down to the fact that I was there, 'standing in my dream'. Through years of discipline, perseverance, study and daring, I had been able to congeal into reality the vision I'd had of a life in pursuit of the aquatic nature of man. Now, every day and every dive was a venture into unexplored territory that redefined the range and ability of our species underwater.

Lying there on the couch and contemplating this, something in the music took me over a precipice. The driving guitar in Coldplay's 'Politik' that had been locked into a dichotomy of twin chords suddenly morphed into a piano that broke free to ride up and over a wave of chord changes, cresting and breaking before re-emerging from the trough. In that moment, something took place in the base of my skull that sprayed a wave of sensation up and around the surface of my cranium, as well as downwards along my spine, and from there out along my ribs and into my arms and legs. It's hard to describe what that sensation was without using ambiguous and oft-abused words like 'opening', 'light' and 'energy'. It was as if a covering had been pulled away from my body, and every newly exposed nerve ending was thrilling at being activated for the first time. Somehow the outer halves of my eyeballs were vibrating, and my cheeks had been drawn upwards to couch my eyes in a kind of soft embrace.

As Chris Martin repeated the closing lines of the song, waves of well-being, immaculate peace and euphoria kept shedding themselves down my spine. Thin seawater tributaries were flowing freely from my eyes, and I was laughing in wonder and gratitude. In all my 27 years, those were the first tears of joy I'd ever shed.

Since then I have experienced this sensation many times, often accompanied by music, when I am meditating outdoors, or in certain social settings. With the right concentration, position and breathing I can sometimes bring it on voluntarily. That there is some kind of physical event happening in the body is without doubt, but even the most technical description of it to Google results only in page links to '*kundalini* awakening' and talk of the release of *shakti* energy that is stored at the base of the spine. It appears to be a phenomena that is unexplained or ignored by Western science. In yoga, the purpose of the physical poses (*asanas*) and flowing movements (*vinyasa*) is to purify the nerve channels (*nadis*) so that energy can travel more freely through the body during *pranayama* and meditation. Although I do not practise yoga itself diligently or accurately, I often liken a freedive without fins to a form of repetitive *vinyasa* flow of arm and leg movements, all performed on one long *kumbhaka* (breath-hold). Is it possible that the hours I've spent repeating those kinds of movements, as well as the breathing exercises and *pranayama*, have had the effect of tonifying major nerve channels in my body in a way that allows them all to be suddenly stimulated by some kind of central circuit-breaker at the apex of my spine?

Interestingly, yogic texts mention that an awakening of *kundalini* energy is often achieved by means of *kevala kumbhaka*, which turns out to be a practice that is almost identical to the seated breath-holds I perform with empty lungs (although they also state that this form of *kumbhaka* 'cures all diseases and promotes longevity', something that is flatly contradicted in my case every time I have a cold or ear infection!). While the language of yogic texts is prone to stray into esoteric and implausible panegyrics, there is a definite similarity between the physical descriptions of yogic states and what I have experienced myself, almost by accident and before having read those descriptions. The *bandha* locks were the first example of this: during my practice of exhale breath-holds they had evolved intuitively as a concrete way of blocking contractions and thereby not dispersing the dive reflex, whereas in yoga they've been practised for thousands of years as a means of retaining energy in a loop between the perineum and the head. Perhaps the most common yogic tool used by freedivers is the *nauli kriya*, in which the stomach is flexed inwards up under the ribcage while the abdominals contract rhythmically in the opposite direction. *Kriya* means cleansing, and this is exactly what it achieves: the rhythmic massaging of the digestive system and organs helps to push waste through and eliminate gas from the stomach, allowing more room for the lungs to expand. The *nauli kriya* also increases the flexibility of the diaphragm itself, which helps to accommodate the collapse of the lungs due to pressure at depth.

The great French freediving pioneer of the 1960s and '70s, Jacques Mayol (upon whom the hero of *The Big Blue* is based), was the first to marry yoga and freediving, and he spent much time studying Eastern disciplines in

India and Japan. On one trip, when visiting a yogi who was a retired university professor who had renounced all titles and possessions to become an ascetic, Jacques described his sport and how he applied yoga to it. The yogi listened carefully; soon afterwards, when they were swimming at a local lake, he disappeared under the water. After lying on the shallow bottom for 6 minutes, by which point Jacques was starting to become nervous, he re-emerged, saying 'You were right, Mr Mayol, this is indeed a shortcut to *samadhi*!'

Jacques Mayol was Umberto Pelizzari's mentor and greatest influence, and in the same way Umberto was my mentor and role model during the first years of my career. This lineage, of which I have strived to make myself worthy, carried with it the inheritance of a bond with Eastern techniques and philosophies. My first exposure to it had in fact begun at an earlier age, when I watched my mother doing yoga on the deck of our boat and tried to mimic her — although the safety harness or my water wings would sometimes get in the way!

Coincidentally, just before the Vertical Blue competition commenced, Linda sent me an article she had written for a yoga magazine that included the words of Sri Ramakrishna (often called Paramahamsa, or Great Swan):

Dive deep, O mind,
Into the ocean of Divine Beauty,
You will discover a new gem
Instant after instant.

*

Even with only 15 competitors and a communal approach in which both athletes and crew helped to get the event running, there were still a lot of last-minute jobs and stress involved, and this continued into the first couple of days of the competition. As a result, I didn't act until the third day, with an easy FIM to warm up. William Winram announced a world-record 84 metres CNF on that day; he continued to announce world-record depths in this discipline for the rest of his time on the island, but turned early in the descent on each attempt.

The following day I announced an 84 CNF as well. It would be my first record attempt with a lanyard and I was nervous, but unlike in Egypt my blood pressure remained normal and I was able to relax completely on my back during the breathe-up in perfect Blue Hole conditions. Twenty seconds from Official Top time I took my last breath and started packing my lungs. Soon after the count reached zero I turned, reached out, and parted the water for my first stroke. Seven of those later and settling into the freefall, I did a quick inventory of my sensations. There were no major hypocapnic signals that would indicate I had over-breathed, so given my initial blood pressure that meant I was right on track. Veteran freediver Eric Fattah had advised me to congratulate myself after the duck dive, as by then the result was already determined, and the deeper I fell the more I empathised with this. It took me a while to find the Velcro on the bottom plate and attach it to my leg, but I was still calm and relaxed as I started my ascent, 1:35 into the dive. 'Twenty-eight strokes,' I told myself (an extra two from how many it would take without a lanyard). After 20 strokes I still felt comfortable, so I started to lengthen the glides and enjoy the rest of the ascent. My safety freediver, Peter Scott, met me at 20 metres and we cruised to the surface together. In training, I had been having difficulty remembering to remove the nose clip during the surface protocol (this is necessary kit when diving with fluid goggles, to prevent water flooding the nose and sinuses). So, as I arrived at the surface this time, I focused all of my attention on doing that one task right before relaxing into recovery breathing (read: panting).

With that dive in a time of 3:20 I reclaimed the world record from Herbert Nitsch. There is no way that I could have expected it at the time, but that would be the last day in the following nine years (at the time of writing) that the world record would not belong to me.

Four days later, the women's record would also be broken by Natalia Avseenko, who overcame a torrent of nerves to swim powerfully to 57 metres and back in 2:34. On the same day I made my first attempt at the Free Immersion record, with the depth set to 107 — one metre more than the record held by Martin Štěpánek. I was the last to dive. Little did I know it, but there would be a surprise waiting for me at depth, and not a pleasant one. In those early days we were using carabiners to drop a single tag down onto the bottom plate before each dive (nowadays, the tags are all attached around the perimeter of the plate before it is set for the first dive). The carabiner that was delivering my tag became stuck on some marker tape just above the plate. When my own lanyard carabiner hit the stuck one, it put tension on the lanyard cable, snapping the wire at the point where it was crimped (as a result, my lanyard designs have improved a lot since then). There was, of course, no tag to be found on the bottom plate, and I spent what seemed like an eternity — but was in fact 5 seconds — rummaging among the used carabiners, trying to find one with a tag on it. When I was satisfied that it wasn't there and it wasn't just narcosis playing with my vision, I started my ascent; at which point, my hand hit the mass of blocked carabiners. I felt something (probably my lanyard cable) brush my foot too, and thinking that it might be the missing tag I reached out to try to grab it. However, I was flailing without reference or adequate vision, and losing precious time, so I continued on my way. The rest of the ascent was uneventful, and the narcosis surprisingly tolerable. Initially the judges gave me a yellow card for not bringing a tag; but when the footage from the bottom-plate camera was reviewed and it became clear that it was through no fault of my own, the card was changed to white and I had my first Free Immersion world record.

I wasn't happy with the ambiguity, though, especially after 'Tag-gate' in 2007, and so on the last day of the event I announced 108 metres. This time, the tag was right where it should have been and the judges' card didn't have any grey edges.

The dive was made more difficult because on the day before, the penultimate day of the event, I had attempted to shift the CNF record by a 2-metre jump to 86, and for entirely different reasons this had been a demanding task as well. I had started the day in a foul mood, and everything seemed to conspire to keep me in it (although it's probably more accurate to say that my foulness inspired reciprocation from others, as well as from what is referred to these days as 'the universe'). I had to find someone to fill a vacancy among the safety freedivers; then was left temporarily without transport to the Blue Hole (my ute was being used as the emergency vehicle). While I was breathing up, I noticed that the Velcro patch on my leg for the tag was coming unstuck, so I borrowed a knife to cut half of it off. The bad run continued right up to the last moment, when I missed the timekeeper's minute call and performed a terrible duck-dive ...

These are all the sorts of reasons that we can sometimes give ourselves for aborting a dive: the lazy/scared monologist in our minds will be mounting his pulpit, ready to spout excuses. At this point, training and a long background of deep dives provides the possibility of turning off the conscious mind and operating completely on autopilot, confident in the actions and contingent decisions programmed into our subconscious. If that analytical mind cannot be shut down, then neither will it be possible to turn off the pestering, pessimistic voice that shadows it — he will follow you all the way down, harping on at you like some cheerless parent-in-law until you either turn early or doom the dive through agitation and increased oxygen consumption. You do, however, need to be able to distinguish between trivial detail (a cut finger that the salt water is making sting) and conditions that actually have an impact on performance (a wry neck preventing you from generating as much power in the armstroke).

As I settled into the freefall on my way to 86 metres, I felt the bad energy that had surrounded my preparation slip away — it was superficial, and therefore stayed on the surface. Beneath everything else, I knew that little had happened that could affect my physiological state. When I turned at the bottom I concentrated, as always, on counting my ascent strokes. Thoughts, both negative — 'you're not going to make it!' — and positive — 'if you make it you'll have a new world record!' — tried to clamber into my consciousness like attention-seeking toddlers, but I used a trick of affecting boredom with them before they even began. 'Whatever you have to say, it's irrelevant now — the dive has already been decided long ago,' I told them, and myself.

I had perhaps never been so happy at the conclusion of a record attempt, precisely because I'd had to overcome an adversary (the most guileful kind — the internal adversary) in order to achieve it. It's hard to overestimate the effect that this kind of success can have: confidence blooms, and competition dives start to feel like just ordinary training. The reverse is also true, of course: every time we succumb to that despairing voice, we fuel our own fussiness and superstition. It's still necessary to distinguish between instinct and anxiety, which unfortunately communicate to us via the same channel, the gastro-intestinal tract; but each time we get it right, we bury the sluggard a little deeper, until his complaining voice is a muffled whisper and all that remains is undisturbed confidence and unclouded intuition.

After finishing the event with four world records, three of them set in the space of just four days, I was told by the head judge, Grant Graves, that this was my 'coming out' as a freediver. I had completely left behind the setbacks and failures of 2006, and in the process had staked out my territory among the sport's elite by claiming two of the three competitive depth records.

*

Before the Vertical Blue competition I had parted ways with Tiziana, so I wouldn't be returning to Sardinia that summer. However my e-mail inbox filled with invitations to teach courses on no-fins freediving in venues across Europe. The discipline was obviously gaining in popularity, and it seemed that in my case the freediving community had conflated success with expertise. I didn't want to disappoint though, so I mapped out an itinerary that connected dots in Holland, Denmark, Sweden, Finland and Italy.

A lot about the way I freedived was intuitive: habits and patterns that led to easier or deeper dives, and thus became permanent. Teaching my method often required examination of what I was doing and attempts to work out the reasons (if any) for it. This is how I came across the peculiar position of my tongue during exhale breath-holds and deep dives that allows me to stay more calm during the urge to breathe. In other cases, there was a more theoretical or analytical basis to what I was doing. For instance, the kick I use when diving without fins often resembles one of the most common errors in surface breaststroke swimming: wide knees that advance beyond the central axis of the body. However, there is a subtle — but decisive — difference between no-fins freediving and Olympic breaststroke. Underwater, the axis of the body remains in line with the direction of movement, whereas in surface swimming it is inclined upwards during the moment of the kick, as the swimmer takes a breath. Thus, the swimmer keeps the upper legs straight to reduce drag on the thighs, and takes advantage of the turbulent water behind the torso for the legs to coil. With full immersion, the water streams unobstructed down the freediver's straight back, and so the legs need to be evenly distributed on either side of this axis: thighs slightly forwards, heels the same distance from the centre line as the knees. There were pretty regular comments on my YouTube videos, from swimmers and swim coaches alike, suggesting that if I improved my kick I would be able to dive much deeper, but after replying to a dozen or so of those I lost interest in repeating my analysis.

The courses in Europe allowed me to share the methods and ideas I had come across, and if they 'stuck' with others then that would imply that they had some kind of universal value. I demonstrated, using a heart-rate monitor, how the heart and metabolism could be slowed down abruptly by blocking the contractions (breathing reflexes) that come on with the increase in carbon dioxide levels. I also showed students the exercises and stretches I had developed to improve the flexibility of my lungs. In particular, I paid a lot of attention to ways to reduce the lungs below their residual volume, by using the mouth like a vacuum pump to suck air out of the lungs after a full exhale. These exercises have now become standard fare for freedivers, and are taught in AIDA and SSI (Scuba Schools International) syllabuses.

Freediving is a sport that can be taught to anyone, from responsible kids through to senior citizens. The only risk is to those with existing heart or lung conditions, so a preliminary medical check-up is essential. In instructing, I get the biggest kick out of watching beginners make those first giant steps (or fin strokes) into the depths. It's fairly common for students to hold their breath for

3 minutes or more after just a few days of instruction, and if they have no difficulty equalising then dives of 15 to 30 metres are within the reach of even newbies. The euphoria new freedivers experience from these kinds of accomplishments is one of teaching's biggest rewards. I still remember my own first dives to those depths, and the swell of terrifying excitement at going that little bit deeper. It's the thrill of holding a firework after the fuse is lit, or playing chicken with an oncoming train. It's the temptation of Icarus, played out in the world of Poseidon. But gradually, with each dive we realise that this sensation is an illusion — there was never really any danger — and it's replaced by a revelation: that we can belong underwater, as a marine mammal, as a sea creature; that here is a world waiting for us to discover it. Grown adults resemble wide-eyed children, giggling into their snorkels, in the face of that discovery.

More than two-thirds of our planet is covered in water. All of it can be our home.

CHAPTER 6

GOING ON ALONE

And coming face to face with one's self

It has been revealed to me that there exists an Ocean of Consciousness without limit. From It come all things of the relative plane, and in It they merge again. These waves arising from the Great Ocean merge again in the Great Ocean. I have clearly perceived all these things.

Ramakrishna

ON CHRISTMAS EVE 2008, Jimmy Montanti arrived after a marathon voyage from Sicily, ready to spend a month training with me and another Italian freediver, Michele Tomasi, who was visiting the island with his young family. Jimmy's luggage was delayed in the trip through Miami, so I lent him clothes and equipment while we tracked it down. On the bag's arrival, he hugged it ecstatically; when he opened it, I saw why. The contents and weight were mostly made up of car-battery-sized blocks of

36-month-aged Parmigiano-Reggiano. The plasticky American Parmesan-substitute I had in the fridge was thrown in the bin, and for the next several weeks we feasted on pasta dishes topped with the crystalline flakes and crumbs of real Italian cheese.

After my experiences in 2008, it was clear that narcosis was a factor I would need to adapt to if I wanted to go deeper. The best way I knew of doing this was through 'hangs'. These are basically static apneas at depth, and I would typically use a heavy weight to give me a free ride down to a depth of between 50 and 65 metres, where I would wrap my leg around the rope and lock my fingers together in front of me. This position allowed me to close my eyes and relax every muscle in my body. It was an evolution of one of the very first exercises I had started doing when I discovered freediving in Utila, Honduras, spending minutes lying motionless in sandy gullies at 10-metre depths. Now that I was doing them at five to six times the depth, the feelings of euphoria were enhanced by the narcosis of high-pressure nitrogen and carbon dioxide in my blood. As these built up during the hang, the narcosis would become more and more intense; but without any tasks to complete, I was able to retain full control of my mind while observing the gradual changes in my body.

First up, my heart rate slowed to one beat every 2

to 3 seconds. It was so slow that instead of the regular 'da-doom, da-doom' sound we're accustomed to hearing, there was actually a pregnant pause between the two parts of each beat. I heard it as 'glung ... gloong ... ..., glung ... gloong ... ...' All of the blood had been shunted in from my limbs and periphery to the core of my torso, raising my internal blood pressure, and my body was compensating for this by slowing the heart's rhythm.

As remarkable as these physical changes were, they were nothing compared with what was happening inside my head — essentially, a stripping back of the sensation of my 'self' to the most basic raw material. The body? That disappeared after a few seconds of being relaxed on the bottom: due to either lack of stimulus or shifting blood, or both, the nerves in my skin and limbs stopped communicating any information back to the brain. This is a common enough experience; floating in a bath or even watching a movie in the cinema can yield the same sensation. Next, the head and face itself were subtracted from the equation. It took a little longer for this to occur, as there are many tiny, overlooked muscles in the face that we don't normally take into consideration but which are often held in contraction. For example, if my mouth and jaw are completely relaxed then my lips will be slightly parted. Shutting my eyelids actually requires a fibril of contraction, so in their most relaxed state my eyes are half-open, the upper lids sagging down over the cornea. Once every fascia of every muscle was completely relaxed, then my face ceased to be a part of my awareness — no more a part of my 'self' in that moment than the surrounding liquid. All that remained, in terms of sensory information being transmitted to the brain, was my vision. With my eyes half-open there was, obviously, no stopping the light-sensitive cells at the back of my eyes from relaying news of what they saw. If anything interesting had been happening in front of me, there would be no way I could 'unsee' it. However, at 60 metres in Dean's Blue Hole there is a muted, dusky light, and nothing at all in the water column. Fish rarely swim into such open spaces, and the walls of the Blue Hole are 100 metres away at that depth — beyond the limit of visibility. In the absence of anything to focus on, my eyes came to rest at the perfectly neutral focal point and remained there, undistracted. Nothing about my field of vision changed for minutes, and this meant that I became 'immune' to what I was seeing.

No body, no face, no taste, smell or sound, and finally no vision. All evidence of physical matter had been stripped away from my awareness. In such a state, the mind has very little to occupy itself with, and immeasurable tracts of time passed without any thought presenting itself to my consciousness. There might, however, be a faint awareness of this fact, an unvoiced notion of 'Ooh, my mind is empty — this is working great!', but on some level even this was still mental activity. Only when this last patina of thought dissolved into the void did the mind itself drop away from my sense of self.

Now my consciousness was naked, stripped of every material and channel that normally kept it occupied. It is not floral prose or exaggeration to say that this is a state of 'pure being'. For in the end, all we are is consciousness. Our thoughts, emotions, memories and hopes are all internal experiences that happen to that consciousness, complementing the external experiences of sound, light and the smell of coffee. My consciousness, the silent witness to everything I experience, doesn't tell my brain to have an idea, or make a calculation: those mental processes happen and we merely experience the results. What we consider to be ourselves (body, mind, memories) is in fact a vehicle for our consciousness, but the consciousness is a silent passenger. Are you your memory of having your wisdom teeth removed? No, of course not. Are you the stream of rambling thoughts you have as you drive to work? No, you're not those either. You are what experiences them: the sense of watchfulness and awareness. That is all.

What's more, this is the only thing that we can know for sure is real. As Sam Harris puts it in *Waking Up*, an impressively objective treatise on spirituality, 'Consciousness is the one thing in this universe that cannot be an illusion ... The birth of consciousness must be the result of organisation. Arranging atoms in certain ways appears to bring about an experience of being that very collection of atoms.'

I'll get back to that freediver, hanging on the end of the line at 60 metres and experiencing nothing other than awareness. But first I'd like to sidetrack into a 'thought experiment' inspired by the experience of this kind of diving. What if we could subtract everything — literally every material upon which consciousness can operate. Not just sentience, but the stored mental material as well. For instance, as I hang on the end of my line, even if I've succeeded in doing away with my body and senses, it is still possible for me to have thoughts, voiced in my head as words, about things that have happened to me, or things I would like to do in the future. This is because I still have the mental software for language, as well as a hard drive full of memories. So let's remove all of that. Now the mind is by definition empty, since it has no words or even images (which could only come from memories) to think with. There is, however, no reason why consciousness itself wouldn't remain. What would that experience be like?

Perhaps the closest we can come to understanding it is the description by Helen Keller, who became deaf and blind at the age of 19 months, of what her life was like before she learnt to communicate by touch. She likened the blur of experience to being 'at sea in a dense fog'. After acquiring her first word, 'Suddenly I felt a misty consciousness as of something forgotten — a thrill of returning thought; and somehow the mystery of language was revealed to me ... Everything had a name, and each name gave birth to a new thought. As we returned to the house every object which I touched seemed to quiver with life. That was because I saw everything with the strange, new sight that had come to me.'

Imagine then, removing from this language-less 'sea of dense fog' even the capacity to feel, taste and smell the surrounding environment, as well as the distant memories of those 19 months of being able to hear and see. What would be left with which to even sense the passing of time? There would be no reference, not even the rhythm of breathing, or the slow heart beat that I experience in the depths. With no content or measure, time would condense/expand into homogeneity. A year, a minute, a lifetime — how would they differ?

It is possible to imagine such a state occurring, and maybe with technology even induce it, by temporarily shutting down access to the areas of the brain that govern sentience, memories and speech. But it is very difficult to imagine just what that state would be like. How, for instance, would it differ from the experience of being a tree, which also lacks sentience or a mental substrate? Does a tree have a similar form of timeless and contentless consciousness?

This is panpsychism, a controversial notion that everything in the universe might be conscious, potentially conscious, or conscious when put into certain configurations. The Sufi mystic Ibn al-Arabi summarised it by saying, 'God sleeps in the rock, dreams in the plant, stirs in the animal, and awakens in man.' I might replace 'god' with 'consciousness', but many would argue that they are one and the same. The point is that there must be a smooth continuum in the degree of self-awareness between rock and man.

But wait — that continuum can go in the other direction, too! If we added to our senses the power of echolocation, we would acquire another layer of information about the world around us: like bats and dolphins, we would perceive the exact dimensions of things as well as their distance from us and even their density, regardless of whether it was night or day. If we had ampullae of Lorenzini (found around the noses of sharks), we could detect electromagnetic fields such as the one surrounding the earth that so many animals use for navigation. And these are just the existing ways presented by evolution with which we could expand our consciousness. Bionic arms have been developed that communicate rudimentary feedback from touch, so that we can not only grip but *feel* through an artificial appendage. Why stop at two arms? Or why not tentacles? And with bluetooth and internet, why would the appendages even need to be connected to the body? Our limbs and nerve endings are envoys from the mind, expanding the scope of our consciousness into the world, but there's no reason to limit ourselves to the attached biological ones we are born with. It is entirely plausible to imagine someone feeling that a surgical instrument, a digger arm or a car tyre is a part of their self to the same extent that the fingers I am pressing against my keyboard are a part of my self.

The Neuralink project headed by entrepreneur Elon Musk is one of several fledgling attempts to do all this, and more. Our memories could be augmented by instant access to all the information stored on the internet (we wouldn't google it, we'd just 'remember' it). Would such an expansion, of mind and body, alter the nature of consciousness itself? In *Waking Up*, Sam Harris goes on to say, 'It is, however, possible to notice that consciousness — that in you which is aware of your experience in this moment — does not feel like a self.

It does not feel like "I". What you are calling "I" is itself a feeling that arises among the contents of consciousness. Consciousness is prior to it, a mere witness of it, and, therefore, free of it in principle.'

Whether you lose all sentience and verbal dialogue, or whether you expand your senses to take in the entirety of the planet and link your mind to all of its computing power, it seems that the hidden mirror that somehow illuminates the experience with awareness will remain unsullied.

*

As transcendent as the experience I was having at 60 metres was, it was still contingent on my physical body, and that body had non-negotiable requirements, such as a supply of oxygen and a distaste for carbon dioxide. These priorities started to make themselves known about 4 minutes into the dive. At first I would stay non-responsive, calm and detached, but at a certain point I would need to check my watch, to have a second gauge on how much longer I could stay submerged. Sometimes I would check my watch again, at what felt like a moment later, to find that nearly half a minute had passed. When thoughts are scarce, time really does lack any sense of scale. Finally, with the onset of breathing reflexes I would slowly start to make my way back towards the surface, pulling softly on the line, my legs trailing limply behind. The longest of these hangs lasted over 6 minutes, around 4 minutes of which were spent motionless at depth.

Could such intimate contact with an unadulterated state of pure awareness enhance our ability to be 'present' in our lives — what is commonly called mindfulness these days? Such an idea is supported by findings about the brain's quality of neuroplasticity: fMRI scans (imaging of brain function) have shown that extensive meditation causes changes to both the structure and function of the brain. If it is so, then this is yet another way in which freediving, which seems to be a shortcut to this state, can positively influence our lives. After all, lying in an octopus's garden and letting the cool water wash away your thoughts has more immediate appeal to sitting still on a cushion while your knees scream blue murder and your nose itches incessantly.

These attempts at finding enlightenment while dangling on the end of a rope like a baited hook alternated with more primal moments, when I would let my reptilian brain take over in the quest for food. One particular afternoon after training, Jimmy and I set out from the northern coast at a place called Chimney Rock, one of the first sites I had ever spearfished on Long Island. That first time, in 2005, I had battled for an hour to remove a grouper from a rocky ledge; then, as I swam towards shore holding it on the spear, a mid-sized reef shark had approached me from behind, concealing itself in my blind spot until it was almost upon me. A wary glance over my shoulder revealed its toothy leer, and in my fright I threw away the fish, watching as the shark tore it from the spear like a shish kebab. From that day on, I always towed a big floating catch bucket so that the fish wouldn't continue bleeding into the water.

Now, Jimmy and I pushed our bucket out through a section of breaking waves in order to reach the reef edge, where the coral and rock fringe of the island bordered a flat expanse of white sand at a depth of 14 metres. We steadily accumulated snappers and grouper as we moved south along the coast. We also accumulated an escort of frustrated reef sharks. Each time we speared a fish and brought it to the surface they would rush to the scene of the crime, incited by the sound of the fish struggling on the spear, then follow the slick of fish blood upwards to our bucket. There the trail ended, and this seemed to flummox and infuriate the sharks, who zoomed around us in circles trying to locate the missing bleeder. We would wait until they cooled down before searching for more prey.

After covering about a kilometre in distance, we turned to retrace our swim back up the coast. The sun was low on the horizon now, and just as we were about to cross the breakers back into the lagoon a large, silver disc-shaped fish swam boldly past us. It was a permit, a game fish prized for both its fight and taste. Reflexively I dived, pulled the band of my Hawaiian sling back, and loosed a spear into the flank of the fish. The permit gave a staccato burst of its tail that carried it down the reef edge in the direction we had just returned from. Jimmy and I sprinted after it in pursuit, mashing our fins into the surface and panting through our snorkels as we tried to keep up. The sharks followed close behind, by now associating any movement on our part with the potential for a free meal on theirs. With the heavy spear projecting at a right-angle from its side, the permit couldn't swim at full speed and we were able to just keep it in sight. Each time it seemed to slow and we tried to swim down to approach it, the fish would find new vigour and accelerate away from us again. This continued for 10 minutes, during which time we covered the entire kilometre of coastline we had just returned from! Finally exhausted, the permit laid itself down in a sandy gully, and with the sharks converging I knew I would have to be quick. I told Jimmy, who was filming with his video camera, to back me up, then swam down to grasp the shaft of the spear with both hands. Silver shapes flashed around the reef, closing in on my position, but it was impossible to keep track of all the sharks — I only hoped that Jimmy was watching in case any of them decided to charge me. The fish struggled against the barb of the spear as I swam with it towards the surface, looking upwards to locate the bucket. Luckily I didn't see what Jimmy was filming as he waited, with the bucket, above me. First one shark, then another, swam directly upwards from beneath me, homing in on the bleeding permit. Each time, one of my fins, which I was whipping to and fro like the tails of trapped eels, would collide with the cheek of the closest shark, causing it to veer sharply away from between my legs. I vaguely felt the collisions with my fins, but my focus was on getting the fish into the bucket; after I'd achieved this, I was alarmed to see just how close the sharks had come. Jimmy continued filming the frenzied scene, laughing all the while.

'What the hell were you doing? You were supposed to be keeping them off,' I fumed in Italian.

'You wait till you see this footage!' he replied triumphantly.

Wearily, we once more swam back along the coastline, dragging the laden catch-bucket behind us as the sun set over the island. The water was dusky and full of brooding shadows. But the ordeal wasn't over yet. As we were swimming through a narrow channel into the lagoon where we started from, a freak wave capsized the bucket, emptying its entire contents of fish and blood into the water. I was ready to call it quits. Like a train of spurned suitors, the sharks had shadowed us desultorily back up the coast, and it would only take seconds for the dispersing blood to reach their nasal ducts. There was no way I was swimming into what would quickly become the centre of a feeding frenzy. Jimmy, however, had different priorities. He let out a primal cry, and in a flash he had righted the bucket and was grabbing the fish bobbing in the water around him and throwing them back in it. I watched, astounded, as he collected every last one before kicking — with the bucket — away from the bloody slick just as the sharks converged on it. We laughed our way back into shore, before staggering on exhausted legs up the beach to begin the business of cleaning and preparing the fish for dinner.

*

In the year 2007, I clinched the no-fins world record, and in 2008 I had added the Free Immersion title. As we headed into 2009, I wanted to improve my diving in Constant Weight (with monofin) to see how close I could get to the world record in that third discipline. The record was then held by French monofin specialist Guillaume Néry, who had taken it from Herbert Nitsch the year before with a dive to 113 metres. Herbert had reserved a place at Vertical Blue in April 2009. Although he was already being heralded as the greatest freediver in the history of the sport, at the start of that year he didn't hold a record in any of the disciplines. Everyone knew that he would be attempting to redress this fact.

After the success of 2008, I felt that if I could make friends with the monofin, learning to use and feel it as an extension of my legs, then 113 metres should be within my reach. It was only 5 metres deeper than the record I had set the previous year in Free Immersion. Between December 2008 and the end of January 2009 I trained mostly with the monofin, improving my personal best from 94 to 111 metres in the space of those two months. Then came one of the worst winters that I have seen on Long Island. For weeks, the winds blew unrelentingly from the east, churning the water of the lagoon, and the Blue Hole that adjoined it, into milky white froth. Worse still, the wind created a current that travelled north up the island, trapping any seaborne material in the south-facing bays. And there was plenty of it. Far out in the Atlantic Ocean there is a vast area called the Sargasso Sea, where surface-floating seaweed blooms in huge volumes. The currents turn it in a massive gyre the size of India, which mixes and tangles with man's plastic flotsam. Somehow, that year the trade winds had pushed great swathes of this seaweed out from the gyre and distributed it across the islands of the Bahamas, piling it up against the northern corners of lagoons such as the one that holds Dean's Blue Hole.

Initially, the visibility was reduced by the cloudy water, and drifts of seaweed and plastic cluttered the surface around our dive platform. As the seaweed kept coming in, it started to form a covering over the Blue Hole, and we had to use our fins to clear a window in this before we could dive. The covering became thicker until it formed a complete lid over the Blue Hole. At this point we had to use a scuba tank to blast a pillar of bubbles up from 5 metres below the platform, opening a gap in the mat of brown weed so that divers could breathe up and start their descent unobstructed. By the depth of 50 metres, the water was pitch-black. This wasn't so much of a problem for the descent, as we could skim against the descent rope with the side of the face or with one hand in order to stay on course. But on the way up, losing the rope was at best disconcerting and at worst a serious hazard. In several dives I finned almost all the way to the surface with no reference line, and burst through the carpet of seaweed to claim a breath of air. Some of these dives ended with sambas, and after one blackout I decided that I would have to rein in my training until the conditions improved. After all, it didn't look like they could get any worse.

I was wrong. The matted lid over the Blue Hole became so thick that islands formed — the surface seaweed had been pushed up so much by all the weed below it that it was drying out on top. Diving under it, I measured the thickness at 2 metres. Birds trotted around these islands, feasting on the entangled shrimp and crabs. Finally — barely a week before the start of the Vertical Blue event — the winds changed and the tide began the job of moving the weed out of Dean's Blue Hole. It was deposited on the beaches, in huge rotting mounds and banks, but was better there than in the water. At last I was able to attempt a training dive to 113 metres in CWT, which would equal the current world record. The dive finished with a samba, but I felt I knew what I needed to do to complete the dive cleanly.

Vertical Blue began, and straight away Herbert announced a world-record attempt of 114 metres Constant Weight. He was having difficulty equalising, though, and on this and the next two days he didn't reach the plate at the target depth. The same applied to me on the third day, when I announced 109 metres and turned just 3 metres above the plate. While 3 metres isn't much, and it's possible to 'ride' the ears a little bit, allowing the thin membrane of the eardrum to stretch with the pressure in order to get a little extra depth, it's a game of Russian roulette. At that depth, a burst eardrum can mean severe vertigo and the inability to swim in a straight line upwards, and normally ends with a deep blackout. At the minimum, it would spell the end of deep diving for a period of weeks while the ear healed. I've always chosen the conservative approach, even when it means turning agonisingly close to the target; but as a result I still have two perfectly intact eardrums. Since the scar tissue of a healed rupture is prone to breaking again, it is definitely an advantage to never suffer this injury in the first place.

On the fourth day of the event (day one of Act Two), Herbert finally succeeded with his equalising. With the record now standing at 114 metres, I felt that it would probably be out of my reach this time. I switched to No Fins, in which I had reached 93 metres in training, although that was a long time ago, back before the seaweed hiatus. On my first attempt at 88 metres I suffered another surface blackout. I still hadn't logged a clean white card dive, and when Herbert broke my world record in Free Immersion with a dive to 110 metres the following day, I felt as if the event was slipping away from me. I returned to Constant Weight, and built up my confidence through dives to 101, 107 and 109 metres; then, on the penultimate day, I had another attempt at 88 metres without fins. This time the dive was clean — enjoyable, even. I ascended to the surface flanked by my

With freediving world record holders Herbert Nitsch and Sara Campbell at Dean's Blue Hole during Vertical Blue 2009. (*Franck Vieljeux*)

safety divers and good Italian friends Marco Cosentino and Antonio Cavallo. My last stroke, at 6 metres below the surface, sent me gliding towards the light, and after two measured hook-breaths (recovery breaths with a pause and squeeze of the exhalatory muscles after the inhale) I tore the Velcro tag from its attachment on my leg and pumped it in the air to celebrate my fifth world record in the purest discipline.

Nonetheless, the event that year belonged to Herbert. He had also made an attempt at 88 metres CNF, aborting it during the descent, but on the last day he sent shockwaves around the freediving community by announcing a depth of 120 metres in Constant Weight. A jump of 6 metres beyond his still-fresh world record was an unprecedented increment in the sport, and there were discreet conversations about whether such an announcement should be allowed to proceed. No one dared deny him the opportunity, however. The next day, Herbert filled his voluminous chest with Caribbean air before slowly meandering downwards, his arms by his sides, at such a slow speed that the idea of a dive to 120 metres seemed absurd. After a full minute he was still only at 40 metres. However, from that point on he started to accelerate as his lungs compressed and negative buoyancy took over, and by 70 metres he was freefalling at 1.2 metres per second (4.3 kilometers per hour or about normal walking speed). Just over 2 minutes into the dive he turned at the plate and began finning powerfully upwards, but by halfway up he had exhausted most of the energy in his legs. When he met his safety divers at 35 metres, they were presented with a bizarre sight. Herbert was ascending with arm strokes only, his legs and fin trailing behind him. There was still plenty of oxygen in his body for him to complete the dive, but his leg muscles had become fused with lactic acid. After a dive time of nearly 4 minutes, Herbert broke the surface and completed a quick protocol to take his twenty-fifth world record and cement his position as the world's number one.

*

The conclusion of Vertical Blue 2009 left me feeling cut short. I was happy with the no-fins dive, but had been hoping for 90 metres; and in the other disciplines Herbert had blown me out of the water. It was now May, and that year the World Championships would be held in November at Dean's Blue Hole (Vertical Blue had made a successful bid to host the biennial event). I was determined not to be shown up again in my own backyard.

My plan was to spend the summer pool training and teaching in Europe before returning to the Bahamas at the start of October to resume depth training before the Championships. It was another summer of criss-crossing the Mediterranean, but I tried to reserve chunks of time in Verona, Sicily and Tenerife, where I could build momentum in my training in the pool. For the first time I swam 200 metres (eight lengths of a 25-metre pool) in dynamic apnea without fins, and all other indexes of speed and efficiency were at their highest.

Towards the end of the summer I was visited in Sicily by my girlfriend of one year, Brittany, an American girl whose relatives on Long Island had introduced us. We shared a common interest in philosophy, and she was beginning a practice of yoga that would see her become an accomplished instructor. I had fallen for her tender and playful spirit, and the fact that her dream had always been to live a simple life on an island seemed to indicate some kind of providence to our meeting. Brittany quit her job in Florida to travel with me, and around this time we decided we would marry, and — why not? — that it would be when we returned to the Bahamas in the autumn. A wiser man might have been suspicious at the apparent urgency to tie the knot, but I could still count the number of long-term relationships I'd had using my thumbs — wisdom would arrive too late.

It wasn't until after the ceremony that I felt as if a guard was let down and I was meeting a different layer of the person with whom I had fallen in love and committed to spend my life. For the next several years I tried to be patient and understanding, believing that what I was experiencing was a recycling of old hurt. I waited for signs that the cycles were receding, like a sea that calms after the storm passes, but there was no respite — the turbulence was self-sustaining. It was inevitable that these marital problems would affect my confidence and peace of mind in freediving. It took a while for the effects to really register, perhaps because I had built up momentum in the progress I was making and, like an ocean-going ship, it took time to turn that around.

In any event, my training prior to the World Championships was building strongly on the base I had created in the pool during the summer months. My dives were quick and powerful, and on every surfacing I felt lucid and in control. It was important that I try to ride this wave of confidence right into the event. It was also important not to give my competitors, Herbert Nitsch and William Winram, any indication of what depths I was achieving in training. In the World Championships each athlete has just one dive per discipline, and the depth attempted has to be announced the night before, without any knowledge of what the other competitors might attempt. It comes down to a kind of poker game, in which you try to decipher what your opponents might announce and calculate whether you can safely attempt a deeper dive. Your opponent is, of course, making the same kinds of calculation, so you also need to be thinking about what your opponent thinks you are going to announce ...

Some athletes wisely avoid these mental contortions by simply announcing a conservative dive without taking anyone else's performance into consideration. However, I had played chess for too long as a kid, and on some level, even if subconsciously, I couldn't escape calculating how the pieces across the board from me might move. I was training with a fellow Kiwi, Kerian Hibbs, and together we devised a system for obscuring the depths I was attempting. The line would be set for 95 metres, regardless of my actual target, and I used the depth alarms on my Suunto gauge to program the actual depth at which I would make my turn. As I surfaced at the end of my ascent, Kerian would shadow me to make sure that none of the other divers in the water around the platform could see my wrist, where the maximum depth was displayed. The technique worked: when the event started, there was no one other than myself and Kerian who knew that I had reached a personal-best depth of 95.8 metres just over a week before the event.

The night before the finals, the announcements were revealed: William Winram had announced 86 metres, while Herbert Nitsch had posted 89 — one metre deeper than the world record I had set earlier that year. I discovered that I'd played the poker game perfectly with my announcement of 90 metres — which, if successful, would earn me my first World Championship gold medal. Although I'd achieved 95 in training, the mental pressure of a record attempt in competition was still a significant factor that I knew I had to accommodate with a healthy margin.

Since my AP (Announced Performance) was 1 metre deeper than Herbert's, it looked as if I'd been able to predict his thinking, and it's possible that this was enough to get under his skin and affect his own dive. I would compete immediately after him, and knowing that might have affected his ability to concentrate on what was already a difficult dive for the Austrian — six metres deeper than his personal best.

While I prepared, I tried not to pay attention to the dives that were happening before mine, but it was impossible not to discern the results from the noises the crowd made. An agonising collective sigh as Alexey Molchanov blacked out on the surface after his dive to 83 metres. Jubilation and applause when William Winram surfaced clean from 86. Winram was guaranteed a medal with this dive; its colour would be determined by the result of Herbert's and my world-record attempts. I waited on the edge of the platform as Herbert dived and the surface team announced his progress from the depth readout on the sonar. A murmur of excitement passed around the crowd when he turned at 89 metres. But he was slow — too slow even for Herbert — in ascending. A few seconds short of 4 minutes dive-time, he appeared on the surface, fighting to stay conscious. His mouth dipped below the waterline, and with that the fate of the dive was decided: a red card and disqualification for the reigning World Champion.

I was already in the water, lying on my back with my feet supported on a float as the line was adjusted to 1 metre deeper. The perimeter of the competition zone was crowded with spectators, their waggling fins and treading feet visible from below like a cluster of tadpoles. On the beach, an even bigger crowd of spectators had gathered; they could easily see everything that was taking place in the water just 20 metres in front of them. I closed my eyes, focused on keeping my breathing shallow and slow, and tried to empty my mind. To relax everything. Without any obvious motive, a part of my brain chose that moment — two minutes before my Official Top — to insist that I consider what would happen if I failed. It was quite adamant that I should reflect seriously on what that would be like. Which, of course, was the worst possible thing for me to think about right then. I tried to placate the voice, telling it that there would be plenty of time after the dive to consider any number of possibilities. Just give me a little bit of a breather for now, will you?

I would find out later that Nitsch, Winram and many other divers strongly doubted that I would make the 90-metre dive. They believed that the pressure of the occasion, as well as the pressure of having overseen the organisation of the competition, would be too much, and I would turn or black out. The voices in my head mirrored the murmuring of my competitors. It was almost as if they were on the same team. In order to succeed, I would need to shut out not only the crowds around me but also my own self. But there is no point in trying to throw your own mind out the door, like an angry bouncer, for it will just come straight back in through a side door or window, each time with renewed vigour. The negative voices in your mind enjoy playing that game. Instead, you have to leave the doors open and let the rabble of dissidents storm in to find an empty house, with no one home to badger or bully. Then, they quickly lose interest.

By the time the dive started, I wasn't even listening to my own mind. Everything was rehearsed, everything was programmed; my body knew exactly what to do. I left home, and let it go do its thing.

Three minutes and forty seconds later, I surfaced. The crowd around the platform was hushed. Only the voice of my surface coach, Kerian, could be heard, giving me cues for the protocol, but I didn't need them. Within three breaths I had completed the protocol and was showing the tag to the judges. It was my first title as World Champion, and the first unassisted dive in history to 90 metres.

Herbert would redeem himself two days later, with a well-calculated dive to 114 metres for the gold medal in Constant Weight. I was 4 metres back on 110, which earned me a bronze medal behind Alexey Molchanov, who dived to 111 metres for silver. As the only male

Showing the tag to the judges after diving to 90 metres CNF during the 2009 AIDA World Championships in the Bahamas.

athlete to climb the podium for both disciplines, I felt as if I had atoned for my poor showing during Vertical Blue at the start of the year. I seemed to have drawn level in the rivalry with Herbert Nitsch. Meanwhile, Alexey's strong monofin dive had revealed him as a future contender, and this event was the harbinger of an even more intense rivalry with the young Russian in years to come.

I finished the year with a depth in No Fins that was 4 metres deeper than that of my closest competitor, William Winram. My training personal best was another 5 metres further than that. Increasingly, I was becoming accustomed to comparing my dives not so much with those of other athletes, but rather with my own preceding performances. How could I tweak my technique in order to be a little more efficient? Is there any way I could refine my equipment? And the biggie: what was my weakest link, and how could I work to turn it into a strong point? In a blog post I wrote:

> Dear weakest link,
> Today I discovered who you are and where you live. Rest assured that I'm going to be coming round very often from now on, to chat and get to know you better. With time, we'll become best friends, in fact we'll be inseparable. Then I'll be able to start calling you 'strength'.
> Yours sincerely, WT

There are moments in which we realise that a skill that we'd really like to possess is actually very difficult, or that we're putting off doing something because we dread it. In those moments, it's important to recognise that we have actually been profoundly empowered. We now possess the knowledge of what needs to be done. Up to that point, without even knowing it, we were being affected by a fear of what we were avoiding. At that point, two paths (briefly) open up: on one, we tell ourselves that we really ought to put more time into it in the future, but for now we're just going to carry on with what we've been doing for a bit; on the second, we turn the full glare of our undivided attention onto that one facet, there in that very moment. That proactive step is the hardest one to take (which isn't to say that the perseverance required afterwards isn't hard, too), but if you never take it then you'll always be at the mercy of your insecurities and perceived weaknesses.

In training, whether it was a drill, a stretch or a diving exercise, I learnt to interpret that feeling of 'Oh my god, this is going to be so hard, why am I doing this?' as the calling card of a weak link. It was my cue to analyse it, isolate it and make a commitment — the type of commitment I knew I couldn't break — to turn it into a strength. Then I began. The process didn't require a competitor, but it was just as motivating as if another diver were neck and neck with me in the depths. I was competing against the notion of my own abilities, trying to outwit the internal sluggard and cynic.

*

Following the closing ceremony of the World Championships, I was broadsided without notice, and passed from joyful celebration to watching my laptop being angrily dashed into pieces against the ground by an inebriated version of the girl I had married. Those pieces would go into the bin, while the pieces of our young marriage were painstakingly reassembled. It was Episode One, and although there is no sense in counting or writing all the following episodes, they were a regular feature and burden in the following years.

CHAPTER 7

THE HECTOMETRE

*Stretching the umbilical cord
to a gossamer thread*

As I drop down into the deep blue I have to let go. I have
to let go of everything that attaches me to the surface and
makes me human: light, sound, identity, and the need to
breathe itself. First I swim, then I sink downwards, my body
becoming heavier from lungs shrinking under pressure. I give
myself up to the sensation that the ocean is drawing me into
itself. In order to completely accept it I must not think about
the coming ascent, which will be much more difficult than the
way down. I cannot anticipate in any way that this freefall into
the abyss will ever end. The crushing pressure silences my
mind, and I fly into the night, a being without thought.

Now is the time! Now is the time to return to life, to air,
to light! This is the test! The extent to which I have dared to
penetrate this twilight realm must be equalled by my desire
to return to the element that sustains life. There I will
breathe the hungry first breath of a newborn child.

**Words spoken in the short film *Hectometer* (2011), directed
by Matthew Brown and produced by William Trubridge**

THURSDAY, 11 MARCH 2010, was a typical spring day on Long Island in the Bahamas. Patches of cloud filed across the low-lying strip of land, creating a comfortable balance between warming sun and cloudy relief. A light southerly breeze ruffled the surface of Dean's Blue Hole. I was training with Arthur Trousdell, who was taking a long holiday to develop his freediving after having been introduced to it by his older brother Michael, just as I had. Arthur would also help out in the safety team for the upcoming Vertical Blue competition.

The time felt right. I made the decision that I had been contemplating all morning, and Arthur helped to set the line for the target depth. Lying on my back on the platform, my head in the shade, I tried to fall asleep. Of course I never do, but the attempt to sleep is what gets me into the most relaxed state possible. I stay like this for at least 10 to 15 minutes, ensuring that every muscle of my body has had a chance to fully unload carbon dioxide and other waste products into my bloodstream. Most importantly, I need this time to ensure that the blood circulating through my veins is fully oxygenated. For example, if I have recently used my arm muscles to pull the line through to a certain depth, that exertion will remove a little extra oxygen from the blood flowing through those muscles, and this deficit will pass downstream into the veins. The deoxygenated blood won't reach the lungs, where it can be topped back up to full levels, for several more minutes. So if I started the dive in this state, there would be slightly less oxygen contained in the blood in my veins, which accounts for two-thirds of our total blood volume (the other third is in the arteries). Relaxation is therefore a way of ensuring that we have stored as much oxygen as possible in the blood and tissues of our body.

From the platform I slipped into the water, using the most sparing movements possible. A family of nerves were picnicking in my chest, feasting on the magnitude of the goal I had just set myself, and this meant that I had to be extra-careful not to over-breathe. I didn't want a countdown for this training dive, so the only sound was the gentle slapping of small waves against the undercut cliffs bordering the Blue Hole. For another 5 minutes I lay on my back in the water, visualising myself as a piece of seaweed and allowing the gentle movement of the water to pass through my body without obstruction.

Another decision was made; I finished my breathe-up with a full exhale, then sucked air deep into my chest, filling my lungs first in their wider base before expanding the ribcage and raising the clavicle to load the upper volumes. Then began the process of 'packing': my mouth compressed more air, one bite at a time, into the lungs, pushing down on the diaphragm and outwards on the ribcage until I felt like an extra in an *Alien* film. Fortunately, this feeling would subside the moment I ducked under the surface and water pressure compressed the air into a smaller volume.

Seven methodical kicks and armstrokes ensued, carrying me down to 25 metres. The first of these were powerful and continuous, pulling me through the phase of positive buoyancy. Then, as the air in my lungs dropped below half of its initial volume and my body became heavier than water, I relaxed the strokes and lengthened the glide phases between them. With the seventh stroke I pulled myself into freefall position, like a seabird tucking its wings into its body as it plummets seawards. My thumbs hooked into elastic bands on my legs so that I could keep my hands close to my sides and relaxed at the same time. 'Shut down,' said the voice in my mind.

This is where the long underwater hangs that I had practised came into play. The accumulated time of several hours that I had spent in a kind of self-induced hypnosis at 60 metres allowed me to slip into that state quickly during my deep target dives.

There were a few initial wobbles in the freefall, but I soon settled in, my motionless and relaxed body falling straight down like a stone into a well. For the next minute and a half I would hold this position, while around me the turquoise blue faded to penumbral light. When I heard my first alarm it felt relatively soon, which was a good sign. I was having no difficulty equalising, and at 1:54 into the dive I stopped my fall, reached out and touched the plate. I was 100 metres down. With no fins. For the first time in my life.

Narcosis settled over me in the ascent, as well as some contractions, although none of them were urgent. Towards the end my muscles were beginning to fatigue, but I'd experienced worse. Finally, I heard a grouper call (a sound made in the back of the throat, that resembles the grunting of a grouper) from Arthur, signalling his presence as he fell in beside me for the home stretch. It made me realise that I'd had my eyes mostly closed and was swimming mainly by feel. Arthur later said that I looked relaxed and calm, with a faint smile.

After 31 strokes and 2 minutes 6 seconds of swimming upwards, I broke the surface and drew my first breath. I looked upwards and away at the sky to the north, savouring the moment, and inhaled again. There would be no surface protocol for this dive — it didn't feel right to spoil the sanctity of such a journey. Instead I turned, smiling, to Arthur, who alone in the world knew what I had just achieved, and gave him a wordless high-five.

*

When I had begun freediving, in 2003, the world record was 60 metres No Fins, and 90 metres with the monofin. The idea of a finless dive to 100 metres might have been beyond the imagination of any freediver living at the time. It had certainly been beyond mine. This year, 2010, I had steadily progressed through the nineties, improving my training personal best with dives to 96, 98 and 99 metres. When I surfaced from the 99-metre dive it had felt so truncated and easy that I'd needed to check the depth on my Suunto gauge to make sure we hadn't made a mistake setting the line. I saw 'Max depth 99.2m' and couldn't hide my astonishment: 'What the fuck? That was a piece of piss!' In that moment, I had known that my next dive would be to a three-digit depth.

*

When we think of the pinnacle of human speed, the image that probably comes to mind is of Usain Bolt striding away from the pack in the 100-metre dash — it's less likely that a picture of the world's fastest cyclist, François Pervis, or the pilot of the 'Budweiser Rocket Car', Andy Green, will be conjured. Likewise, the 'world's greatest jumper' will bring to mind the long-jumper or high-jumper more often than the pole-vaulter or ski-jumper. On the whole, we seem to be most fascinated by what the human body can do with zero assistance. In Ancient Greece, Olympic athletes competed naked, proof of their devotion to the same concept of pure human potential.

So, to the question 'How deep can we dive?', the most fitting answer shouldn't involve gas cylinders, sleds, lift bags or even fins. It should be measured by the unaugmented human body that uses only limbs, hands and feet to propel itself down and up through the water. This is what attracts me most to the discipline of unassisted freediving: it is the truest measure of human aquatic potential. The 100-metre unassisted freedive was likely to be the biggest milestone in the progression of that measure.

All the same, sometimes it's worthwhile to remember what a metre actually is: the distance travelled by light in a vacuum in one 299,792,458th of a second (setting aside the fact that a second itself is an arbitrary division of time). So, 100 metres is just 100 of those. And 100 itself is only a fancy number because we happen to have ten fingers to count on. Metres and multiples of them aren't written into the sea, or anywhere in nature. Yet, as a symbol, the metre can still be used to draw a line in the void and pause for contemplation, although I wouldn't be doing any of that at 100 metres down!

Of course, it's one thing to dive a depth in training, and quite another to do it in competition. On 11 March I was freediving without a lanyard and without the extra task of retrieving a tag from the plate, and both of these factors make a dive significantly more difficult. If I was to attempt such a momentous depth I wanted to be successful the first time, and with Vertical Blue 2010 only a month away I didn't anticipate being ready for it at that event. Instead, my attention turned once more to my ongoing battle with Herbert Nitsch, whose records in Free Immersion (FIM) and Constant Weight (CWT) had been broken by Martin Štěpánek and who would be hungry to return to the top during Vertical Blue. For the first year, Suunto was sponsoring an overall prize, for the athlete who accumulated the greatest total from their best dives in each of the three disciplines. I assumed that I was diving a lot deeper than Herbert without fins (CNF), but I would have to stay close or equal to him in FIM and CWT to have a chance of taking the title.

We both had a slow start to the competition, not diving the first day and turning early on FIM world-record attempts on the second day. On the third day we simultaneously found our groove, me with a CNF world record of 92 metres, waving to my safety divers as I cruised the last few metres to the surface, while Herbert broke the FIM record with a dive to 114 metres. On the first day of Act Two, we were both diving in CWT. I set a new New Zealand record of 116 metres, while Herbert turned early in his world-record attempt at 124. On day five we were once again back in synch, with Herbert logging an excruciatingly long, but clean, world-record dive of 124 metres with the monofin while I broke his three-day-old record in Free Immersion with a dive to 116 metres.

With performances logged in all three disciplines I sat out the next day, while Herbert attempted 118 metres FIM but failed his surface protocol, possibly because he was diving too slowly — the dive time was a massive 4:38! He knew what he had to do to correct that, however, and on the next day he announced 120 metres FIM and then shaved 10 seconds off his dive time to achieve a successful world record. Meanwhile, I had attempted 118 metres CWT but it was my turn to fail the surface protocol.

The event had two more days to go. If Herbert was to win the overall prize, he would have to log a significant dive in CNF. I anticipated that he might have a crack at exceeding my 92-metre record, with something like 93 or 94, and so I sent the judges my AP of 95 metres CNF for the penultimate day. At 3 minutes from the AP cut-off time of 6 o'clock I received one last announcement via e-mail, and saw just how wrong my prediction had been. Herbert had announced 101 metres CNF.

As the organiser of the event, I have to ensure that safety protocols are followed. This includes checking with the judges that they are happy to allow the athletes to attempt the depths they have announced. For Vertical Blue, as well as most other events, any announcement that is more than 3 metres beyond the athlete's personal best can be reduced at the judges' discretion. As far as anyone knew, Herbert's personal best was still 83 metres and he was notorious for hating to do deep CNF dives outside competitions. I messaged the head judge, Grant Graves, to see whether he approved the announcement, and he said to ask Herbert what his personal best was. I was becoming increasingly uncomfortable at being involved in such a process with someone I was competing against, especially when I needed to be preparing for my own world-record attempt.

At 7 p.m. we had a brief conversation on Skype. I asked him what his personal best (PB) was in CNF and he responded '98m' with a winking emoji ;) — I told him that meant the judges could allow his announcement (since it was less than 4 metres deeper than his PB), as long as he could get his safety diver from the 98-metre dive to sign off. He responded that 'it [the dive] wasn't here,' and my following question 'did you have a safety diver?' was left hanging. Soon after that exchange Herbert disappeared from my contacts list on Skype. If he did ever achieve 98 metres in a discipline where he had recently failed while attempting 89, then no one else has ever talked about it, then or since.

Most of the athletes at the event, as well as other AIDA judges, presumed that Herbert's claimed personal best, as well as the announcement itself, were a pretence aimed at trying to rile or unnerve me. If that was the case, it would not prove to be successful. The following day, I surfaced from 95 metres feeling even more fresh than I had after the 92-metre dive, and with a time of 3:56. Herbert dived next; the line was duly set to 101 but no one appeared particularly surprised when he turned early and pulled back up to the surface.

The ease of the 95-metre dive, and a creeping anxiety that someone else might beat me to the 100-metre mark (even though the next deepest athlete was still William Winram at 86 metres), led me to announce 100 metres CNF for the last day of the competition. I had no expectations, and was prepared to turn early if I wasn't feeling in perfect shape. Incidentally, for me this 'go and see' approach is conducive to the most relaxed and stress-free preparation. Having made three consecutive successful record dives in the competition, I was riding a wave of confidence and fully believed that I was capable of the depth. The only niggling concern was whether it would be a good idea to do it then, or to save it for a more fitting occasion. Perhaps this indecision acted through my subconscious to sabotage the attempt: as I rolled over at the start of the dive, some of the air that was packed into my lungs momentarily ascended into my throat before being swallowed into my stomach. On a shallower dive I might have continued, but not knowing how air in my stomach would affect my equalising at great depth, I wasn't about to find out in such a critical dive! I abandoned it.

For the last performance of the competition, Herbert had announced another head-scratcher: 130 metres FIM. This time, however, he didn't even enter the water, stating that there were insufficient supplies of oxygen to mitigate the risk of decompression sickness after his dive. It's possible that he was misinformed, since we finished the competition with enough oxygen for an athlete to have spent an hour decompressing at 5 metres.

This would be the last time I would compete against Herbert Nitsch, and the 120-metre dive would be his last successful world record. Two years later, in June 2012, he suffered a severe accident while attempting to set a world record in sled diving, leaving him comatose and paralysed. When he woke, he was told by doctors that he would be in a wheelchair for the rest of his life, but after weeks of decompression treatment and a self-devised regime of rehabilitation, he made an inexorable recovery in much the same way that he would somehow find his way back to the surface from the longest and deepest dives. Now he has even returned to freediving, although not competitively, and works with the marine conservation group Sea Shepherd.

*

My own attention turned to the Teams World Championships event, which would be held on the subtropical island of Okinawa, 600 kilometres south of mainland Japan. In this event, a national team is made up of three athletes, who each have to attempt performances in three disciplines: Constant Weight, Static Apnea and Dynamic Apnea. One metre of depth, 2 metres of dynamic distance and 5 seconds of static time were each all worth one point: a 100-metre dive would be equal to 200 metres in dynamic and 8 minutes 20 seconds in static apnea. The country with the highest aggregate score across all nine performances of its three team members would win.

I spent May and June in Tenerife, training in the pool at T3 (a state-of-the-art training facility in Costa Adeje), to try to raise my level in both static and dynamic apnea. The New Zealand team would be me, Guy Brew (a pool specialist with an everlasting breath-hold) and

Kerian Hibbs (an excellent all-rounder). If we could all log reasonably strong performances, we stood a good chance of taking gold at the event; however, a single disqualification would typically put a team out of the running.

The competition started with the CWT dives, and having announced the deepest depth — 105 metres — I was one of the first to compete. We were several miles off the west coast of Okinawa, diving in the open sea from a chain of boats straining against a single mooring. Conditions had taken a turn for the worse, with large sea-blown waves that buffeted me on the surface. I tried to time my breathing to avoid getting slapped in the face by a wave during an inhale. Once I finished my final inhale and ducked under, the water congealed back into its familiar timeless calm, and I was on my way. Kerian and I were both successful, but when Guy spent too long in his dive trying to overcome an equalisation block, he had a short surface blackout and received a red card. There was a period of dismay as our title hopes sank quietly out of reach. However, the silver lining was that we could now focus on our own individual performances.

The next event was Static Apnea: my least-favoured of the pool disciplines, although in training in Tenerife I had managed 8:01 and was starting to develop mental techniques to motivate myself through the interminable minutes of self-torture. My first contraction, signalling the urge to breathe, came shortly before 3:00, and from there I battled through to 7:28. It would end up being the second-longest static of the competition, behind my team-mate Guy Brew who astounded the spectators lucky enough to witness his valiant duel with the survival instinct. I was coaching him in the water, letting him know the time at regular intervals as well as ensuring that he was still conscious through the standard system of signal requests (my tap on the shoulder asks 'are you okay?' and his raised finger replies 'yep, still here'). When he passed 7 minutes he was already fighting very hard, his torso bucking like a rodeo bull with each contraction. I assumed that he would soon lift his head to breathe. 'Only 15 more seconds to go to 8 minutes,' I told him, before counting down the remaining time. 'That's 8 minutes there, Guy, good stuff! Uh ... you should probably think about coming up now?' A finger was lifted above the surface and waggled from side to side. He wasn't done yet. The crowd was holding its breath too at this point, and when Guy finally raised his head above the water and the judges stopped their watches at 8:27, there was a roar of exhaled relief and applause.

Controversy surrounds the world record in Static Apnea, and it is confused further by Guinness-record attempts where pure oxygen is inhaled before a breath-hold. The longest performances in competition have been around the 10-minute mark, but these are by athletes with massive lung volumes and incredibly lean bodies, meaning that they have a lot of fuel and very little mass to burn it with. Guy doesn't fit this description, and his astounding breath-hold and long dynamic swims are testimony to his mental control and determination.

The final discipline was Dynamic Apnea. In training I had gone a little over 200 metres a few times, but the water of the outdoor pool in Okinawa was so warm and cloying that I didn't expect to be able to match that. The bloodshift that happens when you hold your breath, even if you're not diving, has the effect of preserving heat in the body's core. If you're already hot to begin with, the effect can be stifling. For a maximal performance I would much rather be shivering than too hot. With this in mind, I told myself that I would only commit to swimming three laps (150 metres) and turning — then I would assess how I felt and whether I was able to carry on. I began my swim slowly, finding relaxation in the first lap while I settled into my practised rhythm of kicking twice with the fin and then gliding for a couple of seconds before repeating the cycle. During the second lap the urge to breathe started to intrude into my relaxation a little, but I told myself I had only one more lap after this. When I arrived at the end of that third lap and turned, I was still feeling very comfortable and the oppressive heating I had feared still hadn't shown up. I cruised through the fourth lap in what seemed like very little time, and turned again.

Suddenly, I was in uncharted territory. In almost all of my training, which is predominantly for depth, I have a set target that I cannot exceed (the bottom plate), as well as a fairly consistent level of ability. I would never wake up one day and decide that I was feeling so good I was going to add 10 metres to my depth. So, as I left the wall at 200 metres I had no reference point and was becoming increasingly perplexed at how comfortable I still felt. My longest dynamic apnea up until then had been 208 metres; I had long since eclipsed that as I continued to kick and glide through the warm water. The world record at the time was 250 metres, or five laps. Either because I had never even considered the possibility of being able to surpass that mark (as dynamic apnea was far from being my forte) or because the uncanny feeling of not having a reference point finally got the better of me, I abruptly popped up to the surface, did a clean and easy surface protocol — and then saw just how close I was to the wall. Another two kick cycles and a small push away from the wall, and I could have broken the record. There is, of course, no way of knowing whether that actually *was* in my reach, but judging by how lucid I was at my final distance of 237 metres, I might have been capable of coming close. Such is the power of entering a performance with no expectations or obligations.

*

I finished the World Championships with the highest individual tally of points, and the feeling that I could do no wrong in my competition dives. This was exactly the place I needed to be in order to attempt what was going to be the hardest challenge of my life to date.

Over the summer, I had begun stirring the pot around an idea that had been simmering since Vertical Blue. I still hadn't mentioned my reaching 100 metres CNF in training to anyone other than my family and closest friends. To prove to my peers and the world that a human body could swim that deep and back on a single breath, I would need to attempt the dive officially. I wanted it to be a stand-alone world-record attempt in Dean's Blue Hole, in order to maximise my chances of success — I didn't feel that there was another venue with similarly stable conditions. I also wanted to ensure that the entire attempt was filmed from start to finish, by technical divers stationed at intervals along the rope, and this would only be possible if my team was in full control of the timing. Making the attempt would not be cheap — the expenses for the crew and gear alone would run to over US$20,000. Crowdfunding was my only option. The only problem was that the concept of crowdfunding didn't exist in 2010. Instead, I devised my own method of fund-raising — auctioning off all 100 metres of the descent line to supporters, using a Facebook image for each metre so that people could bid on them through a comment. The winner of each of the 100 auctions would receive the actual metre of official rope used for the attempt, rolled into a spiral and mounted on a commemorative plaque. Their name or business name would appear on a scrolling list accompanying my descent in the official video, and of course they'd get the T-shirt. The response to this campaign was one of the most touching aspects of the whole enterprise. Family, friends, fans and even freediving rivals all became active in bidding on the rope lengths, which sold for between US$150 and US$500. It was a humbling experience to see that people weren't just paying me lip service — my supporters genuinely wanted me to succeed. It was also, perhaps, the most perilous aspect of the attempt. Should I not be successful, and therefore unable to supply the supporters with a piece of record-dive line or an official video, what then? It would still cost the same, but I couldn't in good conscience take people's money for a task that had not been achieved. I preferred not to consider this contingency, although the prospect of failure was difficult to banish from my mind altogether.

I knew that 10 metres was a decametre, and 1000 a kilometre, so I was curious to find out whether there was a name for 100 metres. I thus discovered the hectometre and decided to name the event 'Project Hector'. I googled *hector* to see its other connotations, and was surprised to discover that there was a species of dolphin by that name found only in New Zealand. I read on to learn that Hector's dolphins were critically endangered, and the subspecies found in the North Island, known as Maui's dolphin, was at extinction's door with less than a hundred breeding adults remaining. I was amazed, and a little embarrassed, that as a New Zealander and an ocean-lover I hadn't yet heard about the plight of this endemic dolphin.

And the parallels with my planned dive didn't end with just the name. Hector's dolphins are a coastal species, preferring shallow waters and almost never diving deeper than 100 metres. Their territory is therefore more or less defined by the zone of water between the shore and the 100-metre depth contour. This is why their numbers have been decimated — those same waters are the richest grounds for human fishing. Over the past 40 years the number of Hector's dolphins has dropped by

These Hector's dolphins drowned in gill nets, before being washed onto a South Island, New Zealand beach.

75 per cent (from 29,000 to 7000), while the number of Maui's has fallen by a tragic 97 per cent (from 1800 to just 50 in 2017). Population models have shown that Maui's dolphins cannot now sustain more than one human-induced fatality every 10 to 23 years.

These catastrophic reductions are almost entirely due to bycatch from set-net fishing and trawling in the dolphins' territory. Currently, the dolphins are protected from set-nets in 19 per cent of their territory, and from trawling in just 5 per cent of it. With such limited protection, and a fishing industry that has been shown to cover up dolphin mortalities (according to the Department of Conservation's Incidence Database, less than 1 per cent of bycatch was reported between 2000 and 2006) and hush government observers, it doesn't take a mathematician to see that the status quo can only lead to the animals' demise. Their only chance of salvation is full protection throughout their territory, out to the 100-metre depth contour. Every year, this is the recommendation made to the New Zealand government by the International Whaling Commission's panel of world experts on marine mammals; and every year, it is ignored.

In any such case, the key to achieving change is the pressure that the public can exert once they are informed about the issue and start to care about it. I decided to make my record attempt a dive for the dolphins, and to ensure that if I was successful then all of the exposure and press attention would be used to sound an alarm for Hector's and Maui's dolphins. In turn, this idea — that I was attempting the dive for a cause far more important than just myself and my ideology around human aquatic potential — would help motivate me to train harder, and to stay the course when circumstances became difficult.

*

I arrived in the Bahamas at the start of October, just over two months before the anticipated date for the record attempt. I made quick progress, and like the previous year I was diving fast and strong after my months of pool training during the summer. Then sickness struck, and for ten days I was out of the water; when I returned, it would take me several days to build back up to where I had left off. In addition, the stress I was experiencing was destabilising my marriage with Brittany. It meant I was lacking in the patience and compassion that was required to prevent a small issue from turning incendiary. And so incendiary the whole thing became, at a time when peace of mind and good sleep patterns were critical.

With the attempt date looming on the horizon I reminded myself to have faith in the process, that 'a smooth sea never made a skilful sailor' and that my personal struggles were nothing compared with the annihilation faced by the dolphins I was diving to save. Slowly, my strength returned and the mucus cleared from my airways. Depthwise I quickly moved through the nineties, and on 19 November did my first no-fins dive of the season to 100 metres. My team for the record attempt was starting to land on Long Island, with safety divers Alfredo Romo and Brian Pucella joining Long Island resident Charlie Beede, and Igor Liberti doing the underwater photography, later joined by Paolo Valenti for topside images. Nic Rowan had made the long trip over from New Zealand, and his moral support and help on the platform during the attempts would prove invaluable. Brian Kakuk and Paul Heinerth, my original deep-safety technical divers from my first record attempt in 2007, returned along with a new underwater cameraman, Jason Sapp. My medic was Tomas Ardavany, who would have a key role in the development of freediving safety protocols in the following years. The team was rounded out by a young and talented film-maker, Matthew Brown, who had made his first trip overseas to create a short film of the event.

In the morning training sessions, I would look around and remind myself that everyone present on the platform had made the effort to be there for me. It filled me with gratitude and confidence, and this helped to dispel the negative internal voices that were ready to chirrup at the first sign of weakness.

The last two weeks of training were what they needed to be: a gradual and systematic final push, like the ascent to a mountain summit from the final, highest camp-site. In my dives I was maxing out all my systems: narcosis was strong in the ascent, my legs and arms were nearing saturation with lactic acid, and after the dive I would continue panting for as much as 10 minutes to purge the carbon dioxide from my system.

Friday 10 December would be the first day of the attempt window. I had decided to use it as a kind of dress rehearsal, with a dive to 96 metres that would be officiated by the AIDA judges Ute Geßmann and Ben Weiss. While this would still be an improvement on my world record of 95 metres, it was nothing like as difficult as the 100-metre attempt to follow. The dive was a success, although probably the least-celebrated of all my records: everyone knew it was just a stepping stone towards that coveted three-digit number.

Two days later, on 12 December, the line was lowered into the Blue Hole until the piece of black tape the judges had used to mark off the distance of 100 metres from the plate was flush with the surface of the water. My dive log has no written notes for this dive, and I remember little about it other than that it was very slow, and excruciatingly close at the finish. Part of the surface protocol involves removing all facial equipment before showing an 'okay' sign to the judges: on this dive, with a mind befuddled from low oxygen, I forgot to take off my nose clip and what could have been a world record was instead a dead duck. Worse still, I had managed to tweak a muscle in my neck during the dive.

That night, I took a dose of anti-inflammatories and (on my mother's advice) propped towels under my back and neck while I slept. It worked, as I awoke rested and mostly pain-free. However, the weather would be next in the unfolding series of challenges. Overnight a cold front had moved across the island, bringing chilly winds and blotting out the sun with low cloud. Almost immediately upon entering the water at 11 a.m., I began shivering. I knew that I would have to keep my breathe-up short; but even so, by the time I rolled over to start the dive the shivering had become so strong that I wasn't able to concentrate on my entry into the water. Just as it had in my first attempt at 100 metres in April, some of the air in my lungs ascended into my throat and was swallowed into my stomach. For a split-second I contemplated continuing; but it would have been foolhardy, so I aborted and rolled back onto the surface with a groan of dismay.

*

Now my problem was time. I had just a few more days before the judges and crew were due to fly out. If I didn't bag the record today, it could come down to the wire on the last day, and the pressure would be immense. I felt as if I already had enough pressure to deal with: at 100 metres down it's 160 pounds per square inch, which is basically equivalent to a guy of my size standing on every square inch of my body.

I couldn't just go back to breathing up, and start the dive again in a few minutes. This carried a risk of 'over-breathing', or beginning the dive with too little CO_2. The last time I'd tried this, in 2006, it had ended in a blackout 12 metres below the surface. I decided to swim ashore, seal myself in the cab of my truck, which was parked by the beach next to the Blue Hole, and turn the heater up to full. I think this was the first and last time I ever used the heater in the Bahamas. I sat there in my wetsuit for about 15 minutes, grilling myself in the hot air and also grilling myself mentally. Could I do this? Was I going to go bankrupt if I didn't? How could I face myself if I let so many people down?

In the end, what pulled me through was the fact that I was doing this for something bigger than myself. Images of the Maui's and Hector's dolphins' rounded shape and Mickey Mouse colours passed through my mind. The fear of failure was replaced with a resolve that I *had* to succeed. That it was *right* that I succeeded. This calmed me and, most importantly, emptied my mind. So it was that my desire to help the dolphins ended up helping *me* on that day, by silencing the negative thoughts in my mind.

I got back in the water, and started shivering again almost immediately; I paid it no attention. My mind was eerily empty. My body was operating on autopilot as I performed my final inhale, started the dive, and swam to negative buoyancy. I remember relaxing as I entered the freefall, and telling myself to 'relax even the potential for contraction'. I remember my depth alarm going off, and pulling the tag from the bottom plate, 100 metres below the surface. I remember keeping my eyes half-closed and telling myself to 'relax' and 'flow' as I set off on the long swim back towards the light. I remember actually enjoying the ascent, commenting to myself how fortunate I was to be able to have this opportunity, and to be able to express myself in this way. I remember coming to the surface, reminding myself to concentrate on doing the protocol correctly in order to ensure a valid dive. And I remember erupting into celebration with my team the moment the judges displayed their white cards. It was as if the sun had come out after a rain, and everything was glistening.

The dive was valid but my surfacing had been tight, with a samba that made my hand tremble as I gave the okay sign. On the internet, some people commented that the tremble made it look as if I'd given the 'okay' sign twice, which would be cause for disqualification. I still had three days of the record window left, and I felt that two full days of rest would allow me to do a better job. I also wanted to demonstrate that round numbers shouldn't define our limits, or give us an excuse to take a 'tea break', as it were. So, on 16 December I dived again to 101 metres, surfacing cleanly after 4 minutes and 8 seconds under the water for my fourteenth world record.

The moment the white card was shown to validate the first no fins dive to 100 meters.
(*Paolo Valenti*)

*

To this day, Project Hector remains one of my sweetest and most humbling successes, because it wasn't just mine. Instead of just striving for myself, I was serving something greater. By making the dive about more than just me, it took my ego out of the equation; it also took the fear of failure out of the equation, and without that anxiety I could occupy the pure 'flow state' of subconscious command.

This lesson can be found not just in sport, but also in business and in day-to-day life. Goals and aspirations that are self-serving only take us so far. But when the incentive is something beyond yourself, it gives you the grace to go further, higher, deeper than you might be physically or mentally capable of. My example is rather mundane when compared with a mother who, in a fit of superhuman force, lifts a car off her child's leg, or with the Fukushima 50, who worked 23-hour shifts with a one-hour nap each day to keep the nuclear reactor cool after the 2011 tsunami in Japan, knowing that it would probably mean an early demise through cancer. However, a goal doesn't have to involve saving the world or a life. Whether making a new product or providing a service that you *truly* believe in, there's no reason why you can't tap into the same source.

Growing up in New Zealand gives the perfect environment to instil this kind of integrity. Until I travelled through other countries later in life, I didn't realise how strong the Kiwi impulse to 'do your best' and 'make a difference' is. It's not just about getting the job done, but about doing it to *your* highest standard. That's why the All Blacks get heckled if they have a sloppy match, regardless of whether they win or not — Kiwis want them to be perfect, because they aspire to perfection themselves. I've noticed a worldwide recognition of this attitude; for someone applying to work overseas, a New Zealand passport is as good a reference as any.

The footage shot during Project Hector was edited by Matthew Brown into the short film *Hectometer*, which attempted to express what it felt like to swim to 100 metres below the sea and back. The words at the start of this chapter, spoken by my friend's daughter Jessica Dinnage, were used as a voice-over and an original score was written by Christopher Ward. The film screened in 2011 at film festivals in Los Angeles, Seattle, Asolo and Camden, as well as at the Doha Tribeca Film Festival where it received a standing ovation when it played before the award-winning documentary *Senna*.

*

Shortly after setting the 100-metre record, in the NZ summer of 2011 I had the chance to meet Hector's dolphins for the first time, at Banks Peninsula close to Christchurch. We watched them jumping and feeding only a few hundred metres from where a fishing trawler was passing, evidence of the overlap in their territory with commercial fishing. As we motored back into Akaroa Harbour we came across a small pod resting in the calm green water, and I put my wetsuit on and slipped into the water to spend time with them. The visibility was only a few metres, so I could only see the dolphins when they made passes close to me, but

A Hector's dolphin's joyful leap, off the coast of Akaroa peninsula, New Zealand.

they were curious enough to do so regularly. Their tiny size, rounded-off fins and airbrushed grey-and-white colouring made even the adults of the pod look like miniatures — pocket-sized orcas, perhaps. They never stayed still long enough for me to see the intelligence and awareness in their eyes, the way I had with dolphins in the Caribbean, but I could feel their inquisitiveness in the way they twisted and played around me, like fidgety water-pixies.

There is almost no similarity between a voluntary breath-hold and drowning. If I were to become hopelessly entangled during a dive, then all my training and ability would count for nothing. Of course, I would try to stay calm and free myself, but once I realised that all hope was lost then I would experience the same terrifying panic as anyone else in that situation. There's no reason to expect that it is any different for dolphins when they are trapped in nets — the signs of desperate struggle on the bodies washed up on beaches, swathed in netting, is clear evidence of this. Not only are the populations of Hector's and Maui's dolphins being destroyed by commercial fishing in their territory, but this is taking place through slow and brutal deaths while the rest of the pod can only watch in confusion and distress.

Other than three species of bat, Hector's and Maui's dolphins are the only mammals that are found exclusively in New Zealand. Yet to date, none of the campaigning, not only by me but also by a host of conservation groups, has resulted in any significant increase in the protection of the species.

Playing with an Atlantic Spotted Dolphin *(Stenella frontalis)* in the waters of Bimini, Bahamas.
(Peter Zuccarini)

CHAPTER 8

MIS-TRIALS

Hamstrung by a nose clip

Sometimes uphill, sometimes downhill,
resham firiri, resham firiri.

Words from a traditional Nepalese song

IN 2015, WHEN I SPENT 20 DAYS hiking in the Himalayan mountains with my father and brother, our guide and porter (both named Narayan) taught us the famous Nepalese Sherpa song that starts with the lines above. Diving is the same: sometimes descents, sometimes ascents; sometimes smooth easy dives, sometimes hard-fought battles on a dwindling reserve of oxygen. You can extrapolate the idea as far as you want: our lives are a constantly changing terrain of hills and valleys, and we do our best to navigate through it. From the top of a peak we sight an even higher peak in the distance, but inevitably our path there will lead through gullies and over ridges, across meadows and through thick bracken.

*

The Vertical Blue event of 2011 was a fairly sedate affair, with only 18 athletes competing. A month before, the Tōhoku earthquake and tsunami had devastated Japan, and the Japanese freedivers (who are normally the most numerous at the competition) had to pull out. In a show of solidarity that is not uncommon in the sport, the other athletes pulled funds together to reimburse two of the women competitors, Misuzu's and Megumi's Vertical Blue fees. One of these generous athletes was the indomitable Natalia Molchanova, who was about to become the first woman to break the 100-metre mark in Constant Weight. A competitive swimmer in her youth, she retired after having children and didn't pick up freediving until 20 years later, at the age of 40. Throughout the next 12 years Natalia was the queen of freediving, reigning over all six disciplines in the pool and sea. Other athletes would focus on a single discipline, and with immense effort they might finally exceed her record; but at the next event she would simply win it back again, with grace and ease. It wasn't that competitiveness was her lifeblood, either. A small and soft-spoken woman, with a kind smile and a love of poetry, most of the time she was simply breaking her own records, amassing a total of 41 during her career. The 100-metre record was one of the few times she faltered, making three attempts all ending in blackouts before she finally overcame the milestone at Vertical Blue 2011.

That Natalia kept on dominating the sport into her fifties, showing no sign of letting up, is a testimony to her mental and physical strength — but also to the nature of the sport, which perhaps favours the slower metabolism and emotional stability that comes with age. I'm often asked how much longer I can expect to continue competitive freediving, and I normally cite Natalia's example of the longevity of athletes in this sport, even though there's no way I could ever match her level of dominance at such ages.

*

As well as Natalia's 100-metre CWT record, I set a new FIM record to 121 metres at that year's Vertical Blue. There was a moment of panic at the base plate when I fumbled with the tag and lost the line for a moment. A quick kick of my legs brought me back within reach, and from there I hauled my way back up to the surface for a total time of 4:13.

After my by-now-customary base-training period in Tenerife over the summer, I travelled to Greece at the start of September for the other main fixture on that year's calendar, the AIDA Individual World Championships. It was held in the oily-calm waters of the Bay of Messinia, offshore from Kalamata. The hills that shelter the bay are dry and dusty rubble slopes, but the waters they contain are among the clearest and calmest in the world. When we caught the shuttle boat from shore to take us 2 kilometres out to where the platform was moored, it felt as if we were sliding across a mirror. Those morning trips gave me time to reflect on how privileged I was to be able to make a life playing in such a beautiful element.

I would have cause for a different kind of reflection during a warm-up competition before the championships, in which I had the second-worst blackout of my career. It was a CWT dive, with an announced depth of 116 metres that should have been routine, but it fell on the one day that the winds stirred the bay up into a choppy mess that played pandemonium with the competition zone. Two-seater paddle-boats were being used to provide the athletes with 'dry zones' where they could store equipment and relax out of the water to avoid becoming too cold. All well and good, but now the waves were breaking clean over the top of these small square rafts, and two of them had begun to sink. By the time it was my turn to dive I was cold and soggy, and not at all relaxed. To add extra insult, the safety crew was slow to move the previous athlete off the line and change the depth; when my lanyard was finally clipped onto it and I heard the call of 'One minute 30 to Official Top!', I couldn't believe that I was being expected to prepare in such little time. I yelled back, 'Are you fucking kidding me?' from where I was lying in the water. There was no reply, so I guessed they weren't. I was livid. Waves were breaking over my head as I tried to condense my final 4 minutes of preparation into just one ... I should have known that there was no way I was going to make the dive; I should have called it off. Anger feeds stubbornness, however, so off I went.

At some point on the way up, my finning speed went from sluggish to swimming-in-molasses. It was 0.69 metres per second: about half of what I should have been averaging in the ascent, and slower than I normally move without fins. Despite the narcosis, I could still perceive that something wasn't right and managed to pick up speed a little, but when I met the safety divers and saw how slowly they were swimming to keep up with me I realised that I was in trouble.

At 20 metres I looked towards the surface (bad sign); at 9 metres I started pulling desperately on the rope (all hope is lost); and at 5 metres I blacked out entirely.

Once brought to the surface I remained unconscious for a further 15 seconds, then began breathing but wasn't fully aware for another minute. The lesson was one that I knew already, but obviously needed to be reminded of: if you can't calm the water inside you, how will you move calmly through the water below? Since then I have been more vigilant regarding those moments when it is better to leave that tag hanging where it is, and save the dive for another day. And, although I have had near-misses with brief blackouts after taking my first breath on the surface, that dive in 2011 was, as at the time of writing, my last blackout underwater.

I rested for three days, did two more easy training dives to build back my confidence, and then the World Championships began. The first discipline was CNF, and my announcement of 93 metres was well clear of the rest of the field. Conditions were good, and I was feeling calm and relaxed. Maybe a little too relaxed ... 5 minutes from my Official Top, I tipped my head back into the water to purge the bubbles from my swim cap and smooth out any ruffles in it. Normally I have my nose clip in place when I do this, but on that day I was still holding it in my hand. Seawater quickly found the twin drains of my nostrils and eagerly set about filling up every cavity connected to them. My nasal chambers, sinuses and Eustachian tubes were all flooded; I jerked my head up, spluttering, to the surface and spent the next several minutes trying to blow the water out from inside my face. Salt water inflames the lining of the airways, causing it to produce mucus, and this had to come out too. Any liquid can cause an obstruction to the flow of air, which leads to equalisation blocks during a freedive. Two minutes before my dive I tested my ears, to see whether they were going to equalise. Rather than the pneumatic 'shhht' sound they usually give, I heard and felt a wet crackle in my middle ear as bubbles of air forced their way through soggy Eustachian tubes. It was over. There was no way I was going to be able to equalise through all that snot and salt water. I abandoned the idea of a gold medal dive, and decided to just 'go and see'.

As expected, equalisation was terrible. Normally I can open my Eustachian tubes spontaneously, allowing air to communicate with the middle ear and equalise its volume, but this time I was having to generate pressure, using my tongue as a piston in a manoeuvre called the Frenzel, in order to pry the tubes open. The air would then shoot through whatever mixture the tubes contained, creating a different variety of fart noise on each occasion. However, after I had settled into the freefall and was squeaking and popping my way down past 40 metres, something happened. Whether it was the movement of all the air that dried the tubes out, or their contents simply drained into a bigger cavity, but equalising started to become easier — and quieter! By the time I was nearing the target depth it was almost back to normal, and when I turned and tore the tag from the base plate I knew that everything was going to be okay. I settled into a dreamy ascent, feeling completely at ease and unhurried. In the final drift upwards from 10 metres I made a cryptic hand sign to the cameras. It was in the bag.

In Constant Weight I had announced 118 metres, which ranked together with Alexey Molchanov's AP, for the same depth, as the deepest announcement for the men. Alexey blacked out on the surface, while I turned early at 112 metres when I ran out of air for equalisation. (Shortly after this event, I would switch to a different method of equalising, called mouthfill, that more reliably ensured available air at depth.) On surfacing, I was so frustrated at having seen the chance of a second gold medal slip from my grasp that I didn't bother with the surface protocol, earning myself a red card (disqualification) instead of a yellow (penalties). Later, when I did the maths, I discovered what my arrogance had cost me. Athletes who turn early are penalised by the difference between their realised and their announced depth, plus one extra point for not collecting the tag. My dive, which at 112 was 6 metres less than the 118 I had announced, would have earned a penalty of 7 points and brought my score down to 105. Which, as it turned out, would have meant a bronze medal.

Lesson number 358: always follow through, even when you're pissed off and don't see the point.

That year the World Championships concluded with Free Immersion — the first time that this discipline had been included in the competition. When the announcements came in, I saw that my 112 metres was well clear of the next diver's target, Polish up-and-comer Mateusz Malina, who had posted 106. I could turn at 110 and still earn gold. I did set an alarm for this depth, but it was easier to sink the extra 2 metres to the plate, although I didn't bother messing about with the tag, which is only worth a one-point penalty.

At the closing ceremony on the beach that night, the two gold medals slung around my neck clinked together as we celebrated and danced next to the Mediterranean. Months of disciplined and abstemious training had come to an end for all the athletes, and with plentiful alcohol on tap the result was carnage. Swedes toppled like pine trees from the stage-turned-dance-floor. Couples and trios found inspiration from Eros in the water and on the beach. Mateusz spent an hour searching the sand for the silver medal that had slipped from around his neck.

*

Although my year had oscillated between hiccups and home runs, I again finished on top of the rankings, with a total of more than 600 points across the six disciplines — the first time that this had been achieved by any athlete. I held world records in two of the depth disciplines (CNF and FIM) but was unhappy with my performance with the monofin in the third (CWT). I resolved after the World Championships to shift my focus to that discipline for 2012. In training I had reached 121 metres, and I felt that with a concerted effort to improve my technique I should be able to close the remaining 3-metre gap to the world record.

From the beginning of 2012 through to May of that year, I didn't log a single deep dive without fins or in free immersion. At each training session I would do a deep Constant Weight dive (115+ metres), breathe pure oxygen to recover and rest for a bit, then do a gruelling sequence of dives to 30 metres with short recoveries between them. To add difficulty in these shallow dives, I started wearing a long-sleeved shirt over the top of my wetsuit, or wore plastic snorkelling fins instead of a monofin while dolphin-kicking. The only break I took was to visit the island of Roatan, Honduras, to which I had been invited by Argentinian dive instructor Esteban

Darhanpe. In the Bay Islands archipelago, Roatan is the posh brother of Utila, where I had learnt to freedive in 2003. Whereas Utila attracts backpackers and boozers, Roatan attracts families, vacationers and boozers. It has perhaps one of the best-functioning marine parks in the Caribbean: the whole island is a marine reserve, with strict and efficient policing. The result is coral reefs teeming with life, none of it in the least bit timorous towards divers.

Esteban had seen the potential of Roatan as a freediving location and wanted to start a school and an international competition in the calm and deep waters off the south-western tip of the island. I was there to help him assess the feasibility, as well as to start to promote the sport on the island. Roatan is an aquaphile's playground, providing every possible way of accessing the underwater world: snorkelling, scuba diving, glass-bottomed boats and even a submarine that can take two passengers down to a depth of 600 metres (2000 feet) to watch giant six-gill sharks feeding on a carcass attached to the submarine. American-born Karl Stanley built the submarine himself after extensive research and consulting, and it has no licence or insurance ('Your only insurance is that I am going with you,' he tells passengers). Yet when I climbed aboard for a scouting dive to 120 metres, I felt much safer than I had in the taxi on the way from the airport. The brief ride took us over the reef and down the face of the wall that drops away from the island, revealing how vertiginously sheer that edge was. At 120 metres I could look up the looming mass of rock and still make out the vague pattern of light piercing through the waves on the surface. Small black silhouettes passed overhead, and I asked Karl what fish those were. 'Tuna, about 60 metres above us,' he replied.

On a later dive we saw a scarred and grizzled sand tiger shark, gliding slowly southwards beside the wall. Its mouth was an eruption of teeth that curled away in rows from its bottom lip. There were bite marks on its gills and back, evidence of the violent struggles these sharks endure in mating. 'Wait a second, I'll see if I can get us a better look at it,' Karl said from the command turret where he was standing behind us. He judged the shark's languid movement, then steered the submarine further down the wall before turning it to face the rock and shutting off the electric motors. Sure enough, the shark's path took it directly between our submarine and the cliff, and if it hadn't been for the thick acrylic window I would have been able to reach out and touch its great barrelled torso.

It wasn't the closest I would come to sharks on that trip. Waihuka Dive Center in Coxen Hole took me out on one of their skiffs to a shark-feeding site several miles offshore. A bucket of frozen fish bait placed on the sea floor was used to draw the reef sharks out. Most of them are returning customers, and can be recognised by hooks hanging from the corners of their mouths, or scars and gashes on their fins. The guides and video crew were all on scuba, and since the bottom was at 20 metres I set up a scuba tank on the sea floor that I could breathe from between periods of swimming free with the sharks. The sharks were almost always aware of my presence and treated me indifferently, with no signs of either fear or aggression.

The idea of sharks as bloodthirsty man-eaters is finally being outed as sensationalism — and not a moment too soon. All over the world, shark populations are collapsing, and one-third of the species are in danger of extinction. Shark-finning, the practice of catching sharks and removing their fins before throwing the carcass back in the water, is largely responsible for this collapse. The market is almost entirely in China, where shark fin soup is a sign of status, served at weddings and business dinners. The fin itself tastes bland and must be flavoured with chicken or other stock.

Sharks have a pivotal role in the food chain that sustains the marine ecosystems. It works like this: without sharks, the larger predatory fish like groupers become more abundant, which in turn reduces the numbers of herbivore fish, like parrotfish, that they feed on. The herbivores are responsible for cleaning algae off the coral, so when they disappear the reef becomes covered in green fur and slime. So fewer sharks equals more reef predators, equals fewer herbivores, equals less coral, and the whole reef ecosystem soon collapses. Although the threat to shark populations is serious, I'm aware that I can't spread my voice too thinly in my efforts to encourage conservation of the oceans and ocean life. This is why I've chosen to use my exposure to support New Zealand's dolphins, not because I hold one order of species to be more worthy than another.

In fact the argument that one species may be sentient or 'conscious' and therefore more important than another that isn't is moot, when species are all mutually dependent. In fact, we're so entwined with other life forms that it can make the boundaries between organisms difficult to define. A huge boulder of brain coral, or a forest of staghorn coral can seem like a single organism to a first-time snorkeller, when in fact it's actually an animal species and an algae species living together in giant symbiotic colonies. They have merged their bodies and resources, and depend on each other for life (when water temperatures rise, the animal polyp expels the algae, and coral bleaching is the result — with climate change this is now happening to huge swathes of coral reef all over the world, especially off the coast of Australia). If the two organisms that make up coral are inseparable then are they really individual?

Each human or animal is arguably a similar colony: the mitochondria that are resident in our cells, and which give them energy, were once entirely separate single-cell organisms that have been incorporated into our cells — they've even kept their own DNA. We have ten times more microorganisms living in our gut than we have cells in our body, and their function is vital to our digestion. Welcome to the ecosystem that we call *Homo sapiens*. On the macro scale, our planet's symbiosis and mutual dependence between CO_2 breathers and O_2 breathers — plants and animals — is really no more than an immense coral sphere, which if viewed from far enough away could appear to an alien as a single organism. It seems nature abhors a boundary as much as it abhors a vacuum. And if it's hard to show boundaries between physical organisms then it makes it difficult to apply discrete boundaries to something as ineffable as consciousness.

Since we still don't know how the brains of mammals create consciousness, we have no grounds for assuming it's only the brains of mammals that do so — or even that consciousness requires a brain at all. Organised groups of animals, such as shoals of fish, or flocks of birds might have a communal consciousness, in addition to their own individual ones.

Such ideas are difficult to square with the notion we generally have of what consciousness is. But when we remove all the toppings and accessories (sight, arms, memories etc) that bind to consciousness then it reduces to that pure state of awareness. As philosopher Thomas Nagel described it: a creature is conscious if there is 'something that it is like' to be this creature. It doesn't require an exertion of will (and in any case neuroscientific research is increasingly concluding that there is no scientific grounds for free will — by studying neural activity our choices/decisions/speech can be predicted a moment before we are even aware of them ourselves). It just needs to be an experience, and an awareness of that experience. My own definition is an awareness of presence and a sense of presence in one's awareness.

Maybe 'what it is like to be' a coral head is similar to what it would be like to be a human without sentience, memories, speech or any of those other faculties. And maybe there is a sensation of what it is like to be an ecosystem, or even the ocean: some kind of sense of presence and awareness without the locus or proprietorship that we feel as humans. Whether this is the case or not, the experience of the ocean itself — that mercurial and bustling mass — can make it very easy to believe in such a thing. When I am freediving I become part of that 'body of water', and (as I said earlier) it is for this reason that in thanking the ocean at the end of my training sessions I feel like I am also thanking myself.

During my time on Roatan I was also invited to swim with the 'semi-captive' dolphins kept by Anthony's Key Resort. I visited the facility first, and saw that the dolphins were kept in pens and only let out to swim in the ocean in small groups of a single sex (to ensure that they would return to be with the rest of the pod). This was obviously an improvement on those hellish concrete prisons called marine parks, but it was still confinement and exploitation for entertainment. I declined the invitation.

*

Back on Long Island, I resumed my training in Constant Weight to try to exceed Herbert Nitsch's last remaining record of 124 metres. I had set a date in May for an attempt, and a crew from the American show *60 Minutes* — perhaps the country's most esteemed TV news-magazine program — had arranged to come to follow my bid at the record. The reporting journalist would be Bob Simon, a 70-year-old 'giant of broadcast journalism', who had reported on the withdrawal of US troops from Vietnam in the 1970s, the Egyptian revolution in 2011 and almost everything in between. During the Gulf War he had been captured by Iraqi forces after crossing a border and imprisoned for 40 days.

When Bob arrived on the island with a small crew of four producers and cameramen, it was hard not to feel intimidated — as if he were there to unearth some kind of hidden truth about me or freediving that even I was unaware of! Once we started chatting, however, his charisma and wit dissolved my guard, and I realised that he was there mostly to have fun and maybe a bit of a holiday. He even had a Kiwi joke up his sleeve! It might have all been a clever ruse, as later I would indeed feel the full power of his journalistic tractor beams focused on me.

My training had continued its Nepalese course of up and down, with, thankfully, a general trend towards an ascent. After two failed dives, with a samba on one and a 2-second surface blackout on the other, I finally completed a clean dive to 125 metres in mid-April, two weeks out from the record attempt. I now knew that I was capable of the depth, but it would be a matter of ensuring that all of my physiological and mental systems were operating at their peaks for the actual attempt.

We had a five-day window for the dive, and I decided to use the first day as a warm-up, to acclimatise to the attention of the cameras and the judges. I dived to 120 metres, surfacing comfortably. After a day of rest, the line was set to 125 metres on 6 May. Bob Simons stood, tall and formal, in the centre of the platform, observing the proceedings like a hawk. For the first time at a record attempt I had my whole family there as well, and my brother, Sam, was managing the instruments on the platform and giving timing readouts. Linda and David watched anxiously from the side of the Blue Hole.

Everything proceeded smoothly, and I was coasting towards the plate at about 1 metre per second when one of my ears jammed and wouldn't equalise anymore. I grabbed the line to stop my fall, and gave three quick jerks — the signal to the surface team to release the counterballast so that I would get a free ride up and save my legs for another attempt the next day. After giving the tugs, I started pulling myself slowly up, knowing that it would take a few seconds for the team to activate the device. However, after pulling for a minute I realised that the rope still wasn't moving upwards. As I hadn't done any free-immersion training that year, pulling on the rope was feeling awkward and I started to become concerned that I wouldn't make it to the surface. I switched back to using the fin, and powered angrily through the last 30 metres in 20 seconds.

'Does anyone *not* know that the signal to release the counterballast is pulling on the rope?' were the first words

I spat out as soon as I had recovered my breath. I continued smouldering and panting in the water, coughing as well from the effect that the unaccustomed arm exertion had had on my lungs at depth. No one answered my question. It was probably a miscommunication between my team and the judges, who were monitoring my movements by feel on the line. Most of my anger really stemmed from having had to abort the dive, and it wasn't fair to take that out on the team.

In an interview later that evening, Bob Simon grilled me on that moment. 'When you came to the surface, you were furious! What made you so mad?' he asked me. I replied that I didn't think I had been that mad, just disappointed at having turned early. 'No, no, that's not what I saw,' he said, before repeating word for word the rebuke I had made to my team. I hesitated, and tried to deflect the question again, uncomfortable with the idea that I could be so hot-headed after a freedive, but Bob wasn't having it. In that dive he had recognised a piece of my character — a shirtiness — that wasn't playing along with the rest of the composed, yogic equanimity I was trying to cultivate. With stern purpose couched in playful mirth, he forced me to confront it there and then. I was silent for a while; the cameras caught my contemplation and then, finally, my admission that, yes, I had been a bit of a dick.

Despite my mood, the first to console me after the dive had been Brian Pucella, who had put his hand on my shoulder and said, 'Good job anyway.' Originally from North Carolina, Brian was a surfer and adventurer who lived onboard his yacht, *Puff*, with his wife and their dog. He was chief of safety for that record attempt, as well as for Project Hector and several editions of Vertical Blue. His loyalty and dedication to Vertical Blue and my own projects had played a large part in their successes. When you're drawing the last breath of air before a dive that will take you to your limit, it makes a big difference to have someone next to you in the water whom you can trust implicitly with your safety should anything go wrong. That was Brian's strong point — but clearly it wasn't always my strong point to appreciate the full value of my crew when my focus was inward and selfish during a record attempt.

*

I would need a day of rest after the aborted dive before feeling ready to attempt 125 metres again. On 7 May the conditions were still favourable. The surface of the Blue Hole was slick calm with a green hue from the overcast light, making it look like a fathomless mountain lake. I was likewise feeling calm and composed as I went

Descending into Dean's Blue Hole, with a tarpon watching from under the overhang.
(*Igor Liberti*)

through my equipment check before entering the water. There was very little sign of any nerves; this might have been because I had been able to shift my focus from the idea of a record attempt to one of 'doing a good dive' — a technically fluent and aesthetically pleasing dive. I thought that if I could achieve that goal, the record would follow.

After a quick and efficient kicking descent to 30 metres I brought my body close to the dive line and relaxed into a freefall that would last almost 2 minutes. This time there was no difficulty with equalising, and my turn at the bottom was calm and fluid. I struck off for the surface at a good speed — 1.6 metres per second to begin with — before starting to slow down as my legs lost strength. It is important for me to 'escape' from the depths at a good velocity to begin with: if I slow down too much, narcosis crowds in on me and I lose the feeling for efficient technique, which slows me down further. As it was, I was able to stay ahead of that effect, and my ascent rate never dropped below 1.2 metres per second. When Brian met me at 35 metres with a grouper call I felt confident, and afterwards he confirmed that I still looked comfortable at that depth. My finning continued almost to the surface, then I brought my arms to my sides and broke through the water to grab the rope in front of me. I was facing away from the platform and the judges, and as I took the first two quick breaths my arms contracted, pulling my body high out of the water. One hand went to my nose to remove the nose clip that I so often forget in the surface protocol. Then the hand shaped an 'okay' sign, and in the very moment that my thumb and forefinger touched together and my hand extended forwards came the realisation of what I had just done. My goggles were still in place over my eyes.

By performing an 'okay' sign before removing all of my facial equipment, I had failed the surface protocol — and with it the record attempt. It had only taken me eight of the available 15 seconds to screw it up; had I taken two more breaths before starting the protocol, I might have been more clear-headed and capable of completing the actions correctly while facing the judges. Letting myself fall back under the water, I let out a groan as I realised how close I had come only to throw it all away with such an avoidable error.

Two days later I would make a final attempt at that elusive record. The depth and dive time were exactly the same, but the pressure would bear down on me a little more on this occasion. I surfaced, after having been underwater for 3 minutes 47 seconds, and grabbed the line high above the water. My whole torso and waist were completely above the waterline as I took full lungfuls of air. I was breathing in great gusts, like the bellows in a forgery, but I was not lucid. After a few seconds my arms started to shake and I fell backwards into the water, continuing to breathe as I stared upwards at the sky. Slowly I began to shake my head from side to side, in exasperation.

When the *60 Minutes* piece went to air, it used the failed attempts to show just how many factors are at play in the sport, and how the success of a dive can hang in the balance of any of them. 'It sounds like a technicality,' commented Bob after describing the failed protocol, 'but he has to prove that his mind is as tough as his body.'

I would have another chance to prove that toughness later in the year, when I would come up against Alexey Molchanov at Vertical Blue, for the first serious face-off since my rivalry with Herbert Nitsch.

*

We had decided to shift the dates for Vertical Blue to November, as this favoured the northern-hemisphere athletes who make up most of the numbers at the event. It would allow them to train over their summer with the goal of peaking at the event in the late autumn. This edition of Vertical Blue would be our biggest so far, with a total of 50 athletes (31 male, 19 female) from 18 countries. I finished my base training in Tenerife early, and by the end of September was back in the Bahamas to prepare for the showdown.

Over the summer Alexey had succeeded where I had failed, diving to 125 metres CWT to claim his first depth world record in the waters of the Red Sea in Egypt. The discipline of Constant Weight came naturally to the Russian, who had been training as a monofin swimmer in the pool since he was a child. His physique was also more adapted to the dolphin kick: a long torso and shorter legs meant that he was able to generate more force in the core and not lose it in the transmission of energy through the legs. These same features became a disadvantage in No Fins, where short levers (arms and legs) transfer less torque to the water.

For now, though, we were both focused on Constant Weight. I had done a number of training dives dolphin-kicking with short plastic snorkelling fins, culminating in one long and leg-slaughtering freedive to 100 metres. It felt almost like it was harder than the same depth without fins! After that I returned to using the monofin, and gradually returned to the world-record mark. Just before Vertical Blue I attempted a personal-best dive to 126 metres. In preparation, I embedded in my mind the idea that my hands would be like blades, scything through the water while the fin powered me from beneath. It worked well, with a strong speed in the ascent and two reports of it being the best surfacing of recent CWT dives. The dive time was 3:38. Now all that remained was to do it in competition.

As is my custom, I sat out the first day of competition to help troubleshoot the inevitable first-day niggles, while Alexey logged a CWT dive of 121 metres to warm up. On day two I surfaced strongly from a dive to 97 metres without fins, and added a 117-metre FIM to my tally on day three while Alexey got on the board in CNF with an 80-metre dive.

The duel began in earnest on the first day of Act Two, when Alexey and I both announced a world-record attempt of 126 metres CWT. Alexey won the coin toss and dived first, surfacing cleanly with the tag after 3:46. I had failed to program my depth alarms correctly, and not knowing where I was in the descent disconcerted me; I turned early at 108 metres. On my next attempt two days later I made the plate, returned to the surface — and blacked out after taking the first breath. Straight afterwards, Alexey dived to 128 metres, attempting to shift the Constant Weight record beyond my reach. In the darkness, more than halfway to the bottom of Dean's Blue Hole, he became confused by the lights beneath the plate and couldn't find the tag — he discovered later that he'd been searching for it on the camera arm! Despite the lost time he still managed to surface and complete the protocol, but without the tag the massive dive couldn't be judged a world record.

With three days of the event left, I still needed a dive in CWT and Alexey required FIM points. We both waited until the penultimate day; then I announced 121 CWT and Alexey 107 FIM. I had decided to take a more moderate approach to the ascent, and my speed was slower but more constant. However, after a certain point it felt uncoordinated and lopsided, as if the blade of my fin was only bending on one side. My vision was also affected, perhaps by the narcosis, and when I surfaced I missed the line on my first two attempts at grabbing it. Despite this, I managed to stay calm and to kick to hold my shoulders above the waterline, and completed the surface protocol without any signs of low oxygen.

Alexey had made a successful dive too, but when the points were added up it was clear that he was out of the running for the overall prize. Although he had the deepest dive in Constant Weight, he was too far behind in the other two disciplines to be able to catch up on the last day. Instead, he chose to again try to improve his record in CWT, with an attempt at 127 metres, but this time he surfaced with a samba and flunked the surface protocol.

Meanwhile, I was attempting to add 2 metres to my Free Immersion world record, with a dive to 123. The Spanish FIM specialist Miguel Lozano was attempting to break the same record, with an announced dive to 122 metres, and went first. A lanky Barcelonan nearly 2 metres tall, Miguel always brought a jovial mood to the platform during training. Now, as Sam shouted out readings for depth and dive time in Miguel's ascent, the mood was more subdued. He was coming up slowly — far too slowly. Even though I was trying to blot the dive out and focus on getting ready myself, I knew that something was going wrong. At 4 minutes Miguel was still 40 metres below the surface. Somewhere around

20 metres he stopped moving altogether, and the safety divers converged to grasp him under the arms and swim him quickly to the surface. It takes longer to regain consciousness after a deep blackout, and while the surface team supported Miguel on his back and started to give him rescue breaths to oxygenate his lungs, blood started bubbling from his mouth — evidence of a lung squeeze suffered at depth.

This was the first lung squeeze of Miguel's career, although other athletes experienced them more regularly. The cause is primarily a lack of adaptation of the lungs to the pressure at depth: if the diaphragm, rigid airways or ribcage are not flexible enough, then at a certain depth the lungs can no longer accommodate the pressure change through a continued reduction in their internal volume — the 'container' that surrounds them will prevent this. At that point, capillaries inside the lungs will begin to rupture, leaking blood into the airspaces. Once on the surface this blood is coughed up, but if there is enough of it then it can start to obstruct the diffusion of oxygen into the bloodstream. A secondary factor contributing to lung squeeze is any sudden or strenuous movements at the maximum depth. These movements, or any strong breathing reflexes, can 'tweak' the lungs, adding extra negative pressure to their internal volume and causing ruptures of blood vessels.

The advent of more efficient training and diving techniques, as well as better equipment, had meant that divers were making much quicker progress through the depths than they had ten years earlier. Whereas I had logged literally thousands of dives over hundreds of days of training before I started exceeding 60 metres, nowadays athletes who had trained extensively in the pool, developing long breath-holds and a powerful swimming technique, might be able to reach this depth within just a couple of weeks of open-water training. However, their lungs weren't fully prepared for the drastic changes in pressure at depth, and at some point they would reach the limits of their chest flexibility. This was when 'lung squeezes' occurred. If the underlying shortcomings weren't addressed, then the squeezes could become worse as scar tissue in the lungs rendered them more susceptible to repeat incidents, and a fear of squeeze itself rendered the divers less relaxed and consequently less flexible at depth.

*

As I lay on my back in the water, preparing for my own dive, I heard the safety team administering to Miguel. Once he had regained consciousness and was moved across to the platform, the depth was adjusted to 1 metre deeper and I was finally allowed access to the line to clip myself on. 'Three minutes to Official Top,' came Sam's call. A few seconds later, I felt some kind of hard surface make contact with the underneath of my body and lift me out of the water. It was the housing of an enormous camera being wielded by someone from a media crew filming Miguel's dive, who had misjudged his ascent. It felt as if a submarine was surfacing underneath me, and I strained to try to maintain my relaxation as the safety divers quickly manoeuvred the cameraman and his equipment away from the competition area.

Thankfully, this would be the last distraction before the dive began. At a dive time of 2:15 I turned smoothly, while plucking a tag from the base plate, and at 4:23 I surfaced, removed my goggles and nose clip, made an 'okay' sign and spoke the words 'I'm okay.' As the judges continued to watch me for the required 30 seconds, Vertical Blue media manager Francesca Koe was doing the commentary for our live internet audio feed: 'You can just tell, his facial expression — he's smiling, he's glad that dive's over!' I reached down to my leg, where I had attached the tag to the Velcro patch, and my smile disappeared. Where there should have been a small rectangle of fur clinging to my leg, there was only the stubble of the male Velcro patch it should have been stuck to.

A groan passed around the spectators crowded around the edge of the competition zone, but I was soon laughing, along with the safety team, at the absurdity of it all. As things had turned out, my record was still intact — although had it been broken by Miguel in his dive before mine, perhaps I might not have been so accepting of the misfortune!

I finished the event with 295 points out of a possible 300, 25 clear of Alexey in second place.

Throughout the event, one athlete had been unable to log any points at all: having burst his eardrum on his first dive, Nicholas Mevoli was forced to sit out the rest of the event while it healed. All the same, he still came to the beach every day to stand quietly by the rocks and offer encouragement and support to those who were about to dive. In 2013 Nick would become one of my best friends among competitive freedivers, and I was able to witness his meteoric rise to an elite level in the sport. Then came the event that rocked the freediving community to its core.

CHAPTER 9

FATAL ERROR

A *dive too far*

> The ocean is like a god for a freediver. You talk to the
> ocean, you pray to the ocean, you love the ocean —
> sometimes you even hate the ocean — but in the end
> you know you cannot live without the ocean.
>
> **Umberto Pelizzari**

IT WAS A WARM LATE AFTERNOON on Roatan when Nick
Mevoli and I put on some basic snorkelling gear and
swam across the tepid lagoon to the reef in front of the
condo apartment we were sharing. We were looking for a
bit of recreational relief after the mental stress of training
and competition dives. We reached the drop-off, where
the coral reef descends vertically down to 20 metres
before a mostly sandy bottom slopes steeply away into
the depths. This edge formed a kind of highway for
the larger sealife such as jacks, dogtooth snappers and

turtles. The devoted management of Roatan's marine park meant that the coral was healthy, and alive with the activity of its myriad denizens. Shoals of blue damselfish hung like a mobile constellation in the midwater above the reef, and would dart downwards in response to any sudden movement.

At first we spent our time taking turns to do lazy dives to the sandy bottom, lying there for a period while the marine life around us resumed its bustling activity. A colony of tiny garden eels would gradually extend their heads and bodies back out of holes in the sand, like stubble growing on a smooth yellow cheek. A nervous stingray skimmed over the surface, with a bar jack riding behind its shoulder for protection. We drifted further along the reef, coming across a turtle resting under a ledge in the side of the coral cliff. A sleeping turtle can hold its breath for an incredible four to seven hours while wedged under overhanging rock or coral; the loggerhead turtle has even been documented as staying underwater for 10 hours, making it easily the most accomplished breath-holding animal on the planet. This particular shell-dweller was a small green turtle, and as I filmed it with my GoPro it started to manoeuvre out from the shelf and use its front flippers to slowly row its domed body across a small gully in the reef. I drifted with it, watching its bird-like eye watching me back. It didn't seem to show any concern as it paddled slowly in a semi-circle around me.

I felt a tap on my shoulder, and turned to see Nick watching. Since I was already filming, I thought that he would swim into the frame so that I could capture footage of him with the turtle. That's probably what I would have done. Instead, he reached for the camera I was holding, and gestured for me to swim into the shot while he filmed. I did so, and spent the next minute or so twisting and sashaying in time with the turtle as we moved across the reef.

Six months later I would tell this story to a gathering of grieving freedivers, as a glimpse into the gentle and selfless character of Nicholas Mevoli. Although we were not friends for long, the year 2013 holds many precious memories of the time we spent together; training, cooking and gradually sharing our thoughts. Nick's deferential way of expressing himself would include phrases such as 'My unsolicited opinion would be ...', and he was someone with whom you could sit in silence and not feel uncomfortable. It seemed as if Nick had been able to isolate our truly mortal enemies — laziness, impatience, indifference and prejudice — and mount a crusade against them in his own psyche; in turn, this kindled a similar change in the minds of those who spent time with him. He was not without his demons,

With Nicholas Mevoli during the 2013 Caribbean Cup, Roatan, Honduras.

but they were controlled to the point where they fed only from his own flesh; to those around him, his language was only kindness. For these reasons, and also because he had experienced some volatile relationships, he was one of the few people to whom I felt I could confide the problems I was continuing to face in my marriage.

*

Esteban Darhanpe, who was organising the inaugural Caribbean Cup in Roatan, had asked me whether I would be okay sharing accommodation with Nick; although I didn't know Nick very well at all at that point, I was sure we would get along. He had brought fresh curry spices from his trip to Honduras by boat via Jamaica, and we took turns at cooking as we trained and competed during the event.

The sport of freediving puts huge oxidative and acidifying stress on the body's systems, so our diet has to address this with alkalinising foods that are rich in anti-oxidants. Basically, this translates to lots of fresh fruit and vegetables. As soon as I get out of the water I'll have a glass of fruit juice mixed with chia seeds; then, when I arrive home, I'll make a smoothie that combines large helpings of fresh aloe, frozen banana and papaya, almond milk, spirulina, cacao, hemp protein, beetroot juice extract and bee pollen. As I drink the thick green gloop, I can almost feel a soothing balance being restored to my body. Half an hour later I have a more solid lunch, then comes the post-prandial nap while my body digests and recovers from training.

In preparation for a deep dive, my diet centres on complex carbohydrates. Compared with fat or protein, carbohydrates are a more oxygen-efficient energy source, as well as the best means of ensuring that the muscles have adequate glycogen stores. Protein-rich and low-glycaemic carbohydrates such as quinoa or oats (my breakfast of choice) are always preferable. But for versatility, there is no beating pasta. My Sicilian friend Jimmy Montanti and his partner, Stella, introduced me to what is now my favourite dish — for flavour, healthiness and ease of preparation. I make it so often that friends refer to it as 'Pasta alla William', even though I try to explain that it is an old Sicilian pesto recipe. It was, in fact, developed during times of poverty after World War I, when meat was scarce — the almonds that feature in the sauce give it a similar kind of body.

It's real name is Pesto Siciliano, and it's made with these ingredients: three large tomatoes (the equivalent in cherry tomatoes is even better); two or three cloves of garlic; one fresh chilli (or more if you're keen); salt (if you like the taste, otherwise your body doesn't need it); a handful of fresh basil; three tablespoons of olive oil; half a cup of almonds; and half a cup of freshly grated aged Parmesan cheese. All you need to do is blend the ingredients, except the cheese and almonds, in a food processor or blender. Add the almonds to the blender last, and stop before they are completely blended. When the pasta is cooked, drain it and add first the cheese, then the sauce, and mix before serving.

In general I avoid land-based animal protein, both at home and at restaurants. You can take your pick of the reasons — animal welfare, ecology or health. It's a clear finding (disputed, of course, by the meat industry) that consumption of beef, pork and chicken in Western and Westernised countries is heavily implicated in the epidemic of 'diseases of affluence' (cancer, heart disease, diabetes), as well as responsible for as much greenhouse-gas emission as the entire travel industry. Not to mention the inconceivable suffering of sentient animals that (in the case of pigs) are more intelligent than the animals we bring into our homes as pets — animals that are protected from similar inhumanities by humane societies.

Of course, some of the practices that bring seafood to the table are just as bad, or worse. For every serving of wild shrimp, as much as 20 times the amount of bycatch (unwanted fish, seabirds, turtles and mammals — many of them endangered) that is trapped in the shrimp nets is thrown back into the ocean, dead. Shrimp farms come at the expense of the coastal ecosystems they replace, which are often mangrove areas vital for the breeding and survival of juvenile sealife. Marine ecosystems all around the world are collapsing, and according to the United Nations' Food and Agriculture Organization, 76 per cent of all fish stocks are depleted or fully or over-exploited.

Nowadays, pretty much the only animal protein I eat is fish I catch myself, from stocks of sustainable species and using a selective method (spearfishing) with no bycatch. Naturally this way isn't an option for most people, especially those who live away from the coast, but making an informed choice that takes into account the provenance of what you're eating is something that we're all capable of. For example, mussels, oysters and farmed tilapia (a group of freshwater fish species) are in most cases sustainable and healthy choices.

There has been a large shift in ecological consciousness around the planet, but it seems as if meat is this decade's 'inconvenient truth'. There's no 'smoking gun' like there is with a car exhaust, and people get more enjoyment out of meat than they do out of transport. It's also an intensely private matter — people can take things personally no matter how delicately you inform them about the damage meat farming is doing. All of this has created a kind of taboo around the subject that extends even into conservationist groups, who don't want to scare away their funders by telling them what they ought to eat (as exposed by the documentary *Cowspiracy*). Proselytising about the topic only seems to make people bare their (mostly herbivorous) teeth and dig their forks deeper into their steaks. For this reason I normally limit myself to being a passive example of my opinions on the subject, and answering any queries that come my way. It seems to me that regarding what we put into our bodies, change must come from within.

*

From the water in Roatan on 28 May 2013, I watched Nick's attempt to be the first American to dive 100 metres CWT. In tough conditions (the rope descended on an angle due to the current), he made the dive in 2:45 with a clean protocol. Upon surfacing he was breathing quickly, but when someone in the water yelled out 'Hook! Hook!' (meaning take a hook-breath), he indignantly replied 'I'm not a hooker!' The judges showed a white card and Nick shook the line with all his might, letting out a cry of triumph towards the skies.

There wasn't a huge difference in appearance between those euphoric displays and the releases of vehement frustration that occasioned his failed dives. In both moments, the intense passion that fuelled him would be purged in a great flood. A month later, for example, when we were both at the AIDA Indoor World Championships in Belgrade, Serbia, I was pulled from my pre-performance relaxation by the sound — heard from clear across an Olympic swimming pool — of an expletive-laden disgorgement that Nick was directing at himself after being disqualified due to a small blackout. It was not the kind of outburst we were used to hearing in a freediving event.

For me, that Indoor World Championship was one of the few strong points in an otherwise mediocre year. The competition was in June, soon after the Caribbean

Cup, but despite minimal pool training I managed a competition personal best of 187 metres in the discipline of Dynamic No Fins (DNF). Afterwards, Nick, Brittany and I embarked on a road trip north through Hungary, with a night in Budapest before driving on through Slovakia to the Czech Republic where we explored the quaintly ordered city of Brno. Needless to say, we stretched out the grace period of indulgence that follows a championship event to be able to sample the fabled draught beers of the region, and they didn't disappoint.

We parted ways with Nick in the airport at Vienna; another memory, that of the bulging, amorphous, yellow fin bag over his shoulder and a gaudy red rollaway case at his feet as he waved from the departures concourse. Two months later, in early September, we were both back to competing at the Depth World Championships, which were being held in Kalamata for the second time. Nick's travelling, frequent competitions and frenzied work schedule in Brooklyn, New York, to pay for it all, were starting to take their toll on him. During training he suffered several lung squeezes, writing about it in his blog, which ended: 'Last night I read a proverb that changed me, "As a dog returns to his own vomit, so a fool returns to his folly." I am tired of being a fool, I will not make the same mistakes and expect different results and, more to the point, I will not push my body until it breaks anymore.' For the rest of the competition he managed to hold himself back, and ultimately reaped the rewards of his circumspection.

My own training had been going well, with a strong dive to 98 metres without fins — my deepest outside the Caribbean. However, when championship day arrived, the 96 metres I'd announced proved to be slightly too much and I momentarily blacked out on the surface. Once again, my posted depth had been well clear of the field and I could have turned at 93 and won despite the penalty points; but this time there had been no indication that I wasn't capable of 96. Frenchman Morgan Bourc'his won gold, with a strong dive to 87 metres. A string of other blackouts and early turns meant that the next-deepest diver was Nick, who, with 65 metres, tied with an Israeli competitor for silver. He wasn't any more content than I was, however, declaring that he didn't deserve the medal; eventually he gifted it to judge and mentor Grant Graves, who had helped him with advice and mental coaching during the event.

In Constant Weight, I dived to 120 metres for the silver medal, behind Alexey who had made a strong recovery after a harrowing incident a week before the championships. A reverse block occurs when, during the ascent, expanding air is prevented from naturally exiting the middle ear back into the nasal chambers, and can cause vertigo. Alexey had experienced one of these and had become alarmed and disorientated, swimming in a spiral around the rope. This led to a very deep blackout 10 metres below the point where safety diver Stephen Keenan was waiting at 30 metres. Luckily Stephen was an incredibly strong diver: he was able to swim down to 40 metres, retrieve Alexey and bring him up to the next safety diver, although he nearly blacked out himself in the process.

Although there was no rupturing of Alexey's eardrums, he had suffered a serious lung squeeze and took days to recover before gradually returning to diving. Many believed that his announcement, only a week after the incident, of a record attempt at 128 metres CWT was rash, but Alexey proved them wrong and made the dive for the gold medal. Afterwards, however, word started to spread that he had made a mistake in the surface protocol. I hadn't seen it myself, but those who had, including crew members and official judges, believed that he had made the 'okay' sign twice before saying 'I'm okay,' which warrants disqualification under AIDA rules.

At that time, the only way for the judges' decision to award the dive to be reviewed — through analysis of the surface camera footage — was if a rival athlete lodged a protest. We (me and two other athletes who would be affected by the decision) decided to give Alexey a heads-up first, as a courtesy, and to give him a chance to exonerate himself if his team had recorded video of the dive. This precipitated a debate, mostly with Alexey's mother, Natalia, and another very vocal member of the Russian team, about the ethics of protesting a fellow athlete. It was easy to see their point — being an agent in the disqualification of another competitor is always going to create a rift. However, protesting was then the only route for correcting a mistake made by a judge that favoured an athlete. Neither protesting nor letting bad judging stand was a satisfactory outcome. We decided that it was the system that was set up poorly, and instead of protesting Alexey's dive made a submission to the judges for a rule change. We stated that quality control for the judging panel shouldn't fall on the athletes' shoulders; there should be automatic review of the surface footage of all performances that were eligible for a medal position. Our submission was accepted (for future events), and now, thankfully, freedivers can concentrate more on what they do best and less on having to look over each other's shoulders.

Two days later, during my Free Immersion gold-medal dive, I literally *did* have someone looking over my shoulder: the vocal Russian team member we'd had discussions with about the protest was filming my performance from inside the competition zone, where other athletes are normally not allowed. Whether this was to try to throw me off, get video evidence if my surface protocol was borderline, or just to take holiday snaps was not clear, but once I'd finished the protocol for the judges I did one for his camera as well, for good measure.

*

Soon after the World Championships, athletes began converging on the Bahamian islands to train in advance of Vertical Blue. Nick was one of these early arrivals, coming directly from yet another competition (his sixth of the year) in Curaçao, where he had taken first place overall. If he had been tired already in September, by this point he was hitting a wall, both with the mental burnout that comes from constant competing and with the recurring physical damage to his lungs that wasn't being given adequate time to heal. Nick was sharing a house in Clarence Town, Long Island, with fellow Kiwi freediver Jonathan Sunnex, who would become an integral part of Vertical Blue in years to come. Johnny Deep, as he is known in freediving circles, was brought up in Hamilton and escaped a life as an electrician for one beneath the waves. Picture a Tarzan-like physique with a mane of brown ringlets and a streak of Māori in the blood, and you wouldn't be far off. The three of us often trained together, and before the event began I watched Nick execute a strong and confident dive to 70 metres No Fins, which equalled the US national record he was hoping to break.

The weather took a turn for the worse just before the event began, with the first of the winter's cold fronts slipping off Florida's mantle to flare out over the Bahamas. The water temperature dropped a couple of degrees, and incessant onshore winds turned the Blue Hole into a milkshake that light could not penetrate. Against this contingency I had ordered a shipment of waterproof penlights that the athletes could mount on the sides of their heads so they could at least see the line in front of them. We felt like astronauts as we flew downwards through the liquid night, with only a small porthole of light with which to see our world.

There's a scene towards the end of the movie *The Big Blue*, in which the character of Enzo (played by Jean Reno) pushes himself too far in his quest to beat Jacques. He surfaces and, while dying in his rival's arms, says, 'You were right. It's much better down there. Push me back into the water.' This scene makes little sense to a freediver. If you are conscious and able to talk after a freedive, there is really no conceivable way that your death would be inevitable. On 14 November, the day that the competition was postponed due to bad weather, Nick posted a YouTube clip of this scene to his Facebook feed.

There was already an air of frustration about the event. I had failed another world-record attempt at 123 metres FIM due to incorrect surface protocol (this time I forgot the nose clip), and Alexey had blacked out attempting 94 metres CNF. But of all the athletes, Nick's frustration was the most evident. Twice during the few days of competition he had turned early when attempting 72 CNF to break the US national record. On 15 November he attempted 95 FIM, but thinking that he had blown his eardrum (as he had the previous year), he signalled the safety divers to assist him to the surface. Sam, who was platform coordinator, would later comment that 'he howled his anger, banged his head against the competition line, and refused any consolation or advice from fellow athletes, medics, and team. He also had a lung squeeze, evidenced by a small soup-spoonful of blood that he spat out at the surface.' This time, however, the ear was intact. On his Facebook feed that evening, Nick wrote: 'Ego is damaged that's all, frustration oozing from my wetsuit this afternoon causing me to be stupid.'

*

'I don't know; I think he'll either turn early again, or black out,' I said in response to a question from Jonathan Sunnex. We were standing on the beach, our toes in the water, looking out towards the platform, where Nick had just begun his third attempt at 72 metres CNF. I hate myself now for making that comment, but I doubt whether anyone present on that day doesn't have at least one thing they regret doing or not doing, saying or not saying ...

It was Sunday 17 November, and I had driven down to the Blue Hole shortly before noon to watch the second half of the day's dives (I wasn't competing myself that day). The weather was improving, although the water remained silted and green from the ground-swell that was pounding the reef. The session was relaxed, with the lowest average depth of the competition to date. On the platform, Nick had been in a good mood while he chatted with Japanese contestant Junko Kitahama before his dive. She was flying out that afternoon, and Nick had given her a warm hug and said, 'I hope I see you again.' Those words would haunt her later.

He had slipped off the platform to start his final phase of breathing before the dive, lying on his back with his feet draped over a swimming noodle and his head supported by an inflatable haemorrhoids pillow (the butt of many jokes — probably why Nick was so attached to it). The dive had started cleanly, and now Nick was on his way down, with the depth readouts Sam was announcing all indicating that he was making good speed. Watching from the beach, we willed him on, knowing that if he didn't have difficulty equalising and made the base plate then he was capable of completing the dive.

'60 metres! Ohhh, turn ...' announced Sam from the platform, to groans of disappointment. 'No, he's going again!' Sam added as he saw the tracer on the depth sounder dip back downwards. 'Come on, Nick,' murmured Carla-Sue Hanson, one of the AIDA judges.

Far below, Nick had turned so that he was feet first, so as to be able to equalise better (it's easier to get air to move into the ears when the direction of movement is upwards). He had done so while avoiding touching the line, which would have disqualified him. The position is extremely awkward, however, and Nick started to fall to one side, moving further away from the line as he drifted slowly downwards. He was also facing in the wrong direction, and when he finally reached the target depth of 72 metres he had to turn and use the narrow beam of his headlight to locate the plate, before tearing off a tag and slipping it inside the hood of his wetsuit. Although he appeared calm throughout, the whole operation took an extra 20 seconds of time in those last 10 metres before the plate.

Back on the surface, Sam was on the point of activating the counterballast to hoist Nick up when he saw him moving again on the sonar. After planting both feet on the base plate, Nick had pushed off with his legs before starting to swim upwards with rapid strokes. On the beach, Johnny and I were shifting from one foot to another. We knew that the extra time at depth could be critical in determining the fate of the dive, but we were willing our friend on. 'Come *on*, Nick,' we both said in unison. 'Be ready for this one,' Sam warned the safety crew, who were preparing to dive to meet Nick.

After being under for 3 minutes 32 seconds, Nick broke the surface. He had returned from the marathon dive completely under his own power. Air had been escaping his mouth at the end of the ascent and the safety divers were ready to intervene, but he kept on swimming. Even though he surfaced away from the line and so couldn't use it to support himself, he kept on treading water until he could reach out and grab it. As he reached, he made an 'okay sign', and said what would be his final words: 'I'm okay.'

The brutality of that obligatory phrase. Nick was not okay. After grabbing the line he blacked out briefly, but only for a few seconds. When he came to, still holding the rope, the people around him were consolatory: 'You were almost there, buddy,' said a safety diver. 'Sorry, Nick,' said Carla-Sue as she showed the red card. Nick continued staring ahead, mostly unresponsive, and it started to become clear that he was having difficulty breathing. His head tilted back, and with a groan he blacked out again. This time, he would not recover consciousness.

Nick was immediately moved onto the platform for resuscitation to begin, but neither Johnny nor I standing on the beach, nor anyone present on the platform, suspected that he wouldn't wake up within the space of a few seconds. Like Enzo's death in *The Big Blue*, it was something that no freediver deemed possible. When the seconds became minutes, and pure oxygen was having no effect on him, I swam to the platform and joined the efforts, helping to maintain the seal around the mask placed over Nick's face, and later preparing a shot of adrenaline for the medic. Nick's heart had stopped beating.

The next phase in the emergency plan was set in motion: Nick was transported to shore and rushed to the emergency van. I drove it as fast as prudence would allow, blasting the horn on every corner; in the back, the safety divers continued their resuscitation attempts.

Nick was a car enthusiast, and might have enjoyed that final ride. I overtook a police car at 110 kilometres per hour; its occupants quickly got the picture and overtook me in turn to escort us the remainder of the short journey to the clinic.

Cardiopulmonary resuscitation was continued at the clinic, but Nick's pulse did not return. When I returned to the emergency room after making a phone call to arrange an air ambulance, there was no longer anyone crouched over him giving chest compressions. Nick was declared dead at 1.48 p.m.

I returned home in a daze. I had never before witnessed death, and neither had I ever lost a close and present friend. In my mind I was still going over everything that had happened, trying to work out what had gone wrong. And what would happen next. I knew that I needed to be the focal point of managing the enquiries, the legalities, the disbanding of the event, the organisation of a tribute, and anything else necessary. Through all of this, there was one recurring question that might never be answered: 'How can someone be here one minute and gone the next? How can consciousness just end?'

Before freediving, Nick's passion had been acting, and he had starred in the independent film *Exist* as a squatter in New York's protest movement. His character,

Top, delivers one especially memorable line: 'I have faith in the fact that we never really die; pieces of us live on in the memories of others.' I suspect that this line was one of his own (the director allowed actors to write part of their script), as he had also once consoled a friend suffering a loss by saying 'True friendship isn't affected by death — it remains intact.'

Ever since that fateful day in 2013, Nick has continued to live on in the hearts and minds of all those he met. Among those closest to him, the phrase 'What would Nick do?' is often used to channel the generosity and selflessness he exhibited.

*

AIDA had overseen close to 30,000 dives in the two decades since its inception, and Nick's death was the first in competition during this period. Neither, for that matter, had there been a mortality in supervised training for any of the three depth disciplines. This track record was often touted as proof of freediving's relative safety compared with other so-called extreme sports such as base-jumping or white-water kayaking. Yet, given the nature and severity of the lung squeezes experienced by many freedivers in the years leading up to November 2013, it is perhaps surprising that Nick was the first to die. Divers were surfacing unconscious, with orange foam issuing from their mouths and requiring tens of minutes on pure oxygen before they started to regain their colour. Others had to be hospitalised. Despite this, there was still a general attitude of complacency towards the problem. 'Take a day or two off and then get back into it,' was a common mentality.

Nick's death forced the whole freediving community to review this way of thinking and training. Individually, athletes realised that lung injuries were not just 'part of the game', and that being blasé or secretive about them would only proliferate the problem. Collectively, the community also made improvements to its practices, starting with a set of additional safety protocols and measures that were devised and first implemented at Vertical Blue in 2014, and shortly thereafter became a standard for all AIDA competitions. Athletes are now forbidden to turn feet first in descent, or to stop and restart, as these awkward movements are believed to contribute to lung squeeze. Post-dive medical checks have become more stringent, and all athletes must report to have measurements taken such as heart rate and arterial oxygen saturation, which can help detect evidence of a mild lung squeeze.

Even for those who never met him, Nick's death was a wake-up call that caused a revolution — a sea change, if you will — in the sport. Although, of course, it could never have been his intention, we still have him to thank for paying the ultimate sacrifice. He was a devoutly Christian man when he died at the age of 32, and it might have pleased him to know that, as in the stories of Jesus and many saints, his death was a message that changed — and maybe saved — the lives of many.

CHAPTER 10

DRY PATCH

Diving for a drink

There is a kind of threshold between shallow and deep.
Between a state of floating, buoyant with the lungs'
volume, and a state of falling into the abyss where this
volume is compressed. As freedivers we must choose
with every dive to pass this point, and surrender to the
freefall. Any hesitation or reluctance will act like a tether
to the surface, that slows or halts our flight.

In the moment we pass this threshold and fall into
heaviness, we leave a part of ourselves behind. We leave
our history and our hopes, and continue as only our
present selves. We leave behind the concept and memory
of breathing, and continue with the deception that we
are aquatic. In that moment, the self separates and we
continue with only what is necessary for our journey.

The less of us we take down, the lighter the load.

William Trubridge, journal entry

FOR ME IN 2014, the load was becoming ever more difficult to shed at the critical moment. It wasn't that my friend's death had caused me to question what I was doing with freediving; rather, it was that everything else in my life was coming up for scrutiny. For one thing, the effect that my marriage was having on my career, and on my mental health in general, could no longer be denied.

In a way, it might have been the same determination to succeed at all costs — the force and resolve that had driven me on to eventually set my first world record after two failed attempts — that kept me in a relationship to the point where it was undermining my own stability. Matters were increasingly becoming out of control, and at times I would have to either escape at short notice to sleep in the car or on the beach, or request intervention from family, friends or even the police. Our beautiful moments of harmony had become the exception. I was running out of oxygen but still clinging to the idea of reaching the surface of our relationship, even though I had no idea how far away that was or even whether such a place existed.

It would be another year before I finally redirected that determination and, instead of trying to make things work, used all of my remaining emotional strength to escape what had become little more than a death spiral.

*

Into this chaotic scenography was thrown one of the most difficult undertakings of my career thus far: the 102-metre CNF Steinlager Live Dive attempt.

Coming into 2014, I believed I knew a bit about pressure and about the stifling weight of expectations. I thought I knew what it meant to have to pick myself up after a failure and step back up to the plate. My mother was the first to point out to me how life has a way of raising the difficulty of its challenges in concert with your ability to cope with them. It's as if life says 'You got that? Think you're hot stuff? Righto then, try your hand at this!' And with that you're served up — or you serve yourself up — a fresh obstacle even more onerous than the previous one. Perhaps this process is only a 'manifestation' of my own, to use a term from self-empowerment circles. After all, I can't remember how many times I've answered in interviews that I 'thrive on a challenge, especially ones that are mental as well as physical'.

In March that year, I had just finished drying myself off after training when a call came through from my sports agent, Jason Chambers, who handles all my sponsorship and media jobs. Jason is a retired MMA (Mixed Martial Arts) fighter who now wrestles sports brands into submission for the stable of athletes he manages. 'Care to do a live-to-air record attempt as part of a marketing campaign for Steinlager beer?' he asked me point-blank. The 'live dive' idea had been on the table between us for some time, with *National Geographic* originally showing interest but backing out when a similar project was hit by tragedy (the planned live-to-air broadcast of a base-jump from Mount Everest was cancelled when five of the project's Sherpas were lost in the most deadly avalanche ever seen on the mountain).

Of course I was interested — especially when Jason mentioned the fee, which would pay for the construction of a lap pool at my house on Long Island, meaning that I wouldn't have to spend time away over the summer for base training. As long as I had several clear months to prepare, I should be able to return to hectometre depth in the No Fins discipline, picking up where I had left off in 2010. Or so I thought. In the three years since my last CNF record I had notched up a mere 20 deep dives in the discipline I was most known for (compared with 50 in 2010 alone). When I took on this new commitment — to freedive to at least 102 metres unassisted — I did feel a slight filament of anxiety. Had I been away from it for too long, chasing that slippery record with the monofin to the point where I would feel naked without it? Would even a single metre prove too large an increment, in the same way that an additional centimetre on the bar might make a high-jumper fail every time?

The first few dives were encouraging, and I quickly found myself back in the nineties. However, from there on my progress was not consistent. A clean dive to 95 was followed with a samba on a 97, then a surface blackout on another 95. Suddenly I couldn't do a strong dive to 93 metres anymore. The filament of anxiety grew strands, like a mass of hair being pulled from a drain. I tried altering elements of the dive: an extra stroke before the freefall to cut some time off the descent; a change in head position to experiment with different streamlining; a slightly quicker rhythm in the ascent. It seemed that nothing could reinstate the ease with which I had been surfacing from these same depths four years previously. I was running out of time before the first event of the year, the second edition of the Caribbean Cup, and to add to my tension I'd heard word that Alexey had been training exclusively without fins in an attempt to beat me at Roatan in my strongest discipline.

When I arrived in Honduras in mid-May, I started with a conservative 85 CNF and added 3 metres with each successive training dive. Then, with the line set at 94 metres, I had a terrible, slow descent and an even worse ascent, and decided to abort at 30 metres from the surface by pulling on the line. Despite the easier ascent this afforded, I still blacked out on the surface for 2 or 3 seconds. It was my last dive before the event, and I was right back at the drawing board.

The Caribbean Cup would be my first competition since Nick Mevoli's death, and as the opening day neared I was feeling mixed emotions. It was as if we'd lost a man overboard and the ship had done a quick turn back to look for him before continuing on in the same direction as before, with the ship's band resuming its song. Were we really ready to move on and start competing again so soon? Was I?

If we were to start again, I wanted to do so with one last glance over my shoulder. It seemed that a fitting way to do this was to complete the final task that Nick had undertaken: the dive that had taken his life. For the first day of the event, I announced 72 metres No Fins. I prepared carefully, wanting this tribute to be as close as possible to the perfect dive we all aspire to. In the freefall I didn't turn my mind off completely, as I normally try to do, but rather let it dwell on what was happening. I took the tag from the bottom, aware of how hard Nick had fought to claim that emblem six months earlier.

Mid-way through the ascent, around the time I was met by the first safety diver, I was overtaken by a surge of the same intense energy I had first experienced in 2008 after doing 90 metres for the first time, the energy that occasionally accompanied meditation, music or even large social gatherings. There was nothing in particular to precipitate it: no thought, experience or action. One second I was swimming at peace; the next, I was overflowing. When bubbles of air ascend in the water column they expand as the pressure decreases, and this effect accelerates as they get closer to the surface: air volume doubles between 30 and 10 metres, then doubles again between 10 metres and the surface. It felt as if something similar was going on in my body: the very sense of being alive was being dilated to beyond what my body could contain. I felt love for my safety divers, for the ocean, for myself. When I surfaced and finally removed my fluid goggles, the safety crew were looking at me curiously; I must have been wearing a rather different expression to what they're accustomed to seeing in my dives. Journalist Adam Skolnick wrote that I 'blinked hard, twice. Then a third time as if waking from a stressful dream.' I might have even been crying — it's hard to tell with goggles full of salt water. No one, it seemed, had deduced the reason behind my announcement — they must have thought that I was starting with a conservative depth because of poor performance in training before the competition.

I stayed with conservative depths — 111 in both Free Immersion and Constant Weight — before returning to No Fins with a dive to 90 metres. On the same day, Alexey made his second attempt at 96 CNF, after his first dive to that depth had ended with a surface blackout. After my dive I put on bi-fins and swam down to watch his final approach to the surface. He was rising quickly and looked to be in full control this time, although it was clear that his arms were starting to run out of energy: between each stroke he would add a dolphin kick of his legs to take some of the load off his upper body. This movement can add a little extra speed and power to the stroke but is ultimately less oxygen-efficient than the regular arm and leg movements of underwater breaststroke, so Alexey was only using it sparingly at the end of the dive, when the lactic acid building up in his arms made them feel like heavy and awkward clubs.

He drifted the last few metres to the surface and completed a clean protocol, removing the tag from where he had stashed it in the hood of his wetsuit to a flare of applause from those watching from the spectator boat. I was clapping too, but was inwardly conflicted. Records are temporary, and no athlete can dominate indefinitely. I often remind myself of these facts because it's easy to become accustomed to seeing your name at the top of the rankings and get sucked into feeling a sense of ownership. No one spells it out more starkly than Bob Dylan, who sang about the 'disease of conceit', and how it will 'give you the idea that you're too good to die' (or lose your world record in my case).

I've always tried to be on the lookout for this pitfall. And yet, when I saw another athlete outshining me in the discipline that I had devoted my career to, it was impossible to hold back the urge to rise to the occasion. My training had indeed been poor, but in the dive to 90 metres I had experimented with an even more minimal breathe-up (slower and more passive breathing before the dive), and this seemed to have paid off with a very comfortable dive. I chose to have confidence in my ability, and announced 97 metres for the following day.

The crew and safety divers had seen me training. 'He doesn't have it,' one of them commented to the others, and I don't blame them for thinking this way. I started doubting myself during the build-up to the dive. The athlete who was diving before me had borrowed the flotation device I use to breathe-up without asking, and then ate into my preparation time by dallying on the competition line to chat with the judge after his dive. It was a windless day, and the spectator boat had started to drift in around the platform, so the safety divers were swimming it back into position. I tried to block all of this out and focus on my breathing: slow and shallow. At 11.10 a.m. I took my last breath, packed 45 times, trying to relax my chest more deeply with each pack so that my lungs could expand to their maximum dimensions. Then I turned and took my first stroke down into the cobalt void below. Most of my diving happens in Dean's Blue Hole, where the shadowed balconies and caves surrounding the hole drink the light out of the water, leaving it dusky and colourless at depth even on a clear day. So it's a pleasant novelty for me to dive in the open ocean where the light rays are unobstructed from any angle, and even at depth the palette is a pure and splendid cerulean blue. When I turned at 97 metres that colour was both the start and the end to the world around me. I was calm and centred. Most of all, I was confident. I started counting the ascent strokes, but soon lost count (my dive log shows 31). At 30 metres I nodded confidently to my safety divers. However, despite my positive mindset the dive was still verging on my limit. When I surfaced, I grabbed high above the water and held myself tight to the rope while I hook-breathed. My hand started to shake as I brought it to my face to remove my goggles. 'Breathe!' shouted Carla-Sue, who was coaching me in the water. 'Keep breathing!' The urgency in her voice told me that I wasn't out of the woods yet, and I did one more strong hook-breath while removing my nose clip. Finally, freshly oxygenated blood arrived at my brain and with the return of lucidity I turned to face the judges and completed the protocol. As I reached for the tag to show it to them, I fumbled it in the water and it slipped out of my reach. The immediate instinct when this happens is to duck under and grab it, but any re-immersion of the airways before the judges have made their decision will earn you a red card so I let the tag go. Luckily the judges saw that I'd had it, and were able to display their white cards to a rousing cheer from the spectators in the water and on the boat.

The CNF title would stay with me for the event, but in the overall standings Alexey had moved ahead. On the same day he exceeded my FIM dive by 1 metre, and then a strong CWT dive on the last day put the overall title out of my reach. For the first time, Alexey had outstripped me in total depth across the three disciplines. In his book *One Breath*, Adam Skolnick writes: 'Will was as graceful as ever and there were smiles all round, but whether he acknowledged it or not, he was aware that observers within the sport, and almost all the athletes present, were certain they had witnessed a changing of the guard. With his victory, Alexey, for years Will's heir apparent, had been declared the new king. Or so went the theory. By the bar, on the dance floor, in the barefoot shallows, and even later at a boozy nightclub on the hill, that's what everyone was buzzing about. Will wasn't so sure.'

With the 102-metre live record attempt scheduled to happen during Vertical Blue at the end of the year, my focus was firmly on the no-fins discipline. There was still a long way to go, but 97 metres had been my deepest competition performance away from Dean's Blue Hole, so I let myself be heartened by that small indication of progress.

*

I threw myself back into training, devising the most gruelling and targeted drills and exercises possible for the no-fins stroke. I'd had a 25-metre lap pool installed in the back garden of my house tucked away in the low-lying bush of Long Island. This meant that I could combine the high-volume workload of pool training, which targets technique and freediving fitness, with more-specific depth work in Dean's Blue Hole.

It's never enough just to do the physical work, though — I must always be analysing my dives and training, looking for an edge or any sign of a potential weak point. As I was going through my dive log, which is created by downloading all the data from the Suunto gauge I wear whenever I'm in the water, I noticed something peculiar. It looked as if, over the years, I had been getting slower and slower in my descent, specifically in the terminal velocity of my freefall. As my lungs shrink and my body becomes more negatively buoyant, I pick up speed the deeper I fall, but eventually the decreases in buoyancy are so small that my speed stops increasing — this is my freefall terminal velocity, which happens at around 80 metres. In 2008, when I was diving with a slightly thicker (and therefore more buoyant) wetsuit, my average terminal velocity was 1.03 metres per second. By 2009 it had dipped below 1 metre per second, and in 2010 it was 0.93 metres per second. However, by the start of 2014 it had dropped even lower, to 0.88 metres per second.

I searched for a possible explanation. It couldn't be my equipment: my wetsuit was now made from thinner neoprene, which should have had the opposite effect of making me sink more quickly. My lung volume hadn't changed significantly over that time (and besides, I would need to be packing in an extra litre or two of air to account for such a drop in speed). This left technique as the culprit — but that didn't make sense, because if anything my technique had improved; I was able to stay more balanced and streamlined while relaxed in the freefall than I could when I was newer to the sport. It was the smooth and gradual decline that eventually tipped me off. I knew that with age we begin to lose density in our bones, and this would make our skeleton, and thus our body, more buoyant. But could such a subtle shift in just one of the tissues of our body have such a marked effect?

According to the data I found, the skeleton of a lean person comprises roughly 15 per cent of that person's body weight, so mine should weigh around 12 kilograms. The average bone density of a white male aged 28 years is 1.06 times as heavy as water. Interestingly, it is a lot more for a black male — 1.2 times the weight of water — which explains why it is harder for black athletes to perform competitively in swimming races, where more of their body remains underwater and creates additional drag. Women have less-dense bones (0.95 the weight of water at 25 years of age), and this is one reason why the fairer sex tends to be more 'floaty'! The studies showed that these bone densities start to decline in the late twenties and do so more rapidly with increasing age. While the change between 25 and 35 years of age is not great, it is still significant. A drop of just 2 per cent, from 1.06 to 1.04 times the weight of water, which is what would be expected for me, would mean that my skeleton would lose about 250 grams of its weight over this period.

Additionally, exercise that involves physical impact (e.g. running and jumping) has been shown to help maintain density throughout the skeleton. In the complete absence of such physical impact, astronauts can lose an average of 1 to 2 per cent of their bone density for *every month* spent in space. Since I spend so much time in the water, where there is little gravity and minimal impact, it's quite possible that my bones were losing density more rapidly than they otherwise would have. When I put my theory to the test by adding a 300-gram lead weight to a collar around my neck, it immediately reversed the decline in my freefall terminal velocity. The descents, which had been stretching out longer than I'd liked, overnight became 5 to 10 seconds faster.

I have to admit that it was disconcerting to see the first evidence of age affecting my training. I've had to keep on adjusting the weight each year, adding 50 grams or so to compensate for my bones gradually changing from the density of a Mars bar to something more like a Crunchy bar. But if this is the only symptom in my sport of the passing of time, then I will count myself lucky!

*

A banner, draped like a heraldic standard from the cliffs beside Dean's Blue Hole, bore the words 'Born to Defy'. Below these were inscribed my name and the depth of the freedive I was committed to attempting: 102 metres.

I moved my toes in the damp sand at the edge of the Blue Hole, shifting my weight from one foot to the other. Why was I here, putting myself through this? After all, I held the world record and no one else had come close to breaking it, or even to reaching the 100-metre mark. Ah, yes: I like a challenge. Maybe it would be more accurate to say that I like the *prospect* of a challenge and I like having triumphed over a challenge, but the part in between where I stand on the beach and look at my challenge emblazoned in writing as tall as I am, knowing that in just under an hour I will have to prove myself worthy of it — that is not the part I like.

My friends at home in New Zealand had been texting me to say that there were similar billboards above State Highway 1, as well as huge vertical banners covering the entire sides of buildings. It was a good thing that I wasn't doing the attempt there, or I would never have been able to escape from the pressure. Steinlager had gone all out for this one, and a small posse of executives and marketers, along with a crew from TVNZ, were on the island to document the attempt. It was 2 December local time (3 December in New Zealand), and the second day of Act Two of Vertical Blue 2014.

It was a windy but sunny day. The Vertical Blue crew were on a short break from the competition, and I could see them checking all the equipment and cameras to make sure that everything was ready for the attempt. I walked back to the athletes' tent, put my headphones on and clicked on a music playlist with the title 'Dec 2'. I carried on listening to the music as I stretched my wetsuit onto my body and gathered the rest of my equipment before being taken by a small dinghy out to the platform. Even after I'd set my headphones aside and slipped into the water, 8 minutes before my Official Top time, I kept a tune in my head, cycling it through my mind to give it something to do that didn't involve thinking about the dive. This was easier said than done, especially since there was another beat to contend with — a rapid *allegro* tempo playing on a muffled drum inside my chest. My breathe-up was still controlled, however, and when I checked in with my body I found it to be in the required state of complete relaxation.

If I could have seen the crowd gathered on the beach, or clasping the floating perimeter of the competition zone, I would have been hard-pressed to find any smiles. Every face was glazed with seriousness. In the function room at Steinlager breweries, employees were gathered around a large TV screen, eyes fixed on the screen and some covering their mouths with their hands. Although my face was turned to the sky and my eyes were closed, I could feel the attention of all those concerned observers: not only the spectators close to me but also the families, office workers, construction crews and students who would be tuning in to the televised feed back home.

While all these people were tuning in to me, I was trying to tune them, and the pressure, out. I wasn't trying to deny it — for pressure denied, whether underwater or in the mind, makes us rigid and eventually more breakable — but simply to detach myself from it. Normally this would be attainable, but today something was holding the door open, letting the pressure leak in. My training in the preceding weeks had, once again, been erratic. On some days I had been able to manage a clean 100-metre dive, while on others I would fail attempting 98. Four days earlier, on the first day of the competition, I had surfaced from what should have been a routine warm-up dive to 93 metres and blacked out during my first inhale. It was a cold day, and a lot had gone wrong in my preparation and during the dive; but still, that dive should have been as easy as a snorkel on the reef. How could I hope to add 10 per cent to a depth I'd failed at, as well as accommodate the extra pressure of it being a world-record attempt? I'd regrouped slightly the following day, with a clean dive to 94 metres, but was I really ready for 102?

It's hard to ask myself that kind of question when success is contingent on a rock-solid confidence in my ability. If the answer is 'no, I'm not up to it', then is that motivated by skittish nerves or by lucid evaluation? If the answer is 'yes', am I just being doggedly optimistic? I chose to shelve the mental debate. After all, I had to make an attempt of some kind — not just to fulfil the sponsorship contract I had signed, but also on behalf of the supporters both at home and on the island who were following me and who believed in me. I was committed to the dive; so I would commit to the idea that it was possible. I did, however, leave myself one escape clause — an 'abort protocol' for if I felt that I definitely wasn't going to make it to the surface. In that case, I would start to use the rope early to pull myself through the remaining metres. It would disqualify me, of course, but should ensure that I wouldn't black out under the water on national television. I told this to Jonathan Sunnex and Moss Burmester, the fellow Kiwis who would be my safety divers, then tried to put the idea out of my mind quickly so that I wouldn't precondition failure. I was going to give it my best shot.

In the middle of the competition square I lay on my back, drawing in my last breath of air, a breath that would need to sustain 4 minutes of underwater exertion to a depth where the ambient pressure would push the cork back down the throat of a champagne bottle. The dive began, and I had those familiar non-sensations of not being an 'I am' that I wrote about at the beginning of this book. The descent went well. At 102 metres I calmly removed the tag and smoothed it onto the Velcro pad on my thigh before starting to ascend. That's when the 'stifled sneezes' started. The squeaks when auntie hugs too hard.

At 60 metres from the surface, hearing those noises escape my throat as my chest contracted, the thought of aborting resurfaced in my mind. I was a long way from Moss and Johnny. The Blue Hole is still dark at this depth, and the rope I was following was a blurry streak like half-erased chalk on a blackboard. I waited, with an empty, unresponsive mind, for the echo of that doubting thought to drift away. My armstrokes continued, although for a brief, terrible moment I felt as if I was doing star jumps on the spot without making any headway towards the surface. Then I noticed a piece of seaweed, suspended in the water column, that I was moving past with reasonable, though not great, speed.

Further along came another squeak, and another thought — like a newsflash: where *were* my safety divers? Straight away there followed the inevitable analysis of that thought: 'If I'm asking myself that question, then it's a sign I'm not comfortable, I'm not going to make it. Okay, so I just had that thought, that's okay ... now let's re-set to an empty mind and stay calm, stay relaxed.' Barely a stroke went by, however, before the next interjection voiced itself in my neocortex: 'It's no good, you're awake now. You're out of the flow state you need for a world-record attempt.' Now I was having to concentrate to maintain the right timing in my stroke, to resist the urge to swim faster. Yet another breathing reflex hit, and I felt this one pull the sides of my cheeks inwards against my teeth. They were now coming with every stroke.

Finally a human shape, Johnny's, descended into my field of vision, turning in front of me and signalling to me with a grouper call. Moss was there too, flanking my other side, and the security of seeing them and knowing that I was now 30 metres from the surface gave me my second wind. I might be able to make it after all. The pressure was dropping, my lungs were re-expanding and my body was becoming more buoyant again, making it easier to keep swimming. I turned my attention to my attention. Am I sharp? Am I still lucid mentally? This was the only way I could truly gauge my oxygen levels, since the urge to breathe and the contractions that were racking my body were all actually due to elevated carbon dioxide. The answers were uncertain, and that was indication enough. I needed to abort now, before I went over the edge into low-oxygen mindlessness, where I could no longer make prudent, reasoned decisions and would just keep swimming until I blacked out. I took another two strokes, just to make sure. The surface was in sight now, for the first time in almost 4 minutes. It was tantalisingly close; if I looked directly up, I would be able to see the dangling feet of the spectators and the masked faces of those who were watching the final phase of my freedive. But it had crystallised now, that unquestionable feeling of urgency combined with a gathering mist in my awareness: I was not going to make it. I shook my head from side to side at my safety divers, and my pride and ambition screamed in agony as my arm reached out to grasp the rope.

Despite aborting the record attempt by pulling on the line and being boosted by my safety divers the final 12 metres to the surface, I still blacked out briefly while taking my first recovery breaths. When I came round, I was surprised to find that no chasm of disappointment had opened up beneath me. I drew comfort from the fact that I had genuinely given it everything I had, and all around me and on the beach the faces were warm and supportive.

The TV crew needed to do an interview straight away, and I thanked my country for the unwavering solidarity I had felt from afar. 'This is just a plot twist,' I promised, 'I feel like I owe New Zealand a world record, and when I do finally reach it it'll be dedicated to everyone who's watching this and to everyone who's sent in their support.' Steinlager were quick on their feet, putting a positive spin on the result with the line, appearing at the end of the attempt video: 'When you push boundaries, success isn't guaranteed. But our support is.' I knew that this was more than just a marketing slogan, and it humbled me to hear those words echoed by the managers who had made the long trip to the Bahamas for the attempt.

*

With the onerous burden of the live attempt out of the way, I could turn my attention to the remaining two days of competition at Vertical Blue. Was there still a chance that I could win the event to salvage something from the training I had put in? It would be a tall order, since Alexey had logged strong dives in two of the disciplines, with 123 metres CWT and 114 FIM, and only needed a good dive in CNF to round this out. However, in this discipline he had been over-reaching himself, trying to exceed his recent personal best at Roatan by diving to 97 metres with no fins. Twice he had attempted this depth, and both times he had blacked out on the surface after long, tiring dives. Conversely, CNF was the only discipline where I had any points at all, from the 94-metre warm-up I had completed before the record attempt. I would need solid performances in the other two disciplines over the last two days. There was no margin for error.

On the penultimate day I announced 120 metres in Free Immersion. I had vacillated over a depth between 118 and 122, and was happy about the final decision as the dive was difficult — I probably didn't have two more metres in me. Meanwhile, Alexey had taken it down a peg with 95 metres CNF. At the end of his ascent he abandoned his leaden arms to dolphin-kick the remaining distance. He managed to make the surface, and fought to keep his head above it as he breathed, holding on to consciousness to finish the protocol. There was a hushed silence while the judges conferred; then a red card was shown. In his struggle to avoid blackout, Alexey had gone over time on the protocol.

So, it came down to the last day and now the ball was in my court. Alexey still had to complete a no-fins dive to be a contender overall, and I was confident that

Alexey Molchanov prepares for a dive during Vertical Blue 2014. (*Daan Verhoeven*)

he wouldn't be attempting 95 again. On my part, I still had to log a dive with the monofin, and calculated that 117 metres would be enough to cover Alexey doing a dive to 94 CNF. In the end he announced 90 metres, and since he was scheduled to dive after me it would all be decided by what happened in my CWT dive.

With all my focus having been on the no-fins record attempt, I hadn't logged a single deep dive with the monofin since Honduras six months earlier. When I strapped the fin to my feet it felt alien, so I did a quick test-dive to 20 metres just to remind myself how to use it. As it turned out, there was no need for concern, and it even seemed as if the time away from CWT had done me good! I touched the plate at 1:47, turned and powered back towards the surface. My whole body felt like a steel blade vibrating at its resonant frequency. The first 50 metres took just 30 seconds, and although I started to slow after that the whole ascent was still only 1:22.

I surfaced, quickly ran through the surface protocol, then tore the tag from my leg to show the judges. Vertical Blue was mine for another year.

At Kanchenjunga base camp in the Himalayas, with Sam and our father, David, 2015. The shade that fringes the icy contours of those mountains is the blue of the open ocean if, when ascending from a dive and still far from the surface, you look sideways across into liquid space.

Performing *Uddiyana Bandha* (diaphragmatic introflexion) on Ocean Beach, Hawke's Bay, New Zealand. The yogic texts talk about experiencing the body as the thin stem of a lotus flower. *(Richard Robinson)*

CHAPTER 11

DOWNWARDS

The greatest adversary: oneself

What we ordinarily think of as mind is an extremely
gross level of mind. In deep meditation or when faced
with immediate danger to our lives, a different type of
mind becomes active. In Tibetan Buddhism it is called
the 'subtle mind'. It transcends time and space as well
as distinctions among all the various type of forms.
It is connected to all life in the natural world.

Dalai Lama

WHEN I ARRIVED IN KATHMANDU to meet my father and
brother in late September 2015, I had competed at four
international freediving events that year, winning ten
gold medals. I had also finalised and signed a divorce
settlement agreement, bringing to an end the see-sawing
relationship of the previous six years.

We were in Nepal to hike the trail to Kanchenjunga Base Camp, supposedly the most difficult base-camp route in the Himalayas — although we didn't find that out until we were already past the halfway point! My father has a great love of wild open spaces, and growing up we would spend our holidays hiking through the Kaweka and Ruahine ranges of Hawke's Bay, sleeping in the well-worn but homely huts managed by the Department of Conservation. Now it had been years since I had spent time in the mountains, or finished any walks that took longer than about a day.

Books about alpinism captivate me, whether they deal with the near-death experiences of climbers like Joe Simpson (*Touching the Void*) or the heroic purity of Reinhold Messner's oxygen-free solo climbs. Perhaps it is the common threads I draw between mountaineering and freediving that keep me enthralled. In his book *Into Thin Air*, which covers the Mount Everest disaster of 1996, Jon Krakauer writes, 'It was titillating to brush up against the enigma of mortality, to steal a glimpse across its forbidden frontier. Climbing was a magnificent activity, I firmly believed, not in spite of the inherent perils, but precisely because of them.' Although I suspect that this isn't mountaineering's only drawcard, it has a carbon copy in freediving, where the minutes spent in a kind of suspended animation allow us to taste our own existence all the more acutely.

Kiwi Everest guide Robert Hall's observation, 'With enough determination, any bloody idiot can get up this hill [Everest]. The trick is to get back down alive', could almost be paraphrased as a description for a freedive — where the descent is in reach of the idiot but the way back up is an entirely different story. At the extremes of each sport, there lies a so-called death zone. The air above 8000 metres of altitude is almost as inhospitable to human life as the underwater world, with an oxygen level just 30 per cent of what it is at sea-level, and there is a similar risk of blackout if a climber pushes the respiratory system too hard. The lungs themselves can also display oedema, where fluid leaks from the blood into the alveolar airspaces, in the same way that it might in a freediver suffering from lung squeeze. Although I wouldn't be going to anything like the extremes involved in that kind of climbing, I was still curious to see how my body, which had become accustomed to warm climes and underwater weightlessness, would respond to the other end of the spectrum.

*

Kanchenjunga is in the far east of Nepal, its peak straddling the border with India. It was once thought to be the tallest mountain in the world, until in 1852 more-accurate trigonometry found that Everest and K2 were both higher. In recent times Kanchenjunga has acquired the highest fatality rate of all 8000-metre-high peaks, and it is also the most sacred of these, with climbers forbidden to actually set foot on the very top of the summit. Compared with the heavily trafficked treks to Manaslu, Annapurna and Everest, the Kanchenjunga trail is far less developed. We started with a steep descent into a valley that was only 900 metres above sea-level, and then climbed progressively (though not smoothly) over the next ten days to the base camp at 5200 metres. The trail followed a river gorge up through Nepalese villages, where 'teahouses' offered the sparse groups of trekkers basic accommodation and carbohydrate-rich meals: nine times out of ten this was *dal bhat* washed down with *Tongba*, an earthy drink made from fermented millet.

At one river crossing we climbed down from the swing bridge to a rocky pool that provided a bracing rinse. It was deep enough that I could hold on to a stone and fully submerge myself while the water flowed around me. In January, I had started the year with a week of training dives with no wetsuit, to a maximum depth of 82 metres, and I had revelled in the intimate contact with the water, and the sensation of my body opening a path through it. Here in the mountains the roles were reversed, with the water moving past my immobile body, but the sensation was almost identical. Sometimes when I freefall into the depths now, I imagine myself lying just beneath the surface in that peaceful Himalayan stream.

As we gradually ascended in altitude I used a pulse oximeter to keep track of how my body was coping with the low oxygen levels. On a rest day in the Sherpa village of Ghunsa, at a height of 3500 metres, my arterial saturation (a measure of how much oxygen the red blood cells in my arteries were carrying) was steady at 92 to 95 per cent, similar to that of our Nepalese guides. The following day, during a steep climb up a scree slope, I decided to test my limits a little. After a burst of exertion, my heart rate peaked at 146 beats per minute while my saturation dropped to just 77 per cent — about the level it would reach 5 to 6 minutes into a static breath-hold. It was interesting to feel the sensation of low oxygen without any of the high carbon dioxide that is inseparable in a breath-hold freedive. I could perceive the drop in my mental lucidity; it seemed almost as if the frame rate of my vision was slower so that I was seeing in flashes rather than in a smooth continuum. Later, on the way back down through Ghunsa, my saturation held fast at 98 per cent, clear evidence that my body had made changes to cope with the thinner air.

Once above the tree line, the colossal rocky summits that the locals dismissed as 'hills' gave way to reveal the true mountains of Nepal. While their lower slopes were a pattern of snow and black rock, the lofty shoulders of those distant peaks were a shiny cream, as if some golden rock had been thrust up from within the mountain to crown its summit. But the colour that took what little remained of my breath away was the blue. The shade that fringed the icy contours of those mountains was exactly the same colour as the blue of the open ocean if, when ascending from a dive and still far from the surface, you look sideways across into liquid space.

Staring up at those giants, and the space they carved out of the firmament, also gave me a sense of perspective about the grandeur of our planet's seas. To think that the massif I was viewing could disappear in the ocean like a pebble in a lake, all the space around it and above it filled with an unthinkable volume of water ...

Even in the clearest water we cannot see more than about 50 metres away — half the length of a rugby field. Imagine, then, that seawater shared the limpidity of the atmosphere, and we could gaze down from the surface to the underwater ridges and valleys of the oceans, seeing schools of tuna flying in formation like migrating birds, sperm whales plummeting downwards towards unsuspecting squid, and clouds of herring being shepherded towards the surface by flashing marlin. In truth, the ocean masks her secrets in a cloak of darkness and opacity, and they can be discovered only in the microcosm of light's purview.

*

While traversing that punishing trail (sometimes uphill, sometimes downhill, but never, *ever*, flat!), I had plenty of time to reflect on the events of the past year, and where I wanted my path to lead on to.

Vertical Blue had been the first of the competitions, but since Alexey wasn't attending and I didn't want to peak too early in a season that would end with the World Championships in Cyprus, I logged conservative dives, although these still netted me gold in all the disciplines (94 CNF, 120 CWT and 115 FIM).

The Caribbean Cup in Roatan followed shortly afterwards. There I focused on CNF, improving my depth for the season to 96 metres. I also experimented, for the first time, with diving with bare eyes. Several other of the top athletes had already made this change, and it appeared that water flowing over the eyelids enhanced the dive reflex, allowing the body to better conserve oxygen. It didn't take long for my eyes to become accustomed to the saltiness of the water and stop stinging, and although my vision was always going to be blurry I could see enough of the line to be able to swim alongside it. In Sulawesi, Indonesia, the Bajau people (known as sea gypsies) live in boats on the water and dive all day without goggles. As a result, from a young age the lenses of their eyes develop a slightly different shape, allowing them to see more clearly underwater. On the last day of the competition, I was tired but decided to try a dive to 92 metres with no goggles, and was amazed at how easily and cleanly I surfaced. From that moment on, all of my deep dives have been made with no covering over my eyes.

After Roatan I travelled to San Andrés Island, a small but densely populated coral island lying 150 kilometres east of Nicaragua's Caribbean coast, although it is part of the territory of Colombia to the south-east. Three competitions in a row was always going to be a little ambitious, but one of my reasons for continuing this tour was that the divorce proceedings begun in April were still being finalised, and I preferred to keep my distance from the Bahamas during that process. In San Andrés I continued increasing my depth in CNF, with a strong dive to 98 metres that took exactly 4 minutes. However, the travel and the relentless competing were draining my reserves, and when I attempted 100 metres on my next dive I started getting strange, insistent contractions, starting at the plate and continuing into the ascent. There was no point in risking a blackout, so I pulled myself to the surface.

Other than the dives I had aborted, all of my competition dives had been clean white card performances. My confidence and depth were building at just the right speed for me to be at my peak during the World Championships in September. First, though, I had to return to the Bahamas, to a difficult period when my arrival back on the island overlapped with the last two weeks of my ex-partner being there. Even dysfunctional relationships have their joys and harmonies — otherwise we would never find ourselves in them to begin with. Parting is never easy, no matter how irrefutable its necessity. One of the things that affects me most is the loss of dreams, in particular those of others'. There is such vulnerable innocence in hopes and dreams that are born of love, and to see this shattered, and to have played a role in that, is especially difficult. Although the parting might be 100 per cent necessary and inevitable, and even though it may lead to other, greater things, the non-realisation of those initial hopes is akin to a death of sorts. Back in 2008, after having said goodbye to my girlfriend Tiziana for the last time, I arrived back home from the airport to find the waffles that, in her heartbreak, she had been unable to finish that morning at breakfast. They lay, nibbled-at and abandoned, a truncated pleasure, haunting me with a reminder of her Italian pronunciation: 'wuffle'.

Now, after returning from San Andrés I stayed in a friend's house until Brittany left and I could finally move back into my own. On arrival I opened the fridge, and there on the top shelf was a large sack of untouched red grapes. It was an expensive treat that she had possibly bought in the hope of a moment's gratification during such a painful time. Instead, it was forgotten among the sorrow. Such details are the minutiae of grief, but they bore holes through the dam holding our emotions back. 'The cure for anything is salt water — tears, sweat, or the sea,' wrote Karen Blixen. I chose the third of these, and threw myself into my training, resolving to 'fall for no one but the sea'.

Once the separation was finally concluded, the rush of freedom and peace of mind was intoxicating. After several weeks of training in the Bahamas, and just before leaving for Cyprus, I performed one of my deepest-ever no-fins dives, as well as an interminably long (4 minutes 50 seconds) FIM dive to 120 metres.

*

The World Championships would pitch me a couple of in-swinging yorkers — or curveballs as the Americans know them. The first was the impressive difference in water density between that part of the Mediterranean and the Caribbean. Not only were the waters of Cyprus more salty, but below 30 metres there was a brutal thermocline where the water temperature dropped from a tropical 28°C to the ice-cream headache that is 17°C. Coldness also makes water more dense, until it drops below 4°C, at which point it starts to expand and become lighter again — which is why ice floats. Water is the only common liquid that has this property, and it's a good thing that it does; otherwise, our planet's oceans would be completely frozen over and life here would have never developed!

Denser water means that the body is comparatively more buoyant, so we sink more slowly. I had expected the effect of the higher salinity, but had completely underestimated that of the temperature. In the briny and frigid depths my freefall slowed to a dawdle, dive times stretched out into narcosis territory, and I blacked out on the surface after a 95-metre no-fins dive that lasted 4 minutes 1 second. That night I looked up the equations for water density, made some calculations and came up with the figure of 300 grams, which I added in lead to my neck weight. On my next dive to the same depth I shaved off 17 seconds, and a few days later I completed a very comfortable dive to 97 metres in only 3 minutes

47 seconds, just before the World Championships got under way.

These training dives were all taking place in the late morning, when the sun was high in the sky and my breakfast was low in my digestive system. So it was another disorienting surprise to get the news, the day before the first day of CNF competition, that the diving would begin at 8 a.m. I had no way of knowing what effect this would have on my performance, so I chose what I considered to be a conservative depth of 94 metres.

That morning I woke at 5 a.m. and ate a small breakfast before starting my stretching routine. In the dawn light I could see that the sky over Limassol had continued to clear. Days before, a biblical dust storm had blown across the short stretch of water from the Middle East, blotting the sky with orange haze and reducing visibility to a stone's throw away. Hospitals had filled with patients with respiratory problems, and the freedivers, to whom clean air is sacrosanct, had wrapped their faces in scarves whenever outdoors. This day, however, the sea and the sky were both rich shades of blue as the shuttle boat took us out towards the deep water and the rising sun.

My 94 metres was the deepest announcement, followed by the 90 announced by defending champion

Morgan Bourc'his. He would dive just before me, and if he didn't make it then that would mean I could turn at 91 and still claim gold. I set an alarm for 91, just in case. From where I was lying, unable to see Morgan's dive, it sounded like the surfacing at the end of his dive was tight, with urgent commands to breathe repeated by his coach, followed by a hasty 'I am okay!' from Morgan. However, he had gone slightly over time in the protocol, and the judges reluctantly showed their red cards. The spectating crowd was conciliatory, giving him a rousing round of applause anyway. 'He made it?' I asked a friend, who replied that it looked like it.

So down I went, thinking that my gauge would have to read 93 for me to still win gold after penalties — in which case I might as well just touch the plate at 94 to be sure. (A reading of 92.9 would be rounded to 92, resulting in 89 after penalties — two for the difference in depth and one for the lack of a tag.) At that early hour of the day, my body was responding to the depth very differently. At the end of the descent, just before the plate, I felt several strong contractions, one of which caused me to lose some of the equalising air from my mouth. 'That's not good,' I thought, before reminding myself that I had done an incredibly fresh 97 metres in training, so there should be at least some margin for error. I was, however, on the alert.

My stroke was quick on the way up, and I felt as if I was staying just ahead of the urge to breathe, like a surfer outrunning a dangerous wave. According to spectators, I still looked good even in the last 10 metres, but the final — and unnecessary — stroke I took, just below the surface, was a sign of trouble. I broke back into the atmosphere, grabbing the line and hook-breathing several times as I fought to stay in control. Then the light went out for a split-second and my head dipped forward. The moment my mouth touched the waterline I came to again and completed the protocol, but it was no use. The gold medal had slipped through my fingers once again. Alexey Molchanov would claim the title this time, with a safe dive to 85 metres. He would rule in Constant Weight as well, with a 122. It was an impressive showing from the Russian, who was attending his first competition since the death of his mother only six weeks before. On 2 August 2015, Natalia — the strongest freediver to have ever lived — had been taken by the sea while performing routine dives to shallow depths in the company of private students in Ibiza, Spain. It was an area of strong currents, and despite extensive searches by boat and submarine her body was never found; we can only speculate as to what became of her. The tragedy rocked the freediving community. Although it was clear that Alexey was still grieving for Natalia's loss, his playful and enthusiastic character had made it through the ordeal unchanged. Not to mention his abilities underwater. In my own CWT dive I again had difficulty on the surface, this time completing the protocol but using half a second too much time. I thought I had compensated for the effect of the early start, with an even more conservative announcement of 115 metres, but it had proved once again to be a hair's breadth too deep.

After two red cards, only Free Immersion remained for me to try and redeem myself. By this time, I had lost all confidence in my ability to determine what depth I was capable of diving at cock's crow. I decided to announce 113 metres, which should suffice for a silver medal, and this time I completed the dive easily in 3:52. As I'd expected, Alexey had announced a deeper target, of 118 metres, but it was his turn to over-reach, with a blackout on the surface that handed me the gold medal.

My goal had been to reclaim gold in CNF, but the medal had now eluded me for two years and I arrived in Nepal without the sense of fulfilment that I had hoped to take away from the World Championships. Gradually, though, that skin of disappointment was scuffed away by the abrasions of the trail, sucked out of me by the leeches lurking in the wet valley foliage and then violently expended into the outhouse toilets when I contracted a persistent case of bacterial dysentery. After a head cold and strained knee ligaments were added to the mix, even making it through the trek became an ambitious goal. Just as in freediving, it was moving back towards sea-level that presented the biggest challenge for me. After years of pushing only against yielding water, the jolts and strains of the rough ground were a sudden shock to my knees. I relished the uphills, where I could lean into the mountain and surge forwards, but every downhill step sent a stab of pain into the side of my knee joints. Anti-inflammatories weren't enough to dull the pain, and at times I resorted to walking backwards for the downhill stretches.

Needless to say, it was all worth the transient discomfort. Not just the incredible views of mountains like Jannu, Chang Himal and, of course, Kanchenjunga, which can only be comprehended when you're breathing the same thin, bright air that envelopes those majestic giants, but also the decisive hiatus it provided to my training and aquatic life. For three weeks, exhales followed inhales with no interruption, and other than dunks in mountain streams I was never underwater. It was the longest I had been absent from either apnea or salt water in 12 years. The wider perspective of the higher ground, the meditative rhythm of walking and the timeless civilisation of the Nepalese all gave me the time and the means to let the internal gyroscope that had been spinning furiously to sustain me come to a rest. Those wheels would soon turn again, but for a brief moment they stood still and let me admire the world around me as well as the one I had created within myself.

By the time we returned to Taplejung, the village we had set out from 18 days earlier, we had covered a distance of 300 kilometres, and climbed (and descended) a total of 10,000 metres — more than the height of Everest. I left Nepal several kilograms lighter and with the dysentery still in my system, and arrived back to a Long Island that had just been ravaged by the worst hurricane in a hundred years — one that had killed, by salt-water flooding, every tree that it hadn't ripped out of the ground. But I returned fresh, and ready for the next challenge. The next depth.

*

It took a while to recover from dysentery, and to regain the body mass and vitality that the infection had drained from me. Eventually, though I resumed training with Johnny, Dean Chaouche and Shiv Madhu. Dean and Shiv had become semi-permanent freediving residents of Long Island. Dean was a young Welshman with fair skin but the curly black hair of Arabic blood. He had stayed in my house during the devastating hurricane, literally holding it together by bracing a door with his body weight for two hours. A wild-haired and whip-smart Indian, Shiv supported life on the island for him and his wife, Emily, by writing software algorithms for the internet advertising companies he founded. During the same hurricane, he stood on the roof of his flooded apartment, filming the carnage with a GoPro.

The four of us developed a sound understanding of each other's idiosyncrasies in the water: how we liked to be positioned in the breathe-up, what the phases of the dive would feel like when monitoring the rope from the surface (every vibration, brush or pull on the line is telegraphed along its length, and can be felt by the person holding it on the surface), what the signs were that one of us was having a tough dive, how best to coach during the surface protocol, and so on. This level of familiarity is vital to safety and the feeling of serenity that comes from knowing that someone else has you covered. Of course there was rivalry as well, but since we were mostly diving at different levels and in different disciplines, this found its outlet in throwing each other off the platform, especially when the victim was in the middle of taking off his wetsuit, with the jacket up over his head.

Steinlager had agreed to support another live attempt at the 102-metre mark with no fins, and this was scheduled for March 2016. From the start, this attempt had a very different feel to 2014, although admittedly most of that was probably self-induced. In the 2014 interview immediately after the attempt, I had promised New Zealand that I would be back to try for the record again, and that when I finally reached the mark it would be dedicated to everyone who had supported me in the process. Or, to paraphrase: 'Sure, I had a blowout this time, but future William will be round in a year or two to take care of the task!' Easy to say then, of course, but when the new date was set 'future William' didn't have quite the same level of confidence as his predecessor, and started to regret such a brazen promise. There were two edges to this sword: the one facing me was the intense pressure that my 'personal guarantee' to the nation had created; but the other was the one I could use to scythe a path forward — the fact that I had no alternative but to succeed. The script had been written, and I must play the part I had cast for myself at all costs. Just like in 2007, I would have to render success *inevitable*.

After mostly base training in November and December, the approach to depth began in January. In short order I reached 90 metres, which seemed to have become a kind of base camp in my no-fins diving. I could easily return to that point without much preparation, but progress beyond was not as easily come by. The first 95-metre dive was tough — no samba, but it wasn't far off. Two days later, and 96 resulted in a surface blackout. It was now February. The pressure needle had gone through the red and was hard up against the barrier at the end of the dial. I took a week's break from No Fins and did a few FIM dives, to 108, 114 and 117, but when I came back to CNF the next dive, to 97 metres, was still tight. Even though I felt comfortable in the ascent and did strong hook-breaths upon surfacing, I could tell that my oxygen level had dipped to just above a samba.

In the evenings, over group meals of pasta and homemade bread, we flung around ideas for how I might bridge the remaining gap to the world-record depth. The first idea was supplementing with creatine phosphate, an energy source mostly used by bodybuilders that doesn't require oxygen to burn. After a 'loading phase' of three days taking creatine I tested another dive, with the identical result. The second idea was to try to induce a stronger dive reflex, just before the dive began, so that my body would shift to anaerobic energy production earlier in the dive and thus save the oxygen for my brain. Coldness is a strong stimulant of this reflex, so in the last 2 minutes of my countdown Shiv used a garden watering can to pour 3 litres of ice-cold water over my face. I could feel the drop in my heart rate as the reflex kicked in and my face was still numb in freefall at 40 metres, but again the 96-metre dive ended with a samba.

With the record attempt only weeks away, it was clear that I didn't have a decent chance of success. To say nothing of success being inevitable. I needed to be diving as I had been ahead of the World Championships the previous year: with clean and confident dives to 100 metres. For now, there was nothing to be done but postpone the attempt until after Vertical Blue. When my agent called Steinlager to see if this was possible I was half-expecting them to pull the pin on the whole project, since they had already paid for billboards publicising March dates. Instead, as always the brand managers at Steinlager were understanding and supportive. 'What matters is that you feel good about it,' was their first response.

We set a new window in mid-July for the attempt, and I breathed a sigh of relief. With Vertical Blue on the horizon my training continued, but there was now less urgency to solve the problem of my drop in form. In March I switched to a program of deep hangs at 60 metres, stretching the dive times out to 6 minutes in search of complete peace and empty-mindedness at depth. After a week of this, I tried another 97-metre CNF dive to see whether developing better relaxation had made inroads on my problems. Yet again, I had a big samba on the surface. It was time to return to base camp, and build a new ascent towards my personal summit. I started with dreamy dives to 90 and 92 metres, then a slightly more difficult 94, but on surfacing from the next 95-metre attempt I breathed and then my head started shaking uncontrollably like a heavy-metal guitarist — another samba.

It was now mid-April. Vertical Blue was just around the corner, and I had still made no progress. To add injury to the insults, my shoulder had developed a strain that prevented me from using it in CNF or FIM, or even from maintaining a streamlined shape in CWT. I was confined to the shallows for another three precious training days while it healed. It looked as if Vertical Blue was going to be a complete write-off for me this year. Funnily enough, I wasn't really that bothered.

When I met Sachiko, even my drive to dive deeper was moved to the back seat. This beautiful dark-haired Japanese girl, a surfer as much as a freediver, and also an actress and a film-maker, was an enigma to rival the deepest ocean depths. She was there to compete in her first freediving event, and every training day I arrived at the Blue Hole hoping to be met by her soft eyes and unfettered smile. By the time the event started I had grown to know her better, which only led to the discovery that there was so much more to know. My family and friends could see a transformation taking place. Suddenly my diving turned a page as well, just as Vertical Blue was getting going. I completed a dive to 116 metres in Free Immersion that was so easy I literally didn't want it to end — I stopped 11 metres from the surface, shaking my head at my safety divers to indicate that I wasn't quite ready to come up yet. This kind of foolery is of course completely unorthodox, and since a shake of the head is normally a sign of difficulty they moved in to assist me. Seeing this, I quickly waved them off before they could disqualify me with a touch, and finished the dive almost effortlessly. On the next competition day I announced 119 metres FIM and it was just as easy.

'It's the oxytocin in your system!' a friend remarked, and this could well have been it. Called the 'love hormone', oxytocin is known to slow down the production of adrenaline and cortisol, the two strongest stress hormones that the body produces. It also inhibits the amygdala, our brain's fear centre. I've never been afraid of the depths I aspire to, but fear of failure and the stress related to that is almost always present. It looked like oxytocin was taking care of all this: I was in love and diving carefree.

Buoyed by the ease of the 119, I announced 122 metres for 30 April. The idea of a world-record attempt in any discipline had been unthinkable just two weeks earlier, but now I was doped on hormones and riding a wave of confidence. My dive log notes that I was not at all nervous and had a perfect descent, with no difficulty equalising to a depth where the pressure would burst the tyres of a freight truck. There I hit my first speed bump, in the form of a tag that just wouldn't stick to the patch on my leg (it was more likely that I was narced and trying to fix it to the wrong area). After a few wasted seconds I started to ascend with tag in hand, but that didn't allow me to grip the line properly so I had another go at attaching it. Perhaps I should just have abandoned it at this point, but I hadn't forgotten the previous FIM world-record attempt in 2012 when a runaway tag had cost me the prize. This time I was not going to let it get away from me.

Finally, the Velcro of the tag gripped the patch on my leg. The whole episode had come at a price, however: instead of the dreamy, blank-minded state I needed to be in for such a deep dive, I was flustered and already having contractions. 'I'm extremely deep, I can't avoid to get panicky here,' I thought to myself, and dedicated the next few strokes to trying to enter back into a state of deep relaxation. But the damage had been done, and more contractions followed. 'Hold on, and try and make it to your safeties,' I told myself, expecting the worst. I was already starting to insert breaststroke kicks between arm pulls, a sure symptom of anxiety and a sign that the dive could end badly.

At last I heard the grouper call of the first safety diver meeting me at 35 metres, but I kept my eyes locked shut, focusing on restraining the urge to breathe, and pulling on the rope with as much control as I could manage. I was almost there, and when I glanced up I could see the square of empty water where I would be surfacing in the midst of the dangling feet of the spectators. It was so close, but seemed so unreachable. I pulled on the rope one more time and shook my head at the safety divers, expecting to feel their hands lifting me under my arms. None came. Ironically, the confusion I'd caused at the end of my 116-metre dive meant that they weren't trusting my head signals! I'd cried wolf once, and now I'd have to fight off the real wolf myself. I pulled on the rope again, did a big breaststroke kick and one final pull, then broke through the surface to hold myself high out of the water. 'Hook!' yelled Shiv from the platform, then 'Keep hooking! Keep hooking!' as I started to tighten on the line, my head shaking. I was taking full lungfuls of air, 5 litres at a time, but starting to slide down the rope. My hand reached for my nose clip but slipped off my nose; I reached again and grasped it, pulling it clear, and now my mind was starting to clear too. I took one last hook-breath, looked

French judge Cedric Palerme in the eye, and completed the protocol.

I had set a new world record, for the first time in five years. It wasn't the no-fins record that I'd been pursuing, but it was a positive sign that that one, too, might soon be within my reach.

One day of Vertical Blue remained, and I felt that if I could avoid the problem with the tag at the bottom plate, then I should be able to manage a greater depth. I announced 124 metres, and spent some time practising the hand movement that would remove the tag from the plate and bring it to exactly the right spot on my leg. This time, there were no hiccups, and after being underwater for 4 minutes 30 seconds I surfaced and claimed my seventeenth world record.

Part of what made these two records memorable was that they were my first successes in the presence of my family. I was able to share the celebration with them, Sachiko and the whole Vertical Blue crew, who had run the event seamlessly to allow me to relax and focus on my diving.

*

The date of the no-fins attempt, in July, was starting to loom on the horizon as I left for the Caribbean Cup in

My first instructor and mentor, Umberto Pelizzari, was guest of honour during Vertical Blue 2016. (*Daan Verhoeven*)

Roatan. My plan was to focus only on CNF there, and try to convert my recent run of form into that discipline so that I would be ready for a dive to 102 metres when I returned to the Bahamas. Once again I started out from base camp: 90, 92, 94 and 97. Each dive was as easy as the last, and the post-dive sambas that had been plaguing my training earlier in the season were no more than an unpleasant memory. On my thirty-sixth birthday I did my last training dive before the competition: at 99 metres, it was also my deepest dive outside of Dean's Blue Hole.

There are six days of diving in the Caribbean Cup, of which I could feasibly use four if I was allowing

48 hours of rest between dives. My deepest target for the event was 100 metres — obviously, it would be foolish to break my record now with the attempt just around the corner. It made sense to build slowly and adjust to the competition scenario in the first couple of dives. This proved to be a wise move, since in the first dive, to 93 metres, there were several vexing issues — including an error in the countdown sequence and a tag that just didn't want to come off the plate — but I came through it easily as I was diving to 6 metres less than my recent training. There was frustration in the second dive as well, as confusion in setting the line meant that I wasn't moved into position until just 2 minutes from my Official Top. But with my duck-dive the aggravation dissolved into the gemlike Caribbean waters, and I had one of those miraculous ascents that seem abridged, as if the 98 metres I had announced had been condensed into only 30. In the final 10 metres I made an 'okay' sign to my safeties, stretched my arms towards the surface and slowly undulated my body in a relaxed dolphin movement, enjoying being gently lifted by positive buoyancy as if a giant hand of the ocean was bearing me skywards.

There was no doubting that I was ready to try 100 metres. The next day, I announced the depth for the first time outside of the Bahamas, and woke ready for the occasion on 30 May. The hectometre is, however, an obdurate temptress, and presented me with a host of adversaries to contend with. Chief among these was one of the largest dive boats on the island, which despite furious signalling from the competition organisers passed right by the official competition zone during my attempt. The timing was such that the wake from the boat hit the dive platform just as I was performing my turn and retrieving my tag. It was chaos on the bottom plate. As I grabbed the line above the plate, the first wave wrenched it and me upwards, dislodging the tag from my grasp. I went for another one, and this time managed to take it, but as I swam upwards the line was bucking up, down, left and right. I felt like I was trying to ascend alongside a skipping rope. Gradually the waves passed, but I was completely unsettled, had lost time in the turn and was worried about pulmonary oedema from the sudden jolt at maximum depth. At 75 metres I aborted the dive, and came up the rest of the way pulling on the rope. It was a great disappointment, but with a day still in hand there was no reason not to take the safer option and avoid the possibility of blackout.

So, on the last day of the event I would have one last chance to return to the hectometre officially for the first time since 2010 — and for the first time ever in a competition.

Even though this wasn't a record attempt, on the morning of the dive I found myself a lot more nervous than I'd been before the recent Free Immersion world records. Even after so many years of freediving, I was still finding it hard to outwit the negative voices in my mind. In essence, the brain is an adaptive organ, constantly evolving itself depending on how we're using it, and for this reason no mental technique will last indefinitely. Our brains become 'immune' to the technique; bored of it. It's similar to how playing your favourite song a hundred times will, by the end, no longer generate the same kind of emotive response. Staying one step ahead in the struggle to control my mind was like an arms race: I had to continuously develop new strategies, mental tricks and mantras.

A lot of these strategies have to do with grounding the awareness in the present moment. It's so easy for your conscious thought to float you downstream into a swamp of speculation about what might or might not happen in the future. I call this 'scenario thinking', and — especially when a world-record attempt is on the horizon — it can infect my every waking hour. Time and time again throughout the day, that toxic swamp burps up questions: What happens if I break the record? Or if I fail? What would I need to say to my sponsors, family, friends? Down the rabbit hole you go, into a whole universe of potential outcomes. Most of these will never come to pass, but the real pointlessness of the whole process lies in the fact that it adds to your background stress, in turn feeding the cycle of obsession with the future. The remedy is to bring your awareness gently back to the present moment, and what you are doing in it. Whether I'm making breakfast, putting on my wetsuit, or breathing on the surface before a dive, I allow that task to occupy my full attention. When I feel the urge to consider possible future worlds, I tell myself that there will be ample time after the dive to think about what happens next.

In Roatan I tried to condense this process into a simple phrase that I could use each time I felt myself slipping off the delicate balance beam that is my awareness of the present. The mantra I came up with there was simply 'What is now is all,' and this became abridged to 'Now is all.'

'Imagine if you black out on this dive, with all these people watching,' my capricious mind would venture as I floated on my back in the competition zone, to which I would reply 'Now is all,' and remember that I was there, in that point of space and time, and nowhere else. 'But wouldn't it be cool if you smashed this dive to 100 the same way you did the last one to 98!' another voice would offer, but the response would be identical and automatic:

'Now is all.' Any investment in those thoughts, positive or negative, would jeopardise the sense of detachment that allowed me to perform at my very best.

The 100-metre dive was won on the strength of that preparation, and everything that followed was a formality. It was a cleaner and quicker dive (4 minutes precisely) than my hectometre record in 2010, and was easily my strongest ever no-fins performance in competition.

CHAPTER 12

10_2

A promise kept

Be quiet now, be still and let that deeper part of you, the
part that has always been and always will be, before birth
and after death, let that take you and bear you up.

William Trubridge, journal entry

WHEN I LEFT ROATAN to return to the Bahamas, part of
me wished that I could have attempted the 102-metre
world record right there and then. I was in the best form
of my career, and the string of successes had made me
feel invincible in the water. Instead, I would have to try
to maintain that form for the next six weeks, and this
prospect made me nervous. I felt like a skipper marooned
in the harbour, desperately willing the favourable wind
to hold out until I was ready to sail.

Dean, Shiv, Johnny and his girlfriend, Sofía Gómez,
would be my safety divers and organisers for the attempt,

with Tomas Ardavany returning as medic, accompanied by neurosurgeon Jani Valdivia. AIDA was sending its president and its secretary, Carla-Sue Hanson and Robert King, as the two official judges. And that was the full crew: there would be no in-water camera operators, as we had developed an underwater drone, capable of moving vertically along two suspended cables at the same speed as the freediver, with lights and cameras for filming the entire dive. These images, as well as above-surface footage on the platform and the beach, would be broadcast to New Zealand on TV One's *Breakfast* program, with my parents as guests on the show in the Auckland studio. I tried to avoid hearing any statistics about how many thousands of viewers would be tuning in, or how the general public rated my chances of success this time around.

I resumed training as soon as I arrived back on Long Island, starting with dives to 90 and 94 metres in order to re-acclimatise to the Blue Hole. Then came my first dives to 100 and 101. These were good, clean dives as well, but my dive time was starting to get slow and I was needing more days — at least two — to recover completely between dives. I knew that I wasn't going to be able to maintain this tempo of diving all the way through to mid-July. At the same time, if I just stopped training and sat at home with my feet up, then the guilt and anxiety I would feel for not diving could remove any benefit I might get from the rest. Perhaps these were legitimate reasons for taking a week off, or maybe I just invented them because I missed Sachiko and wanted to visit her in Japan. When I told Dean and Johnny, they did their best to present their concern impassively but I could tell that they were appalled by the idea. 'You're going to fly halfway round the world *now*? What if you get sick?'

I had to admit that it was a gamble; but then so was staying on the island, where I would risk burnout. One week away would still leave three more before the attempt, and I felt that if I returned refreshed from a time without thoughts of diving, I would be able to fuel that last push towards the summit.

With all the time spent travelling I only had three full days on Okinawa Island, but they were spent sleeping in, eating fine Japanese food and even competing in a dragon-boat race (Sachiko's all-woman crew was missing one oarswoman, so I duly donned a floral dress and filled the gap). When I returned to Long Island I was mentally fresh, and relishing the prospect of one last push for glory. I started back with a sequence of dives to 90, 95 and 100 metres. The last was clean and strong, but still slow. For the next dive I set the line to 102, equal to the planned depth for the record attempt. Nervous about the growing length of my dive times, I tried to swim quicker on this one, and it resulted in my first samba since Vertical Blue. So, after two days of rest I attempted the same depth but allowed myself to swim at a natural pace. This time the dive was clean, but with a time of 4:19 it was scarily long for this discipline. Also, I had started to develop a soreness in my legs that just wasn't going away with rest. When I climbed stairs, or even if I just stood for a period of time, my legs would begin to ache in a way that implied that the lactic acid and other waste products weren't being eliminated from their muscles.

Now that I was reaching my target depths, the rest had become more important than the training, so I focused on doing just enough to maintain my form and confidence, with a deep dive every three to four days. No matter how much rest I took, however, my lower limbs just couldn't purge the lead that was flowing through their veins. To add to the mystery, Dean and Johnny were feeling similar sensations.

Just over a week before the attempt, I tried another training dive deeper than 100 metres and this time I came to the surface struggling, hooked, felt the blackout coming on and swore, before spending 2 seconds unconscious. It was clear that my performance had peaked in June, and now I was on a slow but inexorable decline that even time off hadn't been able to curb. I settled on doing just two dives in the final week, and finished with a promising dive to 101 metres. Encouragingly, the strange heaviness in my legs had finally begun to dissipate. Not so encouragingly, it had been replaced with a much worse bugbear and familiar foe. Stress. It was building: the stress caused by the guarantee of success I had made to an entire nation; the stress of coordinating the record attempt and doing damage control after a blunder by my crew had crippled the underwater drone system; the stress of doing interviews in the build-up.

*

The months of carefully programmed and measured training had ensured that my body was now capable of swimming to 102 metres and back on a single breath. That box was ticked. Whether I was able to accomplish it on the day would now come down to a single organ: my brain. I knew that I would have to use every mental tool in my kit, as well as fashion new ones specifically for this dive. The mantra 'Now is all' was still fresh and functional, but over the days leading up to the attempt I added numerous other devices.

My first step was to pull the carpet out from underneath the very idea of competition stress and nerves. *After Earth* is a pretty basic film, but in it Will Smith's speech on fear outlines a clever method for dissuading it: 'Fear is not real. The only place that fear can exist is in our thoughts of the future. It is a product of our imagination, causing us to fear things that do not at present and may not ever exist. That is near-insanity. Do not misunderstand me: danger is very real, but fear is a choice.'

In freediving the nemesis is not fear of death, but rather fear of failure — in short, performance anxiety. Now, when I felt the fluttering sensation that heralded this anxiety I didn't shy away from it, but instead looked for a concrete source in the present moment: what was happening *right now* that I was afraid of? When I couldn't find anything, this was confirmation that my nerves weren't actually based in the here and now of current reality, but rather in some kind of fantasy set in the future. It was like the moment when you figure out the magician's trick and the whole illusion comes crashing down. Rather than being at the mercy of these nerves, I was able to keep them in control and brush them aside with the cursory thought 'nerves aren't real'.

Nevertheless, sometimes the stress was just too ingrained and visceral for my mind to dispel it completely with a label. On these occasions I could take it in the opposite direction. In a competition or record attempt, it is essentially only the ego that is riding on the outcome. Failure normally involves blackout (on the surface or just below it), when the brain reaches its threshold for low levels of oxygen. Meanwhile, the blood is still carrying enough oxygen for minutes of brain supply — more than enough time for breathing to be resumed on the surface. So it's less the danger of a blackout than the wounded pride of failure that drives the anxiety felt prior to the dive. In a nutshell, I would be stressed out because I might take a hit to my ego. But what if it was more serious than that? What if my life, or the lives of others, actually did depend on the outcome? What if it was *imperative* that I was successful — if I had to dive to turn off the nuclear reactor on a sunken submarine that was ready to blow, for instance? When compared with these kinds of stakes, the fear of simply being embarrassed is laughable. I couldn't imagine how much more anxiety there would be in a life-and-death scenario, but that's not really relevant — I didn't have to experience that. I entertained the idea for long enough to put into perspective just how frivolous this circus-style record attempt really was. How silly was I for letting something so trivial and egocentric affect my emotional state! In the immortal words of Natalia Molchanova: 'Birth and death are important, but freediving competitions are just games for adults.'

In the weeks before the attempt I took evening hikes over the limestone cliffs of Long Island, to try to clear the heaviness from my legs and the cobwebs from my mind. These were also times in which to reflect and draw energy from the sea. On that shore, the progress of the ocean's rows of silent envoys was checked and reflected by the jagged rocks, filling the air with spray and a salty mist. Normally I left my phone at home, but on one occasion it was in my pocket and when it buzzed with an alert I absent-mindedly pulled it out. The alert was a simple message from Twitter, but the way it was worded and the moment in which it was received struck a note of significance: 'Sealife is now following you.'

Of course I have no pretensions that the ocean's sealife gives a damn about my silly jiggling around in the upper percentile of its depths. However, I personally do give a damn about sealife, and I know that with every success I achieve in freediving I secure more power and leverage to be able to influence the issues I care about. 'Do it for the oceans' is one of my greatest motivators, and so even the passing fancy that the ocean's sealife might have noticed my efforts and be 'following' them added to my motivation.

Finally there was one last mental device that I used to program the circuitry of my mind for that last push. The colour orange. I tend to plunder practices like yoga and zazen meditation, taking from them exercises and concepts that I can apply to my training. One of these is the *qigong* visualisation of a ball of energy that is created with specific hand movements and then stored in the body. I imagined this energy as an orange light, since (in traditional colour theory) orange is the complementary colour to the ocean's blue and, I'm told, helps to balance the time I spend in the water. After shaping it like a snowball with my hands, I visualise storing it in the *tanden* (the space between the navel and the perineum that in Eastern martial arts is the seat of the body's energy), to be accessed only during the ascent of the record attempt itself.

Do I believe in such an energy? Not literally, but I do believe in the psychological effects that this kind of visualisation can have. The intention and the action themselves create subconscious cues and contingencies that perhaps allow us to trigger elevated physiological levels. If nothing else, the fantasy that I had a cache of stockpiled energy ready to intervene during the dive gave me just a little extra confidence. And at the end of the day confidence is confidence, even when it is founded upon illusion.

*

Now is all, nerves aren't real, sealife, orange energy, and all the regular techniques of visualisation, positive affirmation and mental anchors ... as that date with the depths drew nearer, my mind had become a kind of one-man army, brandishing an arsenal of weapons with which to eviscerate the hordes of marauding negative thoughts and mutineering apprehensions. I was finally starting to feel that my mind was functioning on a similar level to the way my body had in the training dives past 100 metres. I often tell students in freediving courses that you can't muscle your way to the bottom plate and back, any more than you can get there with meditation alone. Both vehicles need to be firing on all cylinders, and they need to be driven by an inextinguishable flame of motivation.

On the day of the record attempt, I felt as if every part of my being had showed up with its toolkit and lunchbox carefully prepared, ready for action. But still, would that be enough?

The sperm whale takes a final breath and upends its great tail fluke, directing the massive prow of its head downwards into the abyss. That breath must sustain it for an hour and a half underwater, while it descends as much as 2 kilometres below the surface (at that depth, if you opened a pressurised scuba tank, water would flow *into* it through the valve). Nonetheless, the whale is as dependent on the air above the surface as we are. It must return to it, or perish. Whales are capable of conscious thought, according to the 2012 Cambridge Declaration on Consciousness, so they must be aware of their dependency on air. And yet it is the only existence they know. There is no alternative, so it's hard to imagine that for the whale the experience of freediving is anything but natural and peaceful.

That was the kind of dive I aspired to, on that windy July day in the Bahamas. It was the dive that I had aspired to for my whole career, ever since I had stood on that granite promontory in Sardinia on another windy day 13 years before, and committed myself to the pursuit of human aquatic potential. I had spent those years remodelling my physiology, imprinting fluid movement and harnessing the power of my mind for that one goal. Now, if I was to be successful in diving to 102 metres and back unassisted, I would need to channel the calm and ease of a marine mammal.

As I walked down the beach towards the Blue Hole, children were playing in the shallows and I smiled at them, remembering. They were at the start of a journey of exploration into the sea — I was still on that same journey, but a little further along.

Steinlager had labelled the attempt 'Return to the Deep'. In essence, that was also a description of freediving:

a return to the deep oceans after an absence of 400 million years. If you repeat the word 'great' continuously for four years and add 'grandmother' on the end, you will have described your ancestor who lived in the sea. Who breathed the sea. There is no break in that family line; no child who didn't look more or less the same as their parent. The first tetrapods to leave the water breathed by swallowing air into their digestive system, and absorbing oxygen through the gut lining. Pockets of the gut evolved into the lungs we have today. Now, today, I was lying on the surface of the Blue Hole having taken a full breath and swallowed bites of air into my lungs to fill them with all the oxygen they could take. Satisfied that I had taken onboard enough for the dive, I rolled over to face the blue depths below me.

The development of the amniotic egg — an egg with a shell — allowed early land-dwelling tetrapods to prevent the embryo inside the egg from drying out in a dry land habitat, by holding it in a sac of liquid within the shell. Human babies grow for nine months inside a similar amniotic sac: a little bag of ocean within the womb. As I scooped the water aside with my arms and feet, pulling my body downwards, I was back inside the planet's amniote, from which all life has evolved. Perhaps the whole terrestrial escapade had all been a big mistake. Perhaps, realising this, the dolphins and whales had made the migration back from the land to the sea, and were all the better for it. Here was I, attempting to do the same in the course of just one lifetime.

I was freefalling now. As the bubbles of air shrank inside my lungs, the bubble of emptiness expanded in my mind. The taut rope skimmed against the silicone of my swim cap where it was pulled tight down over my forehead, and this allowed me to close my eyes and fly, sightless, into the void.

On the surface, Shiv watched the sonar and announced the depth and time readings. Fifty metres after 1:00. Seventy-five metres by 1:30. The first depth alarm on my Suunto gauge sounded when I reached 82 metres. My mind woke up, pressed the snooze button and went back to sleep. I wasn't there yet.

'Peace and precision.' This simple word pair had come to me in a moment of contemplation years ago, as a distillation of what I must achieve in a freedive. The peace of a resting mind, and the precision of a body that uses the minimal amount of oxygen to move through the water. In the 90-second freefall from 30 metres to the bottom plate at 102, the centreline of my body hadn't deviated more than a centimetre from the vertical axis of the rope, and during that period I could have counted on one hand the number of thoughts that had briefly occupied my mind.

When the final alarm sounded, 7 metres from the target, my right arm slowly reached above my head, feeling for the plate, while my left hand circled the rope. Without looking, without even opening my eyes, I removed a tag from the plate and pulled on the rope, once, to start my ascent. Two minutes had passed since my last breath, and I was more than 2 minutes of hard swimming away from the surface.

I was slow in my ascent, slower even than I had been in training. Initially I was only gaining about 2 metres with every 3-second kick-and-stroke cycle. But gradually I climbed, scaling my own personal Everest, stroke by stroke. 'Now' was the only concept that existed in my mind. There was no anticipation of a record, of surfacing, or even of an end to the slow rhythm of pulsing legs and sweeping arms. I swam as if I had been born swimming and knew no alternative.

By 3 minutes I was at 60 metres and my safety divers were setting off from the surface, on their way to meet me. My eyes were half-open; just enough to perceive the blurry line of the rope in front of me, as well as the gradual renewal of light. If I had been paying attention to my body, I would have noticed my limbs fatiguing, my stomach hollowing with each breathing reflex. But my body didn't need my attention: it had been here before,

(Daan Verhoeven)

had overcome these same barriers and knew what to do without being told.

Now a shape swung into view and turned in front of me. Dean, my first safety diver, had come deeper for today's dive: to 37 metres. Part of my brain was starting to stir — not a part that performed any kind of computation or reasoning, but more a faculty of willpower and concentration. I had to ensure that I stayed present and self-aware in this crucial final stage of the ascent, even if there was still no content to that awareness.

I could now see the surface in my peripheral vision: the judges close to the line; the medic, Tom, standing on

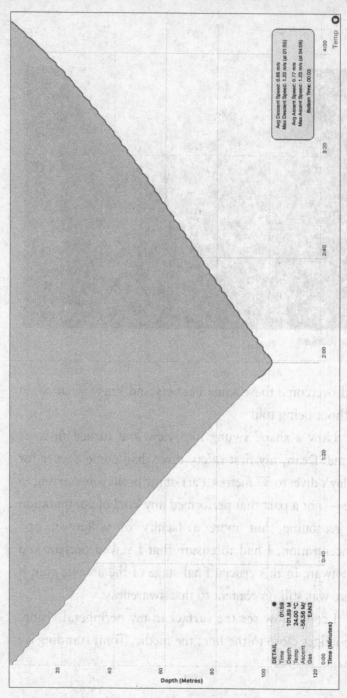

The dive profile of my 102 metre CNF world record, downloaded from my Suunto depth gauge. The gauge is worn on my wrist, so the 'ledges' in the profile indicate armstrokes, when the hands stay at more or less the same depth while the body is pushed forwards. The clean line in the descent after 23 metres describes the freefall phase.

the platform and peering anxiously down through the surface, as if from another world.

The shroud of low oxygen was starting to cloak my mind, but I knew that there was one last thing I had to do, and I knew that I could do it.

My final stroke, the thirty-fifth of the ascent, lifted me the last few metres to the surface, and after a dive time of 4:12 I emerged from liquid to air once more.

I took a deep breath in.

With Sachiko Fukumoto in the warm water of Roatan, Honduras, 2016. The only thing better than discovering the underwater world is sharing it with someone else. *(Lia Barrett)*

EPILOGUE

> Full fathom five thy father lies;
>   Of his bones are coral made;
> Those are pearls that were his eyes:
>   Nothing of him that doth fade,
> But doth suffer a sea-change
> Into something rich and strange.

Ariel's song, from Shakespeare's *The Tempest*

WHEN I ACTED IN MY BROTHER'S PRODUCTION of *The Tempest* in 1997 I played the part of King Alonso, who is shipwrecked on the magician Prospero's island. Now, 20 years later, having returned to the surface from not five but 55 fathoms — though I did not donate my bones to any coral in the process — I know that I have undergone a sea change, and I stand on the other side of the stage.

The sea has changed me, and I continue to change. I believe that the day we stop striving to evolve, or stop considering ourselves as beginners in all things, is the day when our bones really do begin to turn to coral.

I continue to train. The depths still beckon me. On that dive in 2016, when I turned 102 metres down, although my eyes were closed I could feel the pull of untold volumes of water yet below me.

What am I still chasing, one might ask, in that submerged realm? Shakespeare spoke of the lure of 'unpathed waters, undreamed shores'. If George Mallory, who perished somewhere near the summit of Everest in 1924, had been a freediver, he would have justified himself with the words 'because it's everywhere'. My first teacher, Umberto Pelizzari, dived to 'look inside'. These concepts have all rung true for me, too. As did the insight of the elderly Bahamian lady who was asked why she thought I dived, and replied: 'He wants to see what he is.'

I don't have to go deep — sometimes I dive just to be, as Mervyn Peake says, 'at one with every swarm of lime-green fish, with every coloured sponge'. Long after my final record or my final competition dive, I will continue to frequent that 'world of wavering light' where it all began, for me and for life as we know it.

I dive to go home.

GLOSSARY

AIDA (International Association for the Development of Apnea): the organisation created in 1992 that regulates freediving competitions and world record attempts.

AP (Announced Performance): the target depth in metres, declared by a freediver typically the day before competing. The bottom plate with tags will be set to this exact depth for their dive, and it cannot be altered or exceeded. Freedivers submit their AP in secret, and don't find out what their competitors will attempt until the Official Top times list is released by the organiser.

apnea: in freediving, a voluntary breath-hold, typically performed underwater.

breathe-up: the preparatory phase before a freedive begins, during which the freediver is relaxed and concentrating on a specific breathing style or pattern.

counterballast: the system used in freediving to retrieve freedivers attached with a lanyard to the dive line. The counterballast weight is attached to the end of the rope opposite the bottom plate, and is much heavier than the weight used to weigh down the competition line. If it is released then it will drop down and pull the entire competition line, and the freediver, quickly to the surface.

CNF (Constant Weight No Fins): the discipline in which the freediver swims down and up, relying only on their own body for propulsion, and usually swimming with a kind of adapted underwater breaststroke. He or she cannot touch the rope (other than once at the bottom). Any weight worn as ballast must remain constant. The men's world record is currently 102 metres, while the women's world record is 72 metres.

CO_2 (Carbon Dioxide): a naturally occurring gas waste product that results from human respiration, building up in the lungs and triggering the urge to breathe.

CWT (Constant Weight): the discipline in which the freediver swims down and up, wearing fins or a monofin, but cannot touch the rope (other than once at the bottom). Any weight worn as ballast must remain constant. The men's world record is currently 129 metres, while the women's world record is 104 metres.

DNF (Dynamic No Fins): the pool discipline, in which
the freediver swims horizontally as far as possible
on one breath, without fins or any other propulsive
aid. The men's world record is currently 244 metres,
while the women's world record is 185 metres.

DYN (Dynamic Apnea): the pool discipline, in
which the freediver swims horizontally as far as
possible on one breath, using fins or a monofin for
propulsion. The men's world record is currently
300 metres, while the women's world record is
237 metres.

exhale static apnea: as for static apnea, but the breath
is held after an exhale (i.e. with near empty lungs).
This is normally a training exercise only.

FIM (Free Immersion): the discipline in which the
freediver uses a weighted dive rope to pull
themselves down to maximum depth and back
to the surface. Fins are not allowed and, as for
the other depth disciplines, any ballast worn
must remain constant. The men's world record is
currently 124 metres, while the women's world
record is 92 metres.

grouper call/signal: the noise made in the back of the
throat that mimics a grouper fish, and is typically
used by safety divers to signal to freedivers when
they have reached a certain depth in their ascent.

hook-breath ('hook'): a technique of recovery breaths
for after a freedive, with a pause and squeeze of
the exhalatory muscles after the inhale, designed
to return oxygen to the cerebral bloodstream
quickly.

hypoxia: low concentrations of oxygen in bodily tissues,
especially the blood.

hyperbaria: pressure that is greater than atmospheric
pressure at sea level, for example when underwater.

hypercapnia: high concentrations of carbon dioxide in
bodily tissues.

lanyard: the safety device worn by freedivers as a way of
tethering themselves to the dive line, so in the event
of an emergency they can be retrieved by pulling the
dive line to the surface.

lactic acidosis: a build-up of lactic acid in the tissues,
due to prolonged anaerobic activity.

lift bag: a canvas bag that can be inflated at depth
(e.g. from a scuba tank exhaust valve) in order to
provide buoyancy and bring someone or something
to the surface.

narcosis ('narced'): in freediving, the state of
drowsiness, euphoria or confusion caused by the
high pressure in the bloodstream of certain gases
(typically carbon dioxide and nitrogen).

negative buoyancy: when the diver weighs more
than the amount of water they displace, and will
naturally sink in the water column.

neutral buoyancy: when the diver's weight is equal to
the amount of water they displace, and they will
remain at the same depth in the water column. In
freediving this typically occurs at a depth of 10–20
metres, when the lungs have been compressed to
½–⅓ of their size on the surface.

Official Top time: the scheduled time of day after
which a freediver has 30 seconds to begin their
performance.

packing (glossopharyngeal breathing): a technique that
uses the mouth like a pump to force extra air into
the lungs after a full inhale.

positive buoyancy: when the diver weighs less than the
amount of water they displace, and will naturally
rise in the water column.

pranayama: the yogic practice of regulating the breath
through certain techniques and exercises.

rebreather: a breathing system for technical diving,
where the exhaled gas is recirculated through a
device worn on the back that removes the carbon
dioxide and adds additional oxygen.

samba: the name used by freedivers to describe an LMC
(Loss of Motor Control), which is the hypoxic state

that precedes a blackout, and results in involuntary
shaking of the head and arms. So named for the
samba dance that the shaking resembles.

static apnea: the pool discipline, in which the freediver
attempts to hold their breath for as long as possible
while their airways are submerged underwater. It is
typically performed while floating face down in a
pool, and the best times in competition exceed nine
minutes for both men and women.

SP (Surface Protocol): the task that the freediver must
perform after surfacing in order to validate a
competition dive. In AIDA rules, the SP is described
as follows:

After resurfacing the athlete must:

1. Remove ALL facial equipment (mask, goggles
   and nose clip).
2. Give 1 visible 'okay'-sign to the judge.
3. Give 1 verbal 'okay' to the judge by saying 'I'm
   okay' or 'I am okay'.

All the above items must be done in this specific
order within 15 seconds of resurfacing, without
any cues from the jury or officials.

sled diving: the mostly obsolete method of breath-
hold diving, using a weighted sled to descend to
maximum depth, and possibly a lift bag to return to
the surface.

ACKNOWLEDGEMENTS

No one operates in a vacuum, and just as we acquire the tools of our predecessors we also share the advances of our peers. It's unlikely that there is a single freediver — whether training partner, crew member or competitor — who I have dived alongside and not learned from in some way.

So for everyone, named or unnamed, who has been part of this unfolding journey, I extend my gratitude for your contribution.

In particular, I have to thank both my agent, Jason Chambers, who made the writing of this story possible, and Marc Laureano, who has been relentlessly on my case to put pen to paper, and to whom I finally ceded!

Everyone at HarperCollins has done a terrific job with shepherding me towards the finish line of my first book, and I am indebted especially to Alex Hedley for his gentle and respectful guidance, as well as Teresa McIntyre for her assiduous editorial skills, against which my blundering grammar proved no match.

Michael and Frances Trousdell, Georgina Miller, Daan Verhoeven and Pamela Holtzman all gave me invaluable feedback during the drafting phase, and coaxed me through some of the more delicate areas of writing.

And my final, deepest thank you has to be to my family, Linda, David and Sam, who inspired me with their own writings as well as helped to fill the countless holes in my leaky memory.

REFERENCES

Sam Harris, *Waking Up: A Guide to Spirituality without Religion*, Simon & Schuster, 2015

Jacques Mayol, *Homo Delphinus: The Dolphin within Man*, Idelson-Gnocchi, 2000

Adam Skolnick, *One Breath: Freediving, Death, and the Quest to Shatter Human Limits*, Crown Archetype, 2016

Linda Trubridge, *Passages*, 2018 (forthcoming)

EPIGRAPHS

Lord Byron, *The Two Foscari: An Historical Tragedy*, John Murray, 1821

Jacques-Yves Cousteau, *Time*, 28 March 1960

Harold Geneen

Hectometer, Matthew Brown (director) and William Trubridge (producer), 2011

Dalai Lama

Herman Melville, *Moby Dick*, Richard Bentley, 1851

Swami Nikhilananda (trans), *The Gospel of Ramakrishna*, Ramakrishna-Vivekananda Center, 1942

Mervyn Peake, *Titus Groan*, Eyre & Spottiswoode, 1946

Umberto Pelizzari, in *Ocean Men: Extreme Dive*, Bob Talbot (director) and Mose Richards (producer), 2001